INTIMATE MEMORY

SUNY SERIES IN CHINESE PHILOSOPHY AND CULTURE
ROGER T. AMES, EDITOR

INTIMATE MEMORY

GENDER AND MOURNING IN LATE IMPERIAL CHINA

MARTIN W. HUANG

The cover image is a portrait of Zhang Manshu, the concubine of the seventeenth-century writer Mao Qiling, reproduced from the album *Manshu liuying* assembled by the latter in memory of the former. Facsimile reprint (Shanghai: Shangwu yinshu guan, 1930).

Published by State University of New York Press, Albany

© 2018 State University of New York

All rights reserved

No part of this book may be used or reproduced in any manner whatsoever without written permission. No part of this book may be stored in a retrieval system or transmitted in any form or by any means including electronic, electrostatic, magnetic tape, mechanical, photocopying, recording, or otherwise without the prior permission in writing of the publisher.

For information, contact State University of New York Press, Albany, NY
www.sunypress.edu

Book design: Steve Kress Design

Library of Congress Cataloging-in-Publication Data
Names: Huang, Martin W., author.
Title: Intimate memory : gender and mourning in late Imperial China / Martin W. Huang.
Description: Albany, NY : State University of New York, 2018. | Series: SUNY series in Chinese philosophy and culture | Includes bibliographical references and index.
Identifiers: LCCN 2017019639 (print) | LCCN 2017058852 (ebook) | ISBN 9781438469010 (e-book) | ISBN 9781438468990 (hardcover   ) | ISBN 9781438469003 (paperback   )
Subjects: LCSH: Loss (Psychology)—China—History. | Grief—China—History. | Gender identity—China—History. | Memory—China—History.
Classification: LCC BF575.D35 (ebook) | LCC BF575.D35 H83 2018 (print) | DDC 155.9/370951—dc23
LC record available at https://lccn.loc.gov/2017019639

10 9 8 7 6 5 4 3 2 1

CONTENTS

Acknowledgments vii

Introduction 1

1 The Secularization of Memory 15

2 Survivor's Guilt 37

3 Hagiographical Memory 55

4 Wounded Manhood 73

5 Fragments of Anxiety 97

6 Remembering Concubines 113

7 Circulating Grief 135

8 Remembering Sisters 157

Epilogue: A Wife's Remembrances 177

Notes 187

Bibliography 213

Index 221

ACKNOWLEDGMENTS

In the process of writing this book, I have benefited from the help of many individuals. They include Bob Hegel, Daoxiong Guan, Weijing Lu, Huili Zheng, Sarah Schneewind, and Katherine Carlitz. I consider it my good fortune to have Hu Ying, Michael Fuller, and Qitao Guo as my colleagues here at UC, Irvine, whose help and advice have always been the source of support I rely on.

I am grateful to the following institutions for their generous support in the form of sabbatical leave funding and research stipends: the Chiang Ching-kuo Foundation, the University of California President Research Fellowship in the Humanities, and here at UC, Irvine, the Humanities Commons, the Center for Asian Studies, and the Council on Research, Computing, and Libraries.

Portions of chapters 1 and 2 have appeared as parts of the Introduction to the special theme issue of the journal *Nan Nü: Men, Women and Gender in China*, under the title "Remembering Female Relatives in Late Imperial China" (15[2] 2013), which I edited as guest-editor, and my article "Negotiating Wifely Exemplariness: Guilt, Memory and Gender in Seventeenth-Century China," in the same issue. I thank my fellow contributors: Allan Barr, Katherine Carlitz, and Lynn Struve for their contributions, which have benefited my own research on the topic. An earlier version of chapter 4, under the title "The Manhood of a *Pinshi* (A Poor Scholar): The Gendered Spaces in *The Six Records of A Floating Life*," has appeared in the volume *Changing Chinese Masculinities from Imperial Pillars of State to Global Real Men*, edited by Kam Louie and published by Hong Kong University Press in 2015. I thank Kam for inviting me to present an earlier draft of the article at the conference he organized at Hong Kong University.

Finally, my thanks go to SUNY's two anonymous outside readers for their thoughtful comments on the manuscript; although I may not have been able to follow all their suggestions in my subsequent revision, their input was valuable and much appreciated. Of course, any errors remaining in the book are strictly my own.

INTRODUCTION

Barely four months after bidding farewell to his family, the early Qing scholar-official and dramatist You Tong 尤侗 (1618–1704) received the devastating news in the capital a thousand *li* away that his wife had passed away in his hometown more than a month earlier. To mourn his late wife, the distraught You Tong wrote an emotional biographical sketch. Tormented by the guilty feelings of not being at her bedside when she needed him most, You Tong wrote:

> Alas, how sad! I don't know (*zhi* 知) how my wife died. We have been married for forty years. Then she died only one hundred days after I left her [for the capital]. I only know how my wife lived but I don't know how she died. For someone who knows how she died, his sorrow is probably not as deep as someone who only knows how she lived. Then if I don't know how my wife died, how could I really know how she lived? Our son Zhen came to me in his mourning clothes and pleaded: "I know a few things about the life of my mother but I am too distraught to write. My father, how could you bear to desert your children [by failing to keep alive the memories of their mother]?"[1]

Here the emotional intensity of a grieving husband is quite palpable, and the feeling of guilt dominates. Seemingly wondering about his own ability to truly "know" his deceased wife, You Tong emphasized the importance of *zhi* (understanding and knowing), implying he himself was nevertheless the most qualified person to reconstruct and record the "life" of his wife since they had lived together as husband and wife for so many decades. He concluded the sketch with the following passage:

> We were a couple that had gone through all the hardships together and I have never had any concubines (*bingwu qieying* 並無妾媵). Being husband

and wife, we cherished each other as friends. Overwhelmed by my love for my deceased wife (*siqing* 私情; more literally, selfish feelings), I have ventured to pollute the eyes of respected gentlemen with this account of the intimate feelings between a man and a woman (*ernü zhi yan* 兒女之言), hoping that someone could write something [based on this account] to keep alive the memory of my wife, while I would be forgiven given the fact that I, as a visitor [stranded in the capital], have no one to confide in and that my son could only cry in the direction of our hometown. With tears in my eyes, I wrote this, not really knowing what I have just written.²

It had become quite common by the seventeenth century for a grieving husband to write a fairly long and emotional elegiac prose essay to honor his deceased wife in the form of a biographical account. You Tong felt the urgent need to turn her "life" into a scribed text, which was supposed to be endowed with the ultimate power to transcend death and time.

Considering himself the one who knew his wife best, he insisted he was the most appropriate person to author such a textualized life, whereas the tremendous pains of loss turned him into a particularly sympathetic as well as revealing biographer. At the same time, even with such conviction of a uniquely-privileged biographer, You Tong might still feel the pressure to apologize for his outpouring of *siqing* or "selfish feelings." He felt the need to legitimate his elegiac act by suggesting that he wrote this biography at the request of their son, whose filial love for his mother, different from a husband's *siqing* for his wife, hardly needed any apology given the Confucian notion of filiality. There was an obvious tension between the Confucian inhibitions over direct expressions of conjugal attachment and the desire to remember and commit to writing the detailed facts in the life of his wife in a way only he could do.

Despite his somewhat conventional reliance on the filial need of their son as an excuse for writing about the life of his late wife, You Tong's biographical sketch points to what was then an emerging trend—a late imperial literatus' increasing willingness to acknowledge that he was writing about the life of his wife not necessarily for her Confucian exemplariness or even for the purpose of preserving a record of her life for their decedents, but for the sake of his own memory: she was being remembered first of all as someone who had been very close to him. This was a project of personal remembrance based on intimate memory, which was often associated with *si* (the private or even the selfish), a rather reprehensible undertaking, at least in the eyes of the more conservative. It was the intimate, or "eye-polluting" (*chenmu* 塵目; to use a variation of You Tong's own wording) details of the life they shared together that was most worth remembering.

As this study seeks to demonstrate, elegiac biographies such as You Tong's biographical sketch of his wife provide us with a rare opportunity for an intimate look into many aspects of the late imperial husband–wife relationship that so far have remained largely hidden from us. Texts such as this should help us explore the important question how intimate memory sought to find its expression and legitimacy in a culture where manifestations of conjugal intimacy were often viewed with suspicion.

Our understanding of traditional Chinese women has seen great advancement in the recent two decades or so.[3] Impressive strides have been made in recovering late imperial Chinese women's writings, and much light has been shed on the important question of how women viewed and represented themselves.[4] However, in traditional Chinese culture, as in many other premodern cultures, most writings about women were produced by men rather than women themselves. That is, most images of women from traditional China accessible to us today were constructed through the mediation of male consciousness. A careful examination of the nature of this male mediation is crucial to an adequate understanding of the social as well as cultural constructions of women and men as gendered beings during that period.

Probably nowhere is such male mediation more prominent and more complex than in the memorial writings on the deceased women written by their grieving male relatives, such as their surviving husbands. This study focuses on male literati's elegiac or *daowang* 悼亡 (mourning) biographical narratives of their deceased spouses in late imperial China (approximately the sixteenth through nineteenth centuries).[5] It seeks to examine how womanhood was constructed and defined by men in a polygamous society and how such male reflections on womanhood in turn helped define these grieving authors' own manhood in relation to their spouses as well as their male peers, offering us a rare opportunity for a close look at many aspects of the construction of these two different genders in close juxtaposition.

In late imperial China, one of the most likely as well as most legitimate occasions for a man to feel the urge or the need to write about the life of a woman who was very close to him was when she had passed away. This was also the moment he was most likely to feel justified in revealing aspects of her life that he might have qualms broaching on other occasions. On the other hand, if an elegy or epitaph was conceived as a ritual being performed for the benefit of the living along with the apparent subject of its eulogizing—the deceased, it was at least as much about the mourning "self" as about the mourned "other." The way a deceased spouse was being eulogized and remembered is closely related to the self-image the bereaved husband attempted to construct for himself. Our understandings of men and women as different gender beings have to be achieved in close juxtaposition since genders are seldom conceptualized in isolation.

Mourning and remembering are closely associated, or could even be considered two aspects of the same act, as memory is often a result of the absence of its object, while death amounts to permanent absence. Remembering often aims at perpetuating the existence of a person who no longer exists. Fearful that memory will fade—thus the triumph of the eternal absence—one then feels the need to commit memory onto paper to give it a material form in the hope that what is remembered about a person will never be lost again in his or her eternal absence. Thanks in part to its belatedness, the act of remembering/mourning also brings about a distance that enables one to look at the absent person from a new perspective precisely as a result of his or her absence, just as the early sixteenth-century scholar-official and poet Li Mengyang 李夢陽 (1472–1529) famously confessed: "It took the death of my wife for me to really know her."[6] What makes mourning a unique occasion for remembrance is the radicalization of absence—the death of a person makes the bereaved all the more appreciative of the deceased and much more willing to take a different look at someone whose presence was long taken for granted. The belatedness inherent in an act of remembrance injects into the bereaved a special sense of guilt for having previously failed to see or appreciate what in the deceased he or she is now able to see or appreciate. It is this new understanding and appreciation of the deceased, as well as the simultaneous guilty feelings of belatedness, that make the act of elegiac remembrance so intriguing, especially when the mourned and mourner are closely related to each other and when intimate memory assumes a major role in the mourning process.

Browsing through the *wenji* 文集 (collected writings) by many late imperial Chinese literati, one is often struck by the large number of biographical writings devoted to the memories of the deceased female relatives in these collections. Most of them are in the forms of epitaphs (*muzhiming* 墓誌銘), biographical sketches (*xingzhuang* 行狀),[7] sacrificial litanies (*jiwen* 祭文), and occasionally, biographies (*zhuan* 傳).[8] Despite the longstanding Confucian anxiety over women as biographical subjects, as expressed in the Confucian classic *Liji* 禮記 or *The Book of Rites*—"Outside affairs should not be talked of inside the threshold (of the women's apartments), nor inside (or women's) affairs outside it" (外言不入於梱，內言不出於梱)[9]—the late imperial period witnessed a dramatic increase of biographical writings on women.[10] Besides the female exemplar biographies that abound in official and local histories and in the literati *wenji*, individual literati authors also produced many biographical writings on their female relatives, often not necessarily for their exemplariness but for the obvious but important reason that these female subjects were their close kin.

The fact that the male biographer personally knew or was even quite close to the woman he was writing about had important implications: his direct personal knowledge of his female subject could make him more able as well as more inclined to reveal aspects of her life that a typical commissioned biographer or epitaph writer, who tended to follow the Confucian biographical conventions more diligently, might otherwise be unable or unwilling to divulge; his closeness to his female subject complicated as well as highlighted the specific perspectives from which he interpreted the meanings of her life, with the resultant writing more likely to deviate from the norms of the Confucian exemplar discourse. Writing the biography of a woman once very close to the biographer himself tended to increase the possibility of the Confucian biographical and gender uniformity being undermined, as she was more likely to be remembered as an individual rather than a "faceless" abstraction of the Confucian moral precepts for women.

Whereas the perceived intimacy between a grieving husband and his late spouse might present itself as a liability in the eyes of the more conservative in terms of "over-indulgence," a topic to be further explored in chapter 1, such intimacy could cause him to be franker in writing about her, leading to insights into the aspects of the husband–wife relationship otherwise rarely revealed in other kinds of discourses from that period. Precisely because of the special closeness between the male author and his female subject, the uniqueness of his perspective as a husband in shaping her representation became all the more significant in our effort to reach a better appreciation of the gendered implications of male mediation through which most extant images of late imperial women were being constructed. It helps to shed new light on the special dynamic between the autobiographical "self" and the biographical "other" often dramatized in such an intimate act of personal remembrance.

While there was a long and sophisticated *daowang* poetic tradition in premodern China, which was closely related to the *daowang* works in prose this study focuses on, I am mainly interested in the question how a grieving husband tried to construct the life narrative of his spouse(s) based on his personal memories, a task much more likely to be accomplished in various biographical and memorial genres in prose. However, some authors' *daowang* poems are included in discussion whenever they become relevant. The relationship between *daowang* poetry and other elegiac genres in prose is also an important question I explore at some length.

Chapter 1 is an overview of what I would call the phenomenon of "secularization of memory" that took place during the late imperial period as well as the special roles played by intimate memory in this secularization process and the resultant changes memorial writings underwent during that same period. For lack of a better term, I use the word "secularization," which originally refers to the declining influence of a particular religion, to refer to *shisu hua* 世俗化, a much broader Chinese concept, in order to describe this process through which Chinese memorial writings were becoming more plebeian (more ordinary people became represented in these writings) and significantly less constrained by the various rigid moral Confucian precepts. The American theologian Harvey Cox defines secularization as "the liberation of man from religious and metaphysical tutelage, the turning of his attention away from other worlds and toward this one."[11] Sharing aspects of Cox's definition of secularization, the term *shisu hua*, which, in fact, was originally coined to translate the Western term "secularization," has also been employed by Chinese historians to refer to what are considered compatible with those phenomena resulted from the secularization movements in the West. However, the specific social and cultural phenomena in the Chinese historical context thus referred to were not necessarily the results of the declining influence of any particular religion. This broadening of the original meaning of the term "secularization" is, to a certain extent, necessitated by the fact that the kind of dichotomy between the sacred and the secular often seen in Western history was never strong in premodern China since Chinese society was relatively secular to start with. Some Chinese historians have employed the term *shisu hua* to characterize what happened as a result of the waning influence of the strict moral precepts associated with Confucianism in premodern China (whether Confucianism could be considered a religion is still a hotly debated issue) or even the diminished reach of the Communist ideology in post-Mao China.[12] At the same time, the term *shisu hua* has also been used to characterize how certain Confucian moral values began to lose their influence or relevance as the Chinese society became more urbanized and more commercialized during the late imperial period.[13]

A main argument outlined in chapter 1 and further buttressed in the following chapters is that there was something particularly "secularizing" inherent in intimate memory, which, especially when allowed to assume an important role in the mourning process, compelled a grieving husband to remember his late spouse more as a specific and mundane individual, quite different from those saint-like images one frequently encounters in the typical Confucian exemplar discourse, such as the biographies of exemplary women in the standard and local histories produced in late imperial China.[14] She was often remembered by her grieving husband as someone not necessarily perfect but with flaws, thus, rather ordinary. Intimate memory tended to be able to resist more successfully the kind of moralistic abstraction typical of the Confucian biographical tradition, while *daowang* discourse was one of the most important venues where such memory found its expressions despite strong Confucian aversion to conjugal intimacy and especially its public display. This chapter also briefly traces the significant changes some popular genres of memorial writings underwent during that period as a result of the increasingly important role assumed by intimate memory in the mourning process, an interesting phenomenon related to the much-elevated status of *qing* 情 (emotions) in the cultural discourses of the second half of the Ming dynasty and the popularity of companionate marriage in certain circles of the cultural elite at that time.[15] As demonstrated in the discussions of many specific *daowang* works in the following chapters of this study, the importance of the forms memory is capable of assuming cannot be underestimated. The most innovative and most compelling works of *daowang* are often those that successfully challenge and even transcend the conventions of the existing genres of memorial writings.

Chapter 2 is an examination of how the guilt felt by a surviving husband compelled him to delve deep into his memories of his late wife to rethink the issue of what constituted a virtuous wife as he, directly or indirectly, questioned many aspects of the traditional Confucian prescriptions for a woman. His grief and the accompanying sense of guilt as a surviving husband tended to make him more willing to look at things from the perspective of the woman he was writing about. A polygamous husband in mourning was more inclined to demonstrate sympathy for his late wife for the jealousy she might have felt when he took a concubine, while a self-claimed monogamous husband, such as You Tong, as discussed above, attempted to present his claim of monogamy as a proof of his unwavering love for his late wife. In their eagerness to underscore the many hardships their deceased wives had gone through as daughters-in-law, some of these grieving husbands alluded to the tensions between their wives and their own mothers, even casting the latter in a somewhat unflattering light, an act quite remarkable on the part of a son, given the Confucian emphasis on filial piety. Consequently, the self-images conjured up in these *daowang* biographies are often those of a grieving husband who could be unusually sympathetic and sometimes even "indulgent" as well as "indulging," confirming, almost by default, the dangers of conjugal intimacy many orthodox Confucian moralists had repeatedly warned against.

If intimate memory had a tendency to compel some grieving husbands to deviate from the Confucian biographical norms of the exemplary in writing about their deceased wives, chapter 3 focuses on what is seemingly the opposite: the different implications of intimate memory when a grieving husband decided to embark on a hagiographical project on his deceased wife to explicitly celebrate her as a female chastity martyr (*lienü* 烈女), the ultimate female Confucian exemplar. This is a particularly intriguing topic given the rising cult of female chastity during that period.[16] One of my arguments is that the proliferation of the Confucian hagiography of female virtues, a seemingly "sacralizing" trend, paradoxically, might have aided the secularization of memory by providing more biographical "spaces" for those less saint-like women when their male relatives decided to write about them. These biographers of ordinary women could feel more justified in talking less about the Confucian exemplariness of their biographical subjects since there was another special form of biography (hagiography) now readily available to be employed to celebrate those extraordinary female exemplars.

According to Zhang Zhen 張貞 (1637–1712), a late seventeenth-century writer, his wife, before she died, refused food for several days, believing Zhang was about to succumb to his severe illness. She eventually died, but he himself miraculously recovered. Initially, Zhang Zhen wrote a quite moving and intimate biographical sketch of his wife to mourn her, but seventeen years later, apparently having changed his mind, he began to actively solicit well-known literati figures to produce a hagiography of chastity martyrdom for her. In this proposed hagiographical project, however, "forgetfulness" was urged, whereas intimate memory in particular became something to be shunned and deliberately suppressed. The case of Zhang Zhen underscored, by default, the secularizing power of intimate memory in the construction of the image of a wife.

The Ming loyalist writer and scholar Qian Chengzhi 錢澄之 (1612–1693) also attempted to celebrate his late wife—who committed suicide rather than facing the danger of being defiled by bandits—as a female chastity martyr in her biographical sketch. Here, personal memory was appropriated to authenticate the historicity of the image of his wife as a chastity martyr and to enhance his own narrative authority as a Confucian historian, who considered recording such heroic deeds the solemn duty of a historian. Juggling between his private role as a commemorating husband and his public role as an objective historian, Qian tried hard to underscore, with the help of his personal memory, his value as a historical witness. This chapter further complicates the implications of intimate memory in the secularizing process of late imperial memorial writings by showing the diverse roles it could assume.

Chapter 4 is a reading of *Fusheng liuji* 浮生六記, or *The Six Records of a Floating Life*—hereafter referred to as *Six Records*—by Shen Fu 沈復 (b.1761), arguably the most sophisticated, as well as the most complex, work of intimate memory in premodern China. Never before had a grieving husband delved so deeply into his personal memory as Shen Fu did to recollect the intimate details of the life he shared with his late wife; never before had a grieving husband depicted in such a detailed fashion as he did the tensions between other members of his extended family and themselves as a couple, especially the tensions between his father and himself, a daring "unfilial" act on the part of a son, given the unconditional authority enjoyed by parents at that time. Shen Fu's remembrances of his late wife were carefully embedded and framed in his autobiographical reflections on his own past "selves" as he tried to come to terms with his own gender identity as a marginalized literatus. The tremendous empathy he exhibited in recounting the tragic life of his late wife was inseparable from his own experience of emasculation, offering us a rare glimpse into the deep gender psyche of a man dogged by poverty and career failures throughout his life. *Six Records* is a remarkably innovative work of *daowang* in many aspects: its unprecedented length, its intricate chapter structure, its focus on the intimate details of daily conjugal life, its daring exposure of family tensions, and its challenges to the many conventions of traditional memorial writings. It is an elegiac narrative, a memoir as well as an autobiography, all at once.

A few generations younger than Shen Fu, Jiang Tan 蔣坦 (b. 1823) authored a quite different memoir about his wife, titled *Qiudeng suoyi* 秋燈瑣憶, or *The Fragments of Memory under the Autumn Lamp*—hereafter referred to as *Fragments*. As suggested by its title, the memoir is made of random remembrances that do not provide a coherent picture of the couple's married life. Chapter 5 is an attempt to read this memoir in close juxtaposition with Jiang Tan's many *daowang* poems, focusing on his anxieties as a man, husband, and son-in-law, partly caused by his wife's independence and her unusually close ties with her natal family. Compared with Shen Fu's *Six Records*, Jiang Tan's remembrances of his wife present an intricate picture of a very different kind of family tension. His case also gives us a chance to explore some of the new literary functions assumed by these two different elegiac genres, *daowang* poetry and prose memoir.

Given the widespread practice of polygamy among the elite in late imperial China, one should not find it surprising that significant parts of *daowang* writings were devoted to the deceased concubines. Chapter 6 explores the matter of how concubines were mourned and remembered differently and/or similarly by their polygamous husbands. Thanks to the ambiguities associated with the status of a concubine and the great variety of roles she played in a polygamous family (from a slave/maid or a minor wife to someone assuming the full power of a primary wife), she, as the subject of an elegiac narrative, often invited very diverse approaches from her mourning husband when he tried to reconstruct her life. A concubine's relatively low status seems to have given her polygamous husband the license to be more autobiographical about himself in her biography than in that of his primary wife. On the other hand, feeling less constrained when writing about a concubine, he could be much bolder, as well as more innovative, as a *daowang* writer. It is probably not a coincidence that one of the most innovative *daowang* works from the period is *Yingmei an yiyu* 影梅庵憶語, or *The Remembrances of the Convent of the Plum Shadow* (hereafter referred to as *Plum Shadow*) by the seventeenth-century writer Mao Xiang 冒襄 (1611–1693), a lengthy memoir on his deceased concubine, Dong Xiaowan. For the first time, a *daowang* work in prose explicitly advertised itself as a memoir or "words of remembrances" in its title. The emphasis is not so much on her typical "wifely virtues" or her contributions to the "public" interests of a patrilineal family but more on her unique companionship in her husband's various aesthetic pursuits, testifying to the different roles a concubine sometimes assumed in the life of a polygamous husband, not necessarily as a woman whom a man married for the purpose of progeny when his principal wife was deemed deficient in her procreative capacity, a justification usually presented as the most legitimate reason for concubinage. The chapter explores the many different ways concubines were mourned and remembered as well as how such memories were manipulated by their polygamous husbands for very different autobiographical agendas.

By the late imperial period, the development of *daowang* writings had reached such a stage that there was a markedly keener sense of competition among the literati for the honor of being a great "mourner." Chapter 7 examines this increasingly acute self-consciousness on the part of many *daowang* writers. Being perceived as a good *daowang* writer was now an important badge of one's cultural sophistication. At the same time, mourning and writing about one's late spouse were also becoming a cherished occasion for literati networking and social exchanges. A grieving husband was sometimes almost an "eager" mourner, taking special pride in showing off his elegiac talents. Now intimate memories of one's own late spouse were being turned into a cultural object for social circulation to enhance one's literary reputation and expand one's social circles. Some grieving husbands actively solicited condolence writings from their peers and friends and assembled these writings into a special volume, which would then be distributed among his friends to seek more endorsement writings in a seemingly perpetual process of social circulation, whereby the mourned female was sometimes replaced by the mourning male as the focus of celebration in this communal process of commemoration.

Although this study concentrates on a late imperial Chinese man's elegiac biographical writings on his spouse, the last chapter turns to look at his writings on his deceased married sister, in order to better examine how wifely qualities could be conceived of differently when the mourned was a mourner's close female relative rather than his spouse. I understand that it would be helpful if discussions of how mourners wrote about other close female relatives, such as mothers and daughters, could also be included here, but I have confined my discussion in this chapter to a married sister partly due to space constraints, but also because, like his relationship with his wife but unlike his relationships with his mother and daughters, a man's relationship with his married sister tended to be a lateral relationship, and thus a more equitable comparison. Furthermore, as a sibling, a brother was more likely to look at his sister's marriage from her perspective rather than her husband's since her husband—from the brother's perspective—was a member of another family.

Family tension here became a much easier topic to broach, and even dwell on, especially if he felt his sister was not treated fairly in her husband's family. It is here in the writings of a grieving brother that we encounter some of the harshest denunciations of the incompetence and even abusive behaviors on the part of a husband. A brother often found himself torn between his desire to present his married sister as someone he could still relate to as a member of his own family and the reality that she was now a wife and daughter-in-law in another family, drawing attention to the possible conflicts between the interests of the two families. Mourning a married sister, a brother, who was also married himself, was more inclined to rethink the obligations of a man/husband because of his own changed positionality from that of a husband to that of a brother.

Less vulnerable to the Confucian censure for being "selfish" or "indulgent," as in the case of writing about one's own wife, a man might feel less the need to underscore his sister's exemplariness in order to legitimate his writings about her life. This is probably why we have found in Qian Chengzhi's epitaph of his sister such a remarkable life story of a woman who, precisely because of her unremarkableness as a Confucian female exemplar, provides an interesting contrast to the image of a female chastity martyr constructed in the hagiography he wrote for his own late wife. It seems that mourning one's deceased sister gave a literati author a unique opportunity to produce a biography for an ordinary woman without the need to feel apologetic, helping push the process of secularization of memory to its new limits. In fact, Qian showed far more personal feelings in writing about his sister than in writing about his wife, in part because his epitaph of the former was more like a *personal* memoir, while his biographical sketch of the latter was a hagiographical project intended as a *public* tale of a female chastity exemplar. This epitaph throws new light on the very different roles a literati biographer could assume in reconstructing the lives of different women, even when all the women were his close kin.

One of the conclusions of this study is that during the late imperial period—when women were still supposed to be remembered for their Confucian virtues, as in the earlier periods—the particular characteristics that constituted virtues were becoming increasingly contested. For example, what could be celebrated as admirable wifely behaviors began to vary greatly, especially when surviving husbands were the ones doing the remembering. What was worth remembering about a deceased wife could still be her wifely obedience, a conventional female virtue, but, more often, it could also be her ability to provide sound advice to her husband on various matters, from domestic issues to those involving his career. Here her practical wisdom and her decisiveness could become one of the most cherished qualities, which were not necessarily consistent with the typical Confucian expectations of wifely obedience; on the other hand, even her personality flaws could now be part of her husband's cherished memories about her because she was now remembered as a lost companion rather than an exemplary woman. Consequently, the images of women presented in these elegiac works are often far more diverse and much more complicated than what we usually encounter in a typical work of Confucian female exemplar discourse.[17] In these intimate elegiac works, female exemplariness tends either to receive less emphasis or has become a more contested quality.

At the same time, from their writings on their late spouses and sisters, what could we learn about these literati authors' self-images as Confucian men in mourning? First of all, he could be a man emotionally much more complex than he would appear to be on other occasions: in grief, he might be less inclined to present himself as a straight-faced Confucian; his views of women could be very different in that he was now much more ready to appreciate a wife's plight, and thus be more tolerant or even more understanding of her "mistakes" or "flaws." A mourning husband was often a man of conflicting emotions: he could be torn between his attachment to his late wife and his filial obligations toward his own parents,[18] a topic very few men at that time would openly broach on other occasions. Sometimes in showing sympathy for his late wife for the unfair treatment she received in the family, a grieving husband might even present himself as a victim of this same unfair treatment, identifying himself with his wife and revealing aspects of his gender identity otherwise rarely visible, as Shen Fu has done in his *Six Records*. Here *daowang* becomes an act of double grieving: grieving for the loss of his wife and over his own failures as a man and husband.

Intimate memory sometimes helped to considerably complicate the image of an otherwise quite conservative Confucian, as we are to see in the case of the early Qing neo-Confucian essayist, Fang Bao 方苞 (1668–1749). Fang was invariably an orthodox Confucian patriarch when he was writing his "household instructions" (*jiaxun* 家訓) for the members of the younger generation, and a strict Confucian moralist when advising others on how to manage a gentry household. Here female members of the family were more likely to be viewed with suspicion, a source of family disharmony. However, his image changed from that of a straight-faced Confucian patriarch to that of a much more sympathetic husband or brother when he was mourning his wife and his sisters, giving us a rare glimpse into a late imperial man's complex emotional world. A late imperial Chinese literatus, under different circumstances, at different stages in his life and assuming different social roles, could be a man capable of very different views on women. Such inconsistencies are one of the topics this study seeks to explore.

For some literati husbands, mourning and grieving for a deceased spouse became much more than a private act of personal remembrance. It became an important part of a cultured man's carefully choreographed effort of self-fashioning. It was turned into a social act of literati networking. Intimate memory of one's deceased spouse could become a cultural object of social circulation for the purpose of literati self-aggrandizement—a man good at remembering and writing about his deceased spouse was now being celebrated as befitting the refined image of a Confucian gentleman of cultural sensibility.

Remembering and writing about someone who was at once so close, such as one's own spouse, is inevitably also an act of self-expression and self-representation.[19] It seems that by the seventeenth century, this became a much more pronounced feature of literati *daowang* writings in general, culminating, a century later, in Shen Fu's *Six Records*, in which the mourning of a female "other" and the mourner's attempt to vindicate his own male "self" become acts virtually inseparable. Memory, especially intimate memory, is often self-reflexive as well as revisionist in that it could be carefully manipulated for the sake of vindicating and reconstructing the mourner's past and present "selves," highlighting the special dynamic between the biographical and the autobiographical.

The epilogue is a brief discussion of how the early nineteenth-century poetess and woman scholar Wang Duan 汪端 (1773–1839) inscribed her elegiac memory, and how she had to negotiate between the biographical and the autobiographical under the more intense pressure for discretion in a female elegiac author. The epilogue is meant to offer some preliminary thoughts on the matter of how our understanding of gender implications of intimate memory can become even more nuanced when elegiac works by men are examined in careful juxtaposition and comparison with those by women authors from the same period.

In this study of quite limited scope, there are many other kinds of interesting *daowang* works not included in discussion: for example, a substantial discussion of how other important female relatives such as mothers and daughters were mourned or remembered by the literati could go a long way to enhance our understanding of the complicated role of male mediation in the representation of women.[20] However, such discussions must be based on further research, and thus must wait. I hope that this preliminary study leads to more substantial studies that will further enhance our appreciation of the complex roles played by the male literati in the construction of various models of womanhood, as well as how such construction complicated their own self-images as educated males in late imperial China.

CHAPTER 1

THE SECULARIZATION OF MEMORY

Remembering the deceased is an integral part of the mourning process. In late imperial China, such an act of remembrance was often performed through writing thanks in part to the unwavering faith in the power of a written text, either on paper or carved on stone, to perpetuate memory in defiance of time and death. A son, if from a respected or well-connected family, was expected to seek out someone of high social standing to write an epitaph for his deceased father, often based on the materials he himself provided, as a demonstration of his Confucian filial piety.

However, writing about the life of a deceased woman was an undertaking much more problematic. A woman usually required more justification and more scrutiny than a man in order to be deemed worthy of the honor of an epitaph or a biography, since Confucian biographical standards emphasized the public exemplariness of a person, whereas a woman was supposed to belong to the realm of the inner and the private. The seventeenth-century writer and scholar-official, Wang Wan 汪琬 (1624–1690) echoed this view when he wrote:

> Ancient people wrote biographical sketches (*xingzhuang* 行狀; more literally, accounts of deeds) not for the purpose of providing materials for the writing of epitaphs (*zhiming* 誌銘) but for the purpose of submitting them to the Grand Scribe (*taishi* 太史) and the Chamberlain for Ceremonials (*taichang* 太常). People submitted them to the Grand Scribe so that he could come up with biographies and to the Chamberlain for Ceremonials so that posthumous titles could be bestowed. Although people have stopped this practice, we should follow the intention of the ancients. Women are not supposed to have biographies and they are not given posthumous titles. Then why should people write biographical sketches for them? A deceased woman merits a separate epitaph only in the following situations: she is not buried together with

her husband, and she performed extraordinary deeds of chastity martyrdom; she is buried while her husband is still alive or her husband has died long before she does and his burial takes place a long time ago thus an account of her life cannot be appended to her husband's epitaph.... This is why I have refused to write biographical sketches for women. I want to follow the rules of the ancients.[1]

Wang Wan declared that he refused to write any biographical sketches for women because he subscribed to the orthodox view that people should not write biographies for women and that they should write brief epitaphs for them only in exceptional situations, although he did not object to the short account of a woman's life being appended to the epitaph of her husband.

This was a view seemingly shared by a significant group of educated men of the time, including Wang Wan's more famous contemporary, the neo-Confucian savant, Huang Zongxi 黃宗羲 (1610–1695). After his wife passed away, when his son presented him with a copy of her biographical sketch, Huang Zongxi insisted that it was not necessary, because, he was convinced, according to the practices of the ancients, no biographical sketch should be written for a woman.[2]

Such apprehension about women as appropriate biographical or epitaphic subjects can also be found in the early Qing essayist, Fang Bao. Three years after writing an epitaph for a friend's deceased father, Fang Bao was asked again by that same friend to write another one for his recently deceased mother. This time, however, Fang Bao was inclined to turn down the request. Part of the reason for his reluctance was his belief that the mother's life had been relatively easy, so her virtues were not extraordinary enough. Different from the case of a man, a woman, Fang Bao appeared to insist, needed to have demonstrated extraordinary virtues in a difficult life to be considered worthy of an epitaph upon her death.[3]

What is even more significant for the purpose of our discussion here, however, is not so much Fang Bao's initial reservations as the fact that, despite his reluctance, he eventually did agree to write the epitaph for his friend's deceased mother, as requested. In fact, this became a pattern for him and many others: a literatus would repeatedly comply with such requests from others even though he might believe that he should not.[4] The same is true of Huang Zongxi. Despite his adamant insistence that his son should not write a biographical sketch for his mother, Huang Zongxi wrote a quite long one for his own mother.[5] Furthermore, Huang wrote a dozen elegiac pieces for other women, many of which are in the form of epitaph and biographies. Several of them do not have exemplar tagging words, such as *jie* 節 (chastity) or *lie* 烈 (martyrdom), in their titles, suggesting that these female biographical subjects did not necessarily demonstrate extraordinary virtues in their lives.

Cases like these are a testament to the enormous and ever-increasing demand for memorial writings to honor one's female relatives during the late imperial period. Now many, though some of them with reluctance, were simply accepting the reality that women, even when they were not considered extraordinarily virtuous, were being immortalized in written texts, just as it had been the case with men for a much longer period of time, in spite of the traditional Confucian insistence on exemplariness as the sole legitimate justification for the privilege of an epitaph or a biography and the even closer Confucian scrutiny of women as biographical and epitaphic subjects.[6]

This development was part of a wider secularization trend associated with memorial writings in general that began to pick up momentum around the early sixteenth century when more and more seemingly unworthy men and women, sometimes from lower social strata, were becoming epitaphic or biographical subjects. The neo-Confucian essayist and scholar-official, Tang Shunzhi 唐順之 (1507–1560), complained not without bitterness:

> People even as low as those in the business of butchering pigs and peddling wine, so long as they could afford a bowl of rice, would want epitaphs written in their honor. From prominent officials to those who have passed provincial examinations, everyone would have a collection of his writings published after his death. This has become as necessary as a person needs to have food when alive and to be buried in a coffin after death. This never happened in the period of the Three Epochs and [was] still absolutely rare even before the Han and Tang dynasties. Fortunately, most of these epitaphs and collected works usually go to oblivion pretty soon. Even though many books published in the past are no longer extant, those that do survive are still too numerous. Had all published books been kept, there would not be enough space to shelve them even if the earth could be used as a giant bookshelf.[7]

It is interesting to note that Tang Shunzhi deplored these two phenomena in tandem: first, the popularity of epitaphs, and second the increasingly common phenomenon of having one's collected writings published, as these two were closely related, in that biographical writings in printed form such as epitaphs were able to reach a much larger audience. This was largely because they were often circulated as part of the collected writings (*wenji*) by their authors; the publication of such collected writings was greatly facilitated by the rapid expansion of private printing during the Ming.[8]

Now the honor of being immortalized in memorial writings, traditionally reserved for the few, was becoming increasingly available to a significantly larger segment of the society, and women were an important part of that segment.[9] Some women were even beginning to explicitly insist that they absolutely deserved such an honor, requesting in advance that epitaphs be written by skillful writers before they died. The dying wife of an imperial university student pleaded to her husband in this way: "I have devoted my whole life to your family. Don't spend too much for my funeral. However, I would be quite content if you could find a good writer to compose an epitaph to be carved on a piece of stone to be placed in my grave."[10] Before her death, the sister of Wang Shizhen 王世貞 (1529–1590), one of the best-known sixteenth-century literary figures, requested him to write an epitaph for her, partly because of her brother's literary fame (more on Wang's epitaph on this sister in chapter 8).[11]

By the seventeenth century, it was also becoming increasingly common for a mourning husband to commission a biography, in addition to an epitaph, for his deceased wife. The well-known early Qing poet and scholar-official Wang Shizhen 王士禛 (1634–1711) had two biographies written for his deceased wife by two of his friends, Zhu Yizun 朱彝尊 (1629–1708) and Wang Maolin 汪懋麟 (1640–1688).[12] His contemporary, the scholar-official Fang Xiangying 方象瑛 (1632–1685) also asked his friend, You Tong, to write a biography for his late wife.[13] At the same time, some grieving husbands even began to author biographies themselves for their deceased wives, as in the case of the poet and scholar Ye Shaoyuan 葉紹袁 (1589–1646) and the neo-Confucian thinker, Chen Que 陳確 (1604–1677).[14] The early eighteenth-century poet Chen Zi 陳梓 (1683–1759) was so eager to produce a biography for his wife that he decided to write it while she was still alive. He felt particularly proud of himself for writing a biography for a living woman.[15] This was significant because, while it was already somewhat common by that time for an epitaph to be written for a deceased woman, a biography was much less common, and a biography for a living woman written by her husband was rare indeed. Unlike an epitaph, which fulfilled the practical function of being a component of the grave, a biography usually required extra justification in terms of the worthiness of its subject (as implicitly suggested by Wang Wan, discussed above).[16]

This secularization process was significant not only as a phenomenon of plebeianization, as more commoners, especially women, were beginning to enjoy the honor of being biographical or epitaphic subjects, it also started to reshape the way in which a woman was remembered and represented in a memorial text, as her image became less "saint-like" and less dictated by the Confucian biographical rhetoric of the exemplary, with more attention being shifted to the mundane details in her life.

Whereas virtue continued to be an important quality touted in such writings on a woman, what specifically constituted female virtues worthy of the honor of an epitaph or biography was now being deliberately redefined with much more flexibility. The scholar-official Sun Cheng'en 孫承恩 (1485–1565), for example, defended the epitaphs he wrote for many women by contending that a woman was entitled to the honor of an epitaph even if her virtues were not extraordinary and even if she had performed only ordinary deeds (*yongxing* 庸行), believing that average women of mundane virtues nevertheless deserved epitaphs.[17] In an epitaph for the wife of one of his close friends, the influential poet Li Panlong 李攀龍 (1514–1570) offered a spirited defense of her perceived "shrewishness" (*han* 悍) and strong personality as necessary "virtues" of a wife who had to manage the household and advise her husband in various difficult and challenging situations.[18] What had traditionally been viewed as personality flaws in a woman could now be defended even as signs of female virtues

Moreover, virtue was no longer the sole factor acknowledged to have shaped one's memories of a deceased woman. Many other factors, such as her intellectual capability, were also being taken into consideration. The writer and poet Xie Zhaozhe 謝肇淛 (1567–1624) insisted that it was unfair for contemporary historians to apply a different standard when it came to the writing of a woman's biography. According to him, besides moral exemplariness, other factors, such as talent and literary skills, should be taken into consideration when deciding whether a woman merited a biography, just as had always been the case with men's biographies.[19] Circumventing the Confucian biographical imperative on moral exemplariness, many male authors resorted to expanding the notion of "wifely virtue" to include qualities usually not associated with a model Confucian wife, such as intellectual wisdom, literary talent, and even physical beauty. Ye Shaoyuan offered an even bolder and more elaborate theory about the need to take into consideration these other factors in defining womanhood when he mourned and wrote about his deceased wife and daughters (see chapter 2).[20]

As part of a general secularizing trend in biographical and memorial writings, this new enthusiasm for biographies and epitaphs on women was also an important factor contributing to the acceleration of this trend. As some of the authors at that time acknowledged, unlike writing about men, who were more likely to have public careers, when writing about women, biographers and epitaph writers usually had to concentrate on the women's private lives, including seemingly insignificant details of daily life. Expressing his admiration for the famous essayist Gui Youguang's 歸有光 (1507–1571) special ability to convey deep feelings in his writings on women by focusing on the small details in their lives, Huang Zongxi observed that when writing an epitaph for a man, the focus was usually on "important events" (*dashi* 大事), whereas, in the case of a woman, the focus had to be on the "small and trivial things" (*suoxi* 瑣細) that typically characterized her life.[21] This different focus came to be a key gendered feature of women's biographies and epitaphs, whereas Gui Youguang had long been celebrated as an influential master of prose for his special attention to the "small and trivial things" in women's lives.[22]

The shift of focus onto the small and trivial helped secularize the biography of the deceased by directing people's attention to the mundane in the private life typical of an ordinary woman rather than the grand deeds in the public life of a statesman, a standard feature of the biographies of men in official histories. To enhance their narrative authority and justify their decision to author such writings themselves, rather than commissioning someone else to do it, many of these male writers were eager to tout their unique knowledge and personal memories of their deceased female relatives. The overall effect of this new interest in the "small and trivial things" in women's private lives is that the image of a woman presented in these memorial writings started to become more secular as well as more individualized.

While few late imperial biographers and epitaph writers would directly challenge the Confucian biographical imperative on exemplariness, a bereaved husband, for example, might be more interested in those "small and trivial things" because his personal grief and guilt as a survivor often compelled him to mourn and remember his late wife from a different perspective. What endeared his late wife to him was more likely to be the unique and personal attachment between them as husband and wife rather than her supposed exemplariness as a Confucian saint. Some bereaved husbands even suggested that their late wives need not be moral exemplars for them to be fondly remembered. As we have mentioned, Xie Zhaozhe was one of those who pointed out that virtue should not be the sole factor in deciding whether a woman was worthy of a biography. There he was commenting on the biographical practices in histories. He was even more adamant on this point when it came to private memorial writings. In the epitaph he wrote for his own late wife, Xie went out of his way to insist that she had no great virtue for him to eulogize since she was just an ordinary, albeit good, wife.[23] Another scholar-official,

Li Chengzhong 李澄中 (1629–1700), declared in his epitaph for his deceased wife that he was quite content with their married life even though she had not performed deeds of great virtue typical of those famous model wives celebrated in history.[24] Li's contemporary, the scholar Mao Jike 毛際可 (1633–1708), insisted on the need to remember his late mother as she actually was, rather than as a Confucian saint: "I did not dare to attribute the virtues of those exemplary ladies from the ancient times [to my mother] to glorify her life lest [the image of] of my mother presented here would become that of the mother of someone else rather than truly that of mine."[25] Increasingly, people were now accepting and explicitly acknowledging the obvious but somewhat uncomfortable fact that they mourned and wrote about these women simply because they were their close relatives and not because they had been perfect role models when they were alive.

In several of the epitaphs he composed for the female relatives of his friends, and apparently sensitive to the possible complaint about their being full of hackneyed compliments, Sun Cheng'en repeatedly apologized for praising his female subjects with clichés and acknowledged that virtuous women tended to be all similar.[26] However, Sun did not feel at all the same need to apologize when he wrote epitaphs for his own wife and concubine. He was able to present them as women quite different from the stereotypic wives portrayed in his commissioned epitaphs: his own wife was a perceptive woman of great decisiveness, whose advice he very much depended on; his concubine, though subservient, as expected of a concubine, was not a woman known for making wise decisions when it came to raising a child: she doted on her adopted son and eventually died broken hearted as the son grew up to be a good-for-nothing. Failure to properly raise a child was a topic few writers would broach in a commissioned epitaph for a woman from another family. Sun characterized his own concubine as an ordinary woman "with neither great virtue nor serious flaws" (*wushan yi wujiu* 無善亦無咎).[27] Not pretending that he needed to find any other justification, Sun wrote this epitaph simply because this very ordinary woman had been his concubine. I will discuss this epitaph further in chapter 6.

Thanks to their close and intimate relationships with the women they wrote about, these grieving husbands did not feel the need to shy away from mentioning in their memorial writings the personality flaws of the mourned. In the prose elegy he wrote in memory of his deceased wife, Fang Bao did not hesitate to characterize her as "stubborn" (*muqiang* 木強) and "simple-minded" (*gang* 戇).[28] This tendency to admit the "flaws" of one's late spouse when constructing her life-narrative became even stronger by the early nineteenth century: the poet Chen Wenshu 陳文述 (1771–1843), who was known for his encouragement of women's participation in literary activities, wrote a very long biography for his late wife, which was overall quite complimentary but included a long explanation of her becoming an alcoholic, which forced her to ask one of his concubines to take over the management of the household (see chapter 4).[29] By now, ordinary, imperfect women were being mourned and remembered by their husbands just as *ordinary* women despite, or precisely because of, the close relationships and intimate memories shared between the mourner and the mourned.

In addition, as grieving husbands, these authors did not have to worry about the possible accusation of being a detractor in writing about the deceased even if they divulged information on their late wives' shortcomings, something a typical commissioned epitaph writer would be reluctant to do given that the epitaphic tradition dictated that he should only praise the deceased.[30] In his biographical sketch of his late wife, Fang Xiangying, for example, made a special effort to remind his readers that he did not try to embellish her image, since he discussed the flaws in her personality, such as her quick temper and intolerance of others' mistakes, even though the biographical sketch was overall very positive, as well as quite emotional.[31] Significantly, these references to her personality flaws were exactly what her commissioned biographer, You Tong, chose to omit in his biography, which was written at Fang's request and based on the sketch written by Fang himself.[32] By the same token, Chen Wenshu was probably excused for detailing the alcoholism of the woman in his biography precisely because he was both her biographer and her grieving husband.

There appeared to be something quite secularizing about intimate memory itself. When intimate memory was the immediate source a biographer relied on, and especially when the biographer was also the grieving spouse, his biography of the deceased was more likely to become a project of personal remembrance. For a husband/biographer, what was important was to keep alive *his own* memory of a woman with whom he had shared an intimate life together rather than telling a morally edifying story befitting a Confucian saint. Mourning and writing about a woman who was once so close to himself, a mourner/author tended to remember better the specific and the concrete— what the woman was like as an individual—and was much less likely to be constrained by the abstract notion of what an exemplary Confucian lady was supposed to be.

In understanding this historical phenomenon of the secularization of memory (*jiyi de shisuhua* 記憶的世俗化) in late imperial China, we have to be keenly aware of the implications of the secularizing potential inherent in intimate memory. In moments of mourning and grieving, intimate memory tends to insist on remembering loved ones in its own personal way, and seems capable of special resistance to the conforming power of the Confucian exemplar rhetoric. Writing about his female relative, a male literatus, such as Fang Xiangying, had to rely on his personal memories, while in writing about someone whom he hardly knew, as in the case of You Tong composing a biography commissioned by Fang, the biographer's personal memory played almost no role. And yet, as already briefly mentioned in the Introduction and to be explored in more detail in chapter 2, You Tong himself was actually a remarkably revealing and emotional biographer when his own late wife became his biographical subject. When intimate memory entered the mix, it often turned a biography, typically burdened by Confucian conventions and expectations, into a private memoir focusing on shared personal experiences. Further, bereavement appeared capable of dramatically enhancing the unique capacity of intimate memory to personalize the biographies written for loved ones in sometimes heart-wrenching ways.

THE PERILS OF INTIMATE MEMORY

Precisely because of its special capacity to push the limits of Confucian decorum and challenge the boundaries of the long-established biographical conventions, intimate memory provoked strong suspicions from the more conservative. Remembering and writing about one's own wife or the act of *daowang* presented some unique challenges for a grieving husband in late imperial China.

Unlike the case of mourning the deaths of one's other female kin, such as that of a mother, which could always be justified in terms of the Confucian notion of filial piety, a mourning husband remained particularly vulnerable to the criticism that he might have been excessive in grieving over the death of his wife. This was largely due to the general suspicions toward a wife as a result of her problematic status within the structure of a Confucian family, which tended to emphasize patrilineal interests. As an "outsider" married into her husband's family, a wife was often considered a potentially subversive element, possibly causing the disharmony within the family by straining the relationships between her husband and his parents or between him and his male siblings. In household instructions, or *jiaxun*, popular among gentry families in late imperial China were many prescriptions specially designed to prevent, or contain, potential wifely subversiveness, demanding that a husband should always hold the interests of his parents and the large patrilineal family or the "public" (*gong* 公) above the interests of the small family unit he shared with his wife, or their selfish interests (*si* 私).³³ In fact, excessive intimacy (*ni* 暱) and selfishness (*si* 私) were the two "vices" most often associated with husband–wife relationships in Confucian ethical thinking, as Fang Bao argues:

> When the ancient sages formulated the rules of ritual proprieties of husband–wife relationship, the emphasis was on how the couple served [the husband's] parents rather than their selfish concerns with themselves (*ji zhi si* 己之私). This is because, when the wife was obedient, the family became harmonious and orderly. For many people, there was nothing more likely to become trivial and excessively intimate in attachment (*qingni* 情暱) than husband–wife relationship; and yet, the song of wedding ceremony reads: "But [I longed] for one of such virtuous fame to come and be with me" (*deyin laikuo* 德音來括) and "With her admirable virtue, is [*sic*] come to instruct me" (*lingde laijiao* 令德來教), while the last stanza sings: "The high hill is looked up to; the great road is easy to be traveled on" (*gaoshan yangzhi, jingxing xingzhi* 高山仰止, 景行行止.³⁴ However, this is normally what gentlemen expect of their virtuous teachers and friends but not something necessarily easy to fulfill in real life. Then how could one have such high expectations of a bride? Was the song writer being too dogmatic? This is apparently not the case. This is because, if one fails to have such high expectations of a bride, the principle of husband–wife relationship, which is at the core all human relationships, cannot be vindicated.³⁵

Fang Bao is here arguing that precisely because husband–wife relationships could easily go wrong, the standard by which a bride is being judged must be set high from the very beginning of the marriage.

In a conduct book that Ming scholar-official and writer Lü Kun 呂坤 (1536–1618) compiled specially for women, one passage reads:

> There are five ways a wife should serve her husband: in the morning, after completing her toilet, she greets her husband, following the distinctions between a lord and his subject (*junchen zhi yan* 君臣之嚴); she helps her husband wash and prepares food, showing him respect just like a son would toward his father (*fuzhi zhi jing* 父子之敬); Leaving and coming back, she reports to her husband, just like what is supposed to happen between two brothers (*xiongdi zhi dao* 兄弟之道); she points out his mistakes and encourages him

to be virtuous as if they are two friends (*pengyou zhi yi* 朋友之義); when it comes to the intimacy in bed, only then could one talk about the relationship between husband and wife (*fufu zhi ji* 夫婦之際).

This passage is followed by Lü Kun's own comment:

> Among the five principles on husband–wife relation, four are about living in [an] orderly way (*yanju* 嚴居), while only one is on conjugal harmony (*heju* 和居). Unfortunately, people of recent times only know to talk about conjugal harmony for the sake of harmony.³⁶

For some of Lü Kun's contemporaries, an age of moral decline and chaos (*moshi* 末世) was actually characterized by people's prioritizing of the husband–wife relationship at the expense of those between father and son and between brothers. They considered the former a serious threat to the latter two relations, the perceived backbone of an orderly Confucian society.³⁷

Comparing a husband–wife relationship to that between a lord and his subject, or that between a father and son, and likening a family to the imperial court might appear rather far-fetched to people today. However, all these analogies are meant to underscore one thing—the importance of the hierarchical order in a family. What has received constant emphasis in these works of prescriptive literature about husband–wife relationships is the need to be "respectful" (*jing* 敬) and the priority of the hierarchical ordering of a patrilineal family rather than emotional attachment and intimacy between a couple, who constituted only a small unit within a large and extended family. Intimacy is something that needs to be carefully contained. This is partly why *daowang* could become an awkward occasion for a bereaved husband: his grieving and demonstration of attachment to his deceased wife were something that necessitated constant apology, as seen in the following observation made by the early nineteenth-century essayist, Guan Tong 管同 (1785–1831):

> If a husband loves his wife, then there might be too much intimacy of the selfish kind (*sini* 私暱) but not enough strict proprieties; on the other hand, if he does not, then there will be little attachment between them with this important human relationship in jeopardy. Then what is the appropriate approach? One would say that a real Confucian gentleman always cherishes the virtue in other people. If she is not virtuous, he would not be on intimate terms with her for some selfish reason merely because she happens to be his wife; if she is indeed virtuous, he would not refrain from being close to her in order to

avoid suspicions just because she happens to be his wife. It has everything to do with [the moral quality of] that person rather than the predilections of one's heart. If she is indeed virtuous the husband would naturally love her when she is alive and miss her when she is dead. If the husband misses her, then he would try to keep her image and voice alive in his memory by means of writing. Then portraits and works of *daowang* are produced in order to give expression to the feelings of grief and transmit the life of the deceased [to the posterity]. This is all due to genuine human emotions (*renqing* 人情). If such emotions are in accordance with what is appropriate, then a gentleman would not find them reproachable.[38]

Guan Tong's tortuous rhetoric is telling of the ambivalent status of *daowang* writing in the eye of a straight-faced Confucian. The concern that a man might be perceived to be too attached to his wife was often on one's mind to inhibit public expression of deep conjugal feelings. Apology for *daowang* was often made by appealing to the supposed virtue of the deceased wife. Pay attention to the particular rhetoric of Guan Tong: the bereaved husband is justified in grieving for his deceased wife because of the latter's virtue rather than the fact that she was his wife and yet, at the same time, given the predominance of the view that public show of husband–wife love was likely to be frowned upon, Guan is also insisting that a husband should not be concerned with the possible perception of being "selfish" and "indulgent" when he expressed his love for his wife if the latter was indeed virtuous.

Guan Tong's apologetic *daowang* rhetoric must have sounded quite familiar, reminding people of the much better known and less elaborate but, probably, bolder, statement by Li Mengyang much earlier. In defending his friend's seemingly excessive grief in his *daowang* poems after the death of his wife, Li remarked:

> If [he finds his wife] virtuous, then [the husband's] feelings [toward her] would be excessively deep; when excessively deep, they are bound to exceed the limits of ritual propriety; when exceeding the limits of the ritual propriety, his songs are bound to be full of sorrows. This is why it is said that the reason that Zhao reacted to the death of Wen this way was not only because she was his wife (*fei du qi ye* 非獨妻也) but also because he admired her virtue.[39]

On the surface, like Guan Tong, Li Mengyang sought justification for the act of *daowang* in the supposed virtue of the deceased wife, although he was specifically defending his friend's perceived excessiveness—that is, one would feel sad over the death of one's wife, but his sadness would become very deep or even appear excessive if his wife was virtuous. However, at the same time, Li Mengyang was also suggesting, almost by default (*fei du qi ye*; literally: "not only because she was his wife"), that grief, if not deep grief, was at least justifiable because the deceased was the mourner's wife. By allowing both factors to serve as justifications for his friend's apparently extraordinary grief—namely, that the deceased was his wife and, furthermore, she had been exemplary—Li Mengyang was acknowledging, albeit indirectly, that a man's grieving for his deceased wife could still be justified even when the factor of virtue was taken out of the equation. The insistence that a man's grieving was justifiable simply because the deceased had been his wife may not be that remarkable at first glance. What is indeed remarkable, however, is the inference one could draw from Li Mengyang's implicit suggestion that grieving and expressions of such grief over one's late wife did not need her perceived exemplariness as justification. Quite a few grieving husbands of later times made just such claims in mourning their late wives, as I have discussed earlier. Even when ostensibly emphasizing that one's grief over the death of his wife was legitimated by her exemplariness, Li left open the possibilities that besides virtue, other factors, such as *qing* (feelings) might also serve as justifications for *daowang*.

Indeed, *daowang* was an undertaking often full of contradictions for a mourning husband: overwhelmed by his loss and guilt, a mourning husband might feel less inhibited in revealing more about his wife as an individual with whom he had shared an intimate relationship for so many years, therefore, more possibilities of transcending the normative Confucian biographical conventions, and yet, at the same time, the pressure to present her as a moral exemplar, for at least some grieving husbands, may also become more intense precisely because of the special relationship between the mourned and the mourner as well as the perceived moral vulnerability on the part of the latter as a male Confucian mourner. In fact, it is the tension between this need to emphasize the virtue of the deceased and those "other factors" implied in Li Mengyang's apology for *daowang* that constituted the most interesting dynamics of many late imperial *daowang* writings. It is worth notice that Li Mengyang, who played such an important role in the secularization process of memory, as I further demonstrate later, was also one of the early figures in the rise of the cult of *qing* (feelings, emotions), which would reach its apex during the seventeenth century.[40]

The history of *daowang* writings in the late imperial period was also a history of how, in the process of mourning and commemorating, intimate memory found its ways to assert itself despite various Confucian biographical inhibitions. An interesting issue this study seeks to address is how, once presented with an opportunity, intimate memory on the part of a grieving husband was able, especially in the process of mourning, to overcome the strong Confucian suspicion toward conjugal intimacy, and to shed light on those aspects of the late imperial husband–wife relationship that thus far has remained largely invisible to us.

THE CHANGING FORMS OF INTIMATE MEMORY

In trying to come to terms with Confucian anxiety over conjugal intimacy and especially its public display, a grieving husband had to try hard to take advantage of, and sometimes to circumvent the limiting conventions of the established genres of memorial writings. Traditionally, for literati, expressions of *daowang* sentiments largely took the form of poetry, where celebration of conjugal feelings, due in part to its poetic brevity and euphemism, was less vulnerable to Confucian censorship. However, beginning from around the sixteenth century, while large volumes of *daowang* poetry continued to be written,[41] more writers were also turning to various genres in prose to mourn their deceased spouses.

In 1566, the scholar-official and dramatist Li Kaixian 李開先 (1502–1568) published a small collection titled *Daonei tongqing ji* 悼內同情集 (*A Collection of Elegiac Essays on Their Deceased Wives by Those of the Same Sentiments*).[42] The publication of this collection marked an important moment in the development of *daowang* literature in late imperial China: probably a first of its kind, *Daonei tongqing ji* signaled that mourning one's wife in the form of elegiac prose, just like *daowang* poetry, was becoming a common cultural practice shared and cherished among the literati. Moreover, like *daowang* poetry, memorial texts in prose had by now become a cultural artifact literati frequently exchanged and circulated among themselves.

In his preface to the collection, Li Kaixian explained that the rationale for the collection was that the six authors (including Li Kaixian himself) anthologized here shared the same sorrows over the losses of their deceased wives and that most of these authors were close friends with each other. Among the six, some lost their respective wives only a few years apart, and they thus tended to be more empathic with each other: Li Kaixian lost his wife in 1547; his friend and former superior Wang Shenzhong 王慎中 (1509–1559) lost his only three months later; his close friend and *tongnian* 同年 (fellow graduate, who passed the metropolitan examination during the same year), Tang Shunzhi, lost his the following year.

However, the inclusion of Li Mengyang's epitaph was somewhat unusual since he was neither Li Kaixian's personal friend nor someone who had lost his wife recently. Unlike the other five grieving husbands, Li Mengyang belonged to an older generation. Li Mengyang's wife died in 1516, and his epitaph must have been written long before the other authors attempted theirs. Li Kaixian probably never met Li Mengyang in person, although he had always admired him.[43] Consequently, the inclusion of Li Mengyang's writing in the collection underscored the special importance attached to his epitaph: it was included for its exemplary nature. In fact, Li Mengyang's epitaph must have become quite famous by the time Li Kaixian was compiling the anthology, as many of Li Kaixian's contemporaries were already quoting his well-known line—"It took my wife's death for me to really appreciate her"—in their own elegiac writings.[44]

The fame of Li Mengyang's epitaph of his wife is built mainly on the following paragraph containing that remark:

> I said in tears to someone, "It took the death of my wife for me to really appreciate her." That person asked how it could be so. I replied: "In the past when I was studying and serving as an official, I did not pay attention to household matters. Now nothing gets done if I don't pay attention; guests used to come when invited because the food was good; now they don't come any more. Even if they do, the food is not that good. In the past, I did not worry about where things were. Now they are scattered everywhere and are seldom put away and often broken. In the past we never had to worry about running out of vinegar, sauce, salt and beans but now it is no longer the case; chickens, ducks, sheep and pigs used to be fed at regular times but not any more. They have become quite thin; when my wife was alive, one could not hear any bantering inside the house even when the door was not closed during the night. Now one could hear noisy bantering from outside even when the door is closed; in the past I had little clue what dirty clothes look like; now they won't get washed if I don't ask; In doing needlework my wife never asked for help from others nor did she ever imitate those superfluous styles, and yet she could serve as a teacher, but now no one could serve as a teacher any more and all the needlework has to be sent out to be done; In the past, whenever I was bothered by something whether it was related to matters present or ancient, I could always confide in my wife what I could not tell my friends. Now [that she is gone] I have no one to turn to when I come home. That is why I have said that it took the death of my wife for me to really appreciate her."[45]

Li Mengyang's focus on his wife in terms of the "small and trivial things" in daily life is emblematic of the secularization trend that was emerging in elegiac writings at that time. He belatedly wished that he had had a better appreciation of his wife while she was alive, underscoring the paradoxical nature of a painful but simple fact that one usually began to really appreciate the value of another only in his or her absence. It was her eternal "absence" (death) that compelled Li Mengyang to realize even more profoundly the meaning and value of her presence. Mourning, by nature, is a belated realization of the values of someone no longer alive. More interestingly, Li Mengyang's suggestion that his late wife, more than a dutiful wife good at household chores, was also his intellectual companion, must have struck accord among many of his peers, although very few of them had articulated it so succinctly. Wifely virtue was no longer equated simply with abstract Confucian values but, more poignantly, was being appreciated by a bereaved husband in a way only he could.

Many memorials in prose were becoming more emotional, even more lyrical; at the same time, *daowang* poetry was becoming more narrative oriented. Greater numbers of *daowang* poems were being written, often in large sets, in order to capture a more complete picture of the deceased, as many authors of *daowang* prose had been trying to do, an interesting phenomenon of generic convergence (more on this in chapter 5). A related new development of the late imperial *daowang* poetry was that many grieving husbands began to broach some less "poetic" topics in their *daowang* poems, which previous *daowang* poets had seldom touched upon. One of the most innovative seventeenth-century *daowang* poets, Wang Cihui 王次回 (1593–1642) was quite refreshing in composing poems to chronicle his wife's illness and to capture in detail her dying moments, as well as her dying image.[46] In one of his *daowang* poems, he even made reference to the strained relationship between himself and his late wife as a result of what he perceived to be her over-prudence as a Confucian lady,[47] a gesture quite rare among earlier *daowang* poets. Here a wife's Confucian prudence was presented as something problematic. Apparently, these seventeenth-century grieving literati husbands attempted to venture beyond the confines of the convention of *daowang* poetry long established by such early famous poets as Pan Yue 潘岳 (247–300) and Yuan Zhen 元稹 (779–831) in order to expand its generic capacity to deal with more mundane issues in life, while, at the same time, still trying to maintain its traditional claim as a special literary medium for the articulation of conjugal sentiments.[48]

These attempts of innovation in poetry, however, also pointed to its by-now highly conventionalized format and, more significantly, the limitations of poetry in terms of its capacity to situate intimate memory in a fuller social context of mundane daily life.[49] Attempts of similar nature on a more significant scale could also be found in memorial works in prose from that period. However, when it came to the writing of a *daowang* biography, prose as a medium offered much greater potential for innovation. Before discussing some examples of these innovative works that have successfully challenged the conventions of the existing genres, a few general remarks about several common memorial prose genres are in order.

An epitaph (*muzhiming*) was usually made of a prose essay (*zhi* 誌) followed by a brief verse (*ming* 銘) at the end. It was supposed to be carved on a stone slab to be placed in the tomb of the deceased. Besides serving as an account of the life of the deceased, it was expected to contain information on the family background (such as the ancestors as well as the descendants of the deceased). Consequently, more scripted as well as more formal, an epitaph was quite family oriented. An epitaph could also be circulated in the form of a written text on paper and was often included in the collected writings (*wenji*) of its author. In fact, a significant number of epitaphs were written without any intention for them to become a component of the grave of the deceased. For example, several decades after the death of his first wife, Qian Chengzhi sent a request to Huang Zongxi, asking him to write an epitaph for her. In his letter of request, Qian made it very clear what he really cared about was that Huang included the epitaph in the latter's collected writings once he finished writing it.[50] An epitaph's inclusion in the collected writings of a luminary such as Huang Zongxi, a collection that would receive a large readership when published, could most effectively ensure the immortalization of its subject. Often people were able to have access to an epitaph only because it was included in its author's collected writings, rather than as a result of its being excavated from a gravesite. This was especially true during the late imperial period, when private printing and publication flourished. While it was not uncommon for a man to write an epitaph for his deceased wife himself, more often such an epitaph was commissioned. The assumption that an epitaph was expected to be circulated as a text written or printed on paper should in turn have significant implications for its production. In such a case, an author was more likely to write a longer epitaph because the practical concern that it might be too long to be inscribed on a tablet was not an issue. He could thus cover in the epitaph more details on the life of the deceased. Further, the epitaph's assumed audience was much expanded because it was a written text on paper. Despite its scripted nature and other limitations, in the hands of some grieving literati, an epitaph could also be quite revealing about the life of the deceased female relative, as demonstrated in the case of Li Mengyang.

A biographical sketch (*xingzhuang*) was usually produced by the relatives, friends, or disciples of the deceased. Because it was expected to be the primary source upon which epitaph or biography would later be based, its assumed "unfinishedness" added much to its flexibility in terms of format as well as content. It became a favorite choice for many literati when they decided to author a memorial text to honor a deceased relative with the assumption that it would serve as a source of firsthand information. Consequently, to honor a deceased family member, a late imperial man was much more likely to write a biographical sketch than an epitaph or a biography. This is the main reason that one of the most represented genres of memorial writings in this study is biographical sketch, as its "unfinishedness" apparently did not prevent its author from considering it to be his important work and circulating it as such. Some of the most compelling *daowang* prose works were in the form of a biographical sketch.

Sacrificial litany (*jiwen* 祭文) was another popular form of elegiac writing a mourning husband turned to. This was meant to be read aloud during a sacrificial ceremony in honor of the deceased, and could be in either verse or prose. Rather than being biographical, a litany tended to focus on the author's own emotions, as it usually addressed the deceased directly. This is probably one of the reasons that sacrificial litany is the most representative genre of memorial writings in the famous *Wumeng tang ji* 午夢堂集 (*Collected Writings from the Hall of Mid-Day Dream*), a grand book of family mourning compiled by Ye Shaoyuan in memory of his late wife and several of his deceased children. The book contains many memorial writings by various members of the Ye family, as well as their friends and relatives, in honor of those family members who had passed away. With almost all the important genres of memorial writings being represented in the book, the epitaph, however, is conspicuously absent. Perhaps, the mourners' emotions were just too intense to be channeled into the format of an epitaph, which was characterized by its more scripted nature and other generic constraints. By the same token, as we will have opportunities to explore in more detail later, when mourning his late wife, sometimes a grieving husband was more likely to broach those subtle topics in a more private genre such as sacrificial litany rather than an epitaph, with the latter being much more formal and more public in nature.[51]

Despite various restricting conventions associated with these long-existing memorial genres, many late imperial grieving husbands were able to find ways to circumvent the limitations of these genres, as their memorial writings were becoming lengthier as well as less circumspect. One interesting result of the increasingly important role assumed by intimate memory as male literati began to write about the lives of women once very close to them is that the generic distinctions among epitaph, biographical sketch, and sacrificial litany began to collapse. That is, the usual generic differences among these memorial writings sometimes became less distinct under the burden of intimate memory. For example, Qian Chengzhi's epitaph of his diseased sister, as examined in chapter 8, reads more like a biographical sketch, or even a personal memoir, than a scripted epitaph, despite the fact that Qian, on the surface at least, was still trying to follow the conventions of *muzhiming*. This was part of the general secularization movement in memorial writings toward the personal and the intimate during the late imperial period that I have outlined above.

However, the need on the part of intimate memory to assert itself more forcefully and to invent new and more flexible forms of expression for itself was always there. In fact, whenever a grieving husband, in writing about his late wife, was able to move beyond the conventions of the existing genres of memorial writings, the result was almost always invariably refreshing. The neo-Confucian essayist Wang Shenzhong, for example, wrote a memorial essay on his late wife, which he titled "Cundao pian" 存悼篇 (remembering her forever; or more literally: on preserving my mourning sentiments). This quite innovative elegiac essay was included in the afore-mentioned collection *Daonei tongqing ji* compiled by Li Kaixian.

At the very beginning, Wang carefully justified his decision to write this unconventional memorial essay by telling the reader that he had already found someone to write the biographical sketch as well as the epitaph for his late wife, implying that, with these more formal memorial writings already commissioned, he was now in a position to write this rather unorthodox and informal elegiac essay to say what he really wanted to say about his late wife. By presenting his writing as something that could not be classified as belonging to any of the existing memorial genres, Wang freed himself from the constraining conventions associated with these genres and found himself in a much better position to present his late wife from a very personal angle:

> I once said that there were quite a few things about her ladyship that are difficult to understand: she got up early and went to bed late every day and always ready to work, and yet she was never busy doing anything; she was so frugal when it came to buying food that she could almost be considered stingy, and yet she knew little about how to manage household finances; she could be rather cold to others and seldom appeared endearing when she spoke, and yet she was never capable of being arrogant; she was quite nice and lenient towards the maids and yet she never tried to win herself the reputation of a

generous mistress; when she saw good needlework, she would try her best to copy and imitate without stopping, and yet she never decorated her own quilt [with such needlework]; when guests came, she was always anxious to have everything arranged properly as if she were receiving someone very important, and yet she hardly knew who that guest was. . . .

Wang chose to present his late wife as a person of contradictions, and yet it was these apparent contradictions that gave rise to the image of a rather unique woman, a far cry from the stereotype of a model Confucian wife. Throughout the essay, there is very little reference to the kind of female virtues expected of a woman in a typical epitaph or biography of a Confucian wife. Instead, the reader comes away with the impression that the author was writing about a friend, who happened to be his wife, as he characterized their marriage of almost two decades as a friendship of twenty-two years (*xiangyou ershi er nian* 相友二十二年). Presenting one's wife as a friend was an increasingly common phenomenon among the literati during the Ming, as we will see, and here Wang Shenzhong was quite representative.[52]

Wang Shenzhong's short memoir—refreshing and innovative, but still in the form of a short essay—was too insubstantial a piece to be an innovation on a scale that could demonstrate the full narrative potential of *daowang* prose, especially in terms of a sustained focus on the details of the daily life of a married couple. For an innovation of such significance, people had to wait until the mid–seventeenth century, when the writer Mao Xiang produced his famous *Plum Shadow*, a long memoir in honor of his concubine Dong Xiaowan, a former courtesan, detailing their courtship and their nine-year marriage. For the first time, memory was conspicuously advertised as its main narrative focus in the title of a memorial text. By explicitly referring to his writing as *yiyu* 憶語 (literally, words of remembrance) rather than a biographical sketch or an epitaph, Mao Xiang was declaring that he did not have to subject himself to the constraints of the Confucian biographical conventions associated with those traditional memorial genres. It is difficult to overestimate the significance of its much-expanded length as a result. Never before had so many pages been devoted to the minute details of the private life of a couple. The work was long enough (approximately twelve thousand characters) to be considered a stand-alone book; in fact, it has been circulated as such ever since it was written.[53] It was no accident that this innovative memoir had the life of a deceased concubine as its focus: writing about a concubine, whose status within a polygamous family was relatively low and often quite ambiguous, afforded Mao Xiang more freedom in choosing what he wanted to write and how to approach his female subject, with less concern about ritual appropriateness. Such freedom certainly made it easier for him to invent this brand new form, dubbed by some modern scholars as *yiyu ti* 憶語體 (the style of the words of remembrances),[54] dramatically enhancing the narrative capacity of *daowang* prose as well as its flexibility in terms of what intimate memory could reveal (more in chapter 6).

While works of memorial prose in traditional genres—biographical sketch, epitaph, and sacrificial litany—continued to be produced by grieving husbands in large numbers, Mao Xiang's memoir inspired quite a few to further explore the narrative potentials afforded by this new form of memorial prose. More than a century later, Chen Peizhi 陳裴之 (1794–1826), the son of Chen Wenshu, wrote his memoir on his deceased concubine, titled *Xiangwan lou yiyu* 香畹樓憶語 or *The Remembrances of the Tower of Fragrant Garden* (hereafter referred to as *Fragrant Garden*; discussed in detail in chapter 7). However, much more innovative was Chen's older contemporary, Shen Fu's *Six Records*. Although *Six Records* has often been read as Shen Fu's autobiography, a large part of it relates his memories of his late wife. No Chinese writer before Shen Fu had delved so deeply into the ups and downs of his own married life. It is several times longer than Mao Xiang's *Plum Shadow* and divided into six chapters (though only four chapters remain extant).[55] It is a stand-alone book by all counts as far as its length is concerned. As its general title and the chapter titles explicitly suggest, each of its extant four chapters is presented in the form of *ji* 記 (a record). Among all traditional prose genres, *ji* is probably the most flexible: it could be a record of an event (*jishi* 記事), a person (*jiren* 記人), an object (*jiwu* 記物), or a journey (*jiyou* 記遊). The Ming writer Xu Shizeng 徐師曾 (1517–1580) defined *ji* as "what one writes down in case he forgets" (*jizhe, suoyi bei buwang ye* 記者，所以備不忘也), highlighting its function as an aid to memory. Shen Fu's innovation is his use of *ji* to offer a detailed account of married life by concentrating on the subjective emotional experiences of his wife as well as those of his own, as underscored by the respective titles of the four chapters: "A Record of the Joys of the Bedchamber," "A Record of the Pleasures of Leisure," "A Record of the Sorrows of the Misfortune," and "A Record of the Delights of Roaming Afar." Very few writers prior to Shen Fu had used this flexible prose form of *ji* to focus on emotional experiences. Its special affinities with memory seems to have afforded him great leeway in deviating from all the conventions of existing memorial writings.

What is especially remarkable about this work is the degree to which Shen Fu was able to explore in unprecedented detail his loving relationship with his wife and the tensions and conflicts within the extended family (a topic often shunned in traditional memorial genres) and how he and especially his wife were unfairly treated by the other members of their family (including his own parents), while never showing hesitations in defending her. His lament over the tragic fate of his wife was carefully embedded in his musings over his own failures in life as a poor literatus (*pinshi* 貧士), placing in full social context and significantly complicating the otherwise familiar *daowang* theme made famous by the Tang poet Yuan Zhen almost a thousand years ago: "Sad was everything for a couple suffering from poverty" 貧賤夫妻百事哀.[56] In so doing, Shen Fu appears to have elevated to a new height the art of personal memoir and *daowang* near the end of the long secularization process of memorial writings in premodern China, just before the influence of the Western culture began to pour in. As an innovator, Shen Fu might have been ahead of his times. *Six Records* waited more than half a century—until the late nineteenth century, when Chinese culture was beginning to be seriously challenged by Western influences—to be discovered and published. Its belated discovery and publication might suggest that its publication in Shen Fu's own times would probably have scandalized the reading public, due in large part to his frank and detailed account of the intimate private life of a couple as well as the family tensions confronting them. It could be argued that in the development of traditional Chinese *daowang* literature, it was in the *Six Records* that the secularizing potential of intimate memory found its most complex and most sophisticated expression. In many ways, *Six Records* could be considered the pinnacle of the late imperial *daowang* literature, despite being a work that defied the expectations of any existing genres of memorial writings—or perhaps precisely for this reason.

It is no coincidence that the two most innovative works of prose in the history of Chinese *daowang* tradition, Mao Xiang's *Plum Shadow* and Shen Fu's *Six Records*, both of which explicitly advertised themselves as long narratives of personal memory, are intimate memoirs narrativized in full social contexts. A grieving husband's choice of a particular form to reflect on his late spouse mattered significantly in terms of how her "life" could be re-constructed and how his own image as a male mourner could be projected, a topic to be explored in more detail in subsequent chapters.

CHAPTER 2

SURVIVOR'S GUILT

The sudden void left by death often compels one to look at the life of the deceased from a very different perspective. In the case of a deceased wife, her grieving husband is more likely to feel a sense of guilt for not better appreciating her while she was still alive, as famously captured by Li Mengyang's line: "It took the death of my wife for me to really appreciate her." This chapter is an examination of how the feeling of personal guilt on the part of a literati husband in mourning his late wife shaped his memories of her and how the image of his late wife he constructed could, as a result, significantly complicate as well as deviate from that of a model wife celebrated in the Confucian female exemplar discourses of the time. Such complications and deviations, at the same time, contributed to the rise of the new image of a husband, who was often loving, understanding, and even sometimes indulging, a far cry from what a straight-faced Confucian husband was supposed to be.

Zhu Bangxian 朱邦憲 (1527–1572), a poet of some reputation, did not do so well in the civil examinations. Although his father was a *jinshi* degree holder and had served as the prefect of the Fuzhou prefecture, Zhu Bangxian achieved only imperial college student status. Zhu Bangxian was known for his chivalrous personality and enjoyed friendships with many luminaries, such as the scholar-official Wang Shizhen and the poet Wang Chideng 王穉登 (1535–1612), both of whom wrote biographies for him.[1]

Zhu Bangxian married three times in his life (not counting two concubines), remarrying twice after the deaths of his first two wives, Tangshi and Shenshi. Zhu wrote biographical sketches for both of them. According to these biographical sketches, the two wives shared many similar female virtues: neither of them was talkative or laughed a lot (thus, having good womanly manners); both had tremendous respect for his mother, who, however, was a very strict mother-in-law. Concerned that his mother's health might be negatively influenced, the first wife, Tangshi, had to kneel down repeatedly to beg her to go easy whenever she was upset with a servant or a maid; the second wife, Shenshi, too, often had to kneel down with her husband when his mother was punishing the latter for neglecting his study. Tangshi took good care of the son of her husband's concubine, née Lu, as if he were her own child, while Shenshi also treated the children of Tangshi as if they were her own after the death of Tangshi.[2] In a word, both were virtuous wives whom he loved and missed. The two biographical sketches are quite moving, but, full of familiar tropes of an exemplary wife, they seem quite conventional. For example, Zhu mentioned that his first wife Tangshi treated the son by his concubine as if he were her own, a wifely virtue many polygamous literati liked to promote in a woman. He also mentioned how his second wife Shenshi sold her own jewelry in order for him to afford food and wine to entertain his friends while keeping his mother from hearing of it. A woman selling jewelry to buy wine for her husband to entertain his friends became a common trope in a grieving Confucian husband's account of the virtues of his late wife, ever since the Tang poet Yuan Zhen's *daowang* poems on his late wife Weishi became popular, as captured in one of his famous poetic lines: "To buy wine I begged her to sell her hairpins" 泥他沽酒拔金釵.[3]

In addition to the two biographical sketches, Zhu Bangxian wrote a sacrificial litany for his second wife, Shenshi, which was anything but conventional. Unlike epitaph and even biographical sketch (which is intended to be "source material" for a future epitaph writer and formal biographer, thus more flexible and less scripted), whose assumed audience tended be more public in nature, a sacrificial litany is usually meant to be a direct communication between the mourner (here the mourning husband) and the mourned (his deceased spouse). Consequently, much of the concerns characteristic of an epitaph, such as its female subject's contributions to the "public" interests of the patrilineal family, may not figure prominently in a sacrificial litany, where the focus is more likely to be the author's personal relationship with the deceased. Of course, a sacrificial litany, due in part to its ritualistic function (to be read aloud at a sacrificial ceremony), can also be grandiloquent and unspecific, especially when written in verse. However, in the hands of some, sacrificial litany could become a powerful vehicle for venting intensely personal feelings, as in the case of Zhu Bangxian. The image of his second wife presented in Zhu's sacrificial litany is quite different from the one constructed in his biographical sketch, compelling the reader to re-read the latter from a far-different perspective. The litany is short enough to be translated and quoted below in its entirety:

After you married me, you served my mother, Cai ruren, with great filiality, raised the son of my previous wife with care, and supervised the maids and servants with kindness and proprieties; you helped my mother manage the household with great skill. You won praises for your great virtue from everyone. It could be said that you did not let me down (*wu fu yu yu yi* 無負於予矣). You were my second wife and we were about the same age. Your health had not been well and you fell sick quite often; on average, you were bed-ridden three months out of every twelve months. I neglected my study because I had to administer medicine to you and take care of you when you were sick. If you lay in bed sick for ten days, I could hardly have any sleep during those ten days. I was so tired that I myself fell sick. All said that I really loved you. It could also be said that I did not let you down (*wu fu yu jun yi* 無負於君矣).

I was stubborn and blunt. I could often speak something that ended up upsetting you. You knew I spoke without bad intention, but you could not take it well (*buneng shunshou* 不能順受). You lost your mother when you were very young. You once said to me: "When one's mother is not one's own birth mother, one's life would be hard although one would not necessarily suffer from lack of food or clothing. I would treat your son [by your previous wife] as the elder brother [of my own son]." You shed tears over this.

When the concubine was pregnant and consequently I could not send her back, although you did not try to stop it [her being allowed to remain in the family], you were quite unhappy. Furthermore, you had some deep worries, which you could not talk about and which I could not ask about. You still kept these worries within yourself when you died. All this was where I let you down (*ci jie yu suo fu jun zhe ye* 此皆予所負君者也). Alas! Between the two of us, who let the other down more (*liangen xiangfu shuduo* 兩人相負孰多)? This was something we both knew, but we could hardly tell others. Very sick, before you died, you said to me with eyes wide open: "I am about to die. I could not bear to say good bye to you even though I probably could to our son." I know that you had no regrets about [marrying] me.

Now my mother is sixty-one and I am thirty-two. With all the children clinging to me, I had no better solution but to marry again, finding Zhang to replace you. This was where I let you down the most (*yu suo da fu jun zhe ye* 予所大負君者此也). When you first married me, you told me not to forget my previous wife [who had passed away]; now in the underworld you should know that I would never forget you. Besides, Heaven knows about everything, and retribution is exacting. Since you never mistreated your stepson, how could your own sons be mistreated by others?[4]

Reading the litany and the biographical sketch side by side, we find the image of Shenshi became considerably complicated. First of all, the Shenshi as revealed in the litany is by no means consistent with the obedient wife who carried out her duties without any complaint, as suggested by the initial impression one gets from reading the biographical sketch. Note the standard phrases Zhu employed to describe her in the biographical sketch: "respectful, obedient and graceful, she tried her utmost to fulfill her duties as a daughter-in-law" (*jing, shun, wan, mian, quju fuzhi* 敬順婉娩, 曲舉婦職).[5] However, as we learn from the litany, she was actually not that *shun* 順 (obedient), as she could become easily upset if her husband spoke too bluntly (*buneng shunshou* 不能順受) and, more importantly, she apparently let her husband know her unhappiness when he took a concubine, a serious flaw on the part of a wife in the eyes of many Confucian polygamists. Although Zhu Bangxian insisted that she was very nice to the children of his previous wife, he failed to mention how she treated the children by his concubines, a silence that becomes all the more conspicuous in contrast to his praising elsewhere of his first wife, Tangshi, for her virtue of not being jealous when he took a concubine.[6]

In the litany, we are told that Zhu often took care of Shenshi because she was sick, forcing him to neglect his own study. This makes us wonder whether this might have played a role in his being often punished by his mother for not spending enough time studying. Should this be the case, the mention in the biographical sketch that the two of them had to kneel down begging his mother for forgiveness, in addition to being presented as evidence of her obedience toward her mother-in-law, might also suggest the possible tension between her and his mother: after all, it was her constant illness that prevented her husband from devoting himself fully to his study. This should make us reread more carefully a curious passage in the biographical sketch:

> Being a devoted Buddhist, my mother sometimes practiced fasting. My wife always tried to prepare food for her in person, even when she was sick herself, and once she said to me: "Mother is old. It would be difficult for her to sustain good health without tasty food. What can be done about it?" And yet she did not dare let my mother hear this comment.

Apparently not approving the Buddhist practices of her mother-in-law, Shenshi believed that given her old age she should not fast. Zhu Bangxian mentioned this episode probably as a proof of Shenshi's filiality as a daughter-in-law deeply concerned with the health of her mother-in-law, and yet it may also point to the tension between them, especially now we have learned that

Shenshi, being sick all the time, might have become a burden on the family. Her frequent illness might also be a contributing factor to her husband's repeated examination failures, which must have been a huge disappointment to his mother given how hard she had tried to have him study diligently.

More intriguingly, Zhu tells us in the litany that Shenshi had some deep worries, but she seldom talked about them, while he never asked her about them either. We are never told exactly what they were, but, according to him, these worries had caused her health to deteriorate rapidly. Zhu's reluctance to even speculate in the litany about what Shenshi's secret worries were could lead people to suspect that they might be related to the tension between her and his mother. However, in the biographical sketch, he did tell us that Shenshi was in constant fear that she might incur displeasure from the mother-in-law. The picture presented here is hardly that of a harmonious family, an unhappy situation Zhu Bangxian may have inadvertently revealed in his attempt to draw attention to the hardships his second wife had experienced and to his own guilty feelings over it.

Thanks in part to the unique generic nature of sacrificial litany (*jiwen*), the reader here is made to feel that he or she is almost eavesdropping on a very private conversation between a guilt-ridden husband in mourning and his deceased wife in the underworld. It is this positioning of an eavesdropper that makes the reader even more keenly aware of the private and intimate nature of this memorial text. Zhu Bangxian was pleading directly with his late wife that he had not let her down as a husband when she was alive, even though he could not help feeling, at the same time, that he had let her down after her death. After all, he remarried once again! Or it could be read as an endeavor on Zhu Bangxian's part to convince her and himself as well that if he ever indeed let her down, he did it with great reluctance and was forced by circumstances beyond his control. For example, the somewhat unflattering reference to her getting upset over his taking a concubine (something he probably did under the order of the mother): according to Zhu Bangxian's epitaph written by his fellow townsman, the scholar-official Pan En 潘恩 (1496–1582), Zhu took two concubines, who were the respective birth mothers of several of his sons.[7] Lushi became his concubine while his first wife, Tangshi, was still alive. Zhushi, the birth mother of two of his nine sons, was very likely the concubine referred to in the litany. It was possible that Zhu Bangxian might have promised Shenshi that he would send Zhushi back to her home if she did not become pregnant after his mother instructed him to take her as concubine to ensure he had many sons (perhaps because his being his father's only son was a source of great anxiety for his mother).[8] However, this became impossible upon her pregnancy. Consequently, he had to let her stay and become his concubine, thus letting Shenshi down. The word for "letting down" (*fu* 負) appears five times in this brief litany, underscoring his guilty conscience as a surviving husband.

The promise of never forgetting his wife was a pledge a polygamous husband, who insisted on his own version of conjugal faithfulness, would sometimes make to ensure that he could not be accused of being unfaithful when he did something that might be perceived by some to be disloyal. Here, memory could purportedly perform the magic of redemption: so long as he promised he would never forget his deceased wife, he could remarry or take more concubines without worrying about the blame of disloyalty. Zhu Bangxian, of course, married Zhang only after Shenshi had died (his taking a concubine did not count as marriage because a concubine was not considered a wife).[9] However, his confession that this was where he let her down the most is very telling as far as his guilty feelings are concerned, because she would probably not be too thrilled to learn that he remarried so quickly. Although a husband's remarrying after the loss of his wife was virtually taken for granted by many in late imperial China, the fact that Zhu Bangxian nevertheless felt the need to defend himself after he had decided to marry another woman, Zhangshi, bespeaks, in a way, the depth of the attachment between this husband and his late wife.[10] Indeed, the entire litany could be understood as its author's attempt to redeem himself by seeking forgiveness from his deceased wife as guilt and grief continued to gnaw at his heart. His sense of guilt might have turned him into a husband more "indulging" than he would have otherwise allowed himself to appear: he showed more understanding of his wife's jealousy as she languished in a polygamous marriage. Jealousy is presented here as something that could be justified or, at least, tolerated, even though concubinage had been considered by many at that time to be a man's inviolable rights.

On the other hand, Zhu also appears to suggest that both he and his wife were guilty of *fu* (letting someone down), as he was simultaneously trying to persuade her and himself that he had at least tried his best not to let her down. His rhetorical question—"Between the two of us, who let the other down more?"—is intriguing, in that they likely both knew the answer to this question but could not reveal it to others. The generic feature of a sacrificial litany appears to have granted him a special privilege of privacy: this is a private conversation between a couple—his personal plea to his deceased wife. His refusal to tell the reader exactly who had let the other down more, as well as what his wife's secret worries were that caused her early death, underscore the intimate nature of this litany and the limits beyond which the reader, an eavesdropper, would not be allowed to intrude into their private world. However, by preserving this litany as a memorial text in his collected works, which was expected to be read by many, he was also trying to carefully fashion his own image as a loving and grief-stricken husband. Besides his late wife, the apparent addressee of this litany, its actual audience had to be someone other than his late wife, who, already dead, ironically, could never have been its actual audience. This might remind us of Tang dynasty *daowang* master Yuan Zhen's confession in his sacrificial litany to his late wife: "Alas! Listing one's official titles and virtues, composing various elegies and performing sacrificial rituals, all these are done by the people who are still alive. They have nothing to do with the dead!"[11]

A scholar and minor official, Ye Shaoyuan is another mourning husband whose writings about his late wife point to some of the most interesting trends in the development of *daowang* literature in the seventeenth century. Here I focus mainly on Ye's biography of his late wife, Shen Yixiu, and the lengthy sacrificial litany he wrote one hundred days after her death. Compared with Zhu Bangxian, Ye Shaoyuan was even less inhibited in terms of what he felt he could reveal about the private life he shared with his late wife. In his writings, Ye showed less qualms about exploring the kinds of family tensions only vaguely suggested by Zhu Bangxian in the latter's litany addressed to his second wife. If Zhu had demonstrated clearly his deep attachment to Shenshi, Ye Shaoyuan simply adored Shen Yixiu, not always for the reasons many of the more conservative would agree with.[12]

Ye Shaoyuan appears to have full confidence in his late wife as a worthy biographical subject when he chose to present his memories of her in the form of a formal biography (*zhuan* 傳) rather than a biographical sketch, as in the case of Zhu Bangxian. In other words, by calling his own memoir of his wife a *zhuan*, Ye Shaoyuan was proclaiming that he need not seek validation by deferring to someone else to produce a formal biography for his late wife. His memories, if presented as a biographical sketch, would have served only as "raw materials" needing to be processed or filtered by an epitaph writer or formal biographer. Few bereaved husbands before Ye Shaoyuan had demonstrated such confidence in their late wives' worthiness as biographical subjects by composing a *zhuan*.

Ye's confidence, it seems, was based on his carefully reasoned attempt to rethink female exemplariness as part of his overall *daowang* endeavor: he was implying that his late wife was worthy of a formal biography in part because she was now being judged by the new standards of female exemplariness he was proposing. In his preface to *Wumeng tang ji*, Ye Shouyuan argued that in judging a woman, in addition to virtue, two other important qualities, talent and beauty, should also be taken into serious consideration. Just as there were three kinds of cultural immortality (*san buxiu* 三不朽), a Confucian man was supposed to seek, namely, immortality as a result of great virtue (*lide* 立德), immortality as a result of great public service (*ligong* 立功), and immorality as a result of great writings (*liyan* 立言), a woman should also be able to achieve immorality as result of her virtue (*de* 德), beauty (*se* 色), and talent (*cai* 才). However, people, according to Ye Shaoyuan, usually found it difficult to define a woman's talent, while they were even more reluctant to talk about her physical appeal. Consequently, these two qualities had been neglected, with the usual emphasis being placed solely on virtue when it came to defining womanhood.[13]

Intellectual ability and beauty are indeed the qualities associated with his late wife that Ye Shaoyuan paid special attention to in his *daowang* writings. According to him, his wife was an excellent poetess and a woman of erudition, with whom he could converse on almost any topic, from how to deal with daily household necessities to profound existential questions such as that of life and death, and from various interesting issues in the classical books to the unusual events of the current time. Ye told us that the two even shared their criticism of the famous Han dynasty scholar Liu Xiang's 劉向 (77–6 BC) readings of the Confucian classic *Zuozhuan* 左傳 (*The Zuo Commentaries*) and Ban Zhao's 班昭 (ca. 45 to ca. 117) *Nüjie* 女誡 (*Precepts for Women*): "[Expressing] our disdain for Liu Xiang's interpretations of the *Zuo Commentaries* and [sharing] our low opinions of what is preached in Ban Zhao's *Precepts for My Daughters*" (*bi Zhonglei Zuozhuan zhi du, lou Huiji Nüjie zhi chuizhe ye* 鄙中壘左傳之讀，陋惠姬女誡之垂者也).[14] Here their displeasure with Ban Chao's *Nüjie* is particularly noteworthy given its crucial role in setting the Confucian standards for women's education as a must-read for almost every young literate woman in late imperial China. This was probably not surprising since the image of Shen Yixiu he was reconstructing here from his memories could hardly be what would fit within the prescriptive parameters laid out in Ban Zhao's *Nüjie*.[15] Granted, the mention of his late wife's dissatisfaction with this famous Confucian etiquette for women, which was made in juxtaposition with her critical view of Liu Xiang, the famous scholar of Confucian classics, might be intended to showcase her impressive intellectual competence in general, but this was nevertheless quite remarkable, drawing our attention to her different view on what female model behaviors should be. By mentioning this as part of the common intellectual interests the two shared as husband and wife, and by underscoring the intellectual compatibility between them,

Ye Shaoyuan attempted to present his late wife as a special woman who could not be fully appreciated in terms of the traditional roles prescribed for women.

Furthermore, Ye Shaoyuan did not shy away from praising his late wife for her physical appeal. "I am not grieving for Wanjun [his wife's style name] because she was a beautiful woman. However, intelligent within and beauty without, she was indeed an extremely exquisite lady."[16] From the perspective of this grieving husband, her beauty could be appreciated only in terms of her superior intellect:

> She had a thorough understanding of all the profound principles behind events ancient and present as well as the difficult issues in many different books. Calm and straightforward, she possessed an air of self-assuredness and detachment, reminding people of a tall pine tree in the cold air. . . . With dark eyebrows, a pair of beautiful eyes, and a slender and delicate figure, she never understood the need for rouge and powder or jewelry; detesting make-up, she always wore plain clothing without having any ornament on her hair when participating in the gatherings with other women. And yet she liked to talk and laugh (*hao tanxiao* 好談笑) and was quite humorous (*shan huixie* 善詼諧). She was a good wine drinker. . . .[17]

This is a far cry from the image of a submissive and self-effacing woman one expects to encounter in a typical biography or epitaph of an exemplary Confucian lady, who was supposed to refrain herself from laughing casually or talking freely in front of others (*bugou yanxiao* 不苟言笑), exactly the kind of image Zhu Bangxian had tried to present in the biographical sketches he wrote for his two deceased wives, as discussed before.[18]

All the emphasis on her intellect and beauty did not necessarily mean Ye Shaoyuan believed that his late wife was any less exemplary when it came to the more conventional female virtues as defined by the Confucian tradition. Highlighting the hardships a woman suffered in her married life was almost a convention in elegiac celebration of her as an exemplary wife, as if hardship and suffering were somehow considered a necessary condition for female virtue. Absence of such hardship and suffering in the life of his friend's mother was apparently an important reason behind Fang Bao's reluctance to write an epitaph for her in the aforementioned case.

An important part of Ye Shaoyuan's lengthy sacrificial litany on Shen Yixiu is about the hardships she suffered during their married life. A primary rhetorical feature of this litany is that many of its paragraphs begin with a similar sentence pattern: "People thought she was . . . but they did not know. . . ."

It emphasizes how much she was misunderstood by people as having had an easy life and, thus, the importance of his own privileged knowledge about her as her husband and her worthiness of his elegiac tribute. One of the purposes of this elegiac narrative was to demonstrate that her life was far more difficult than it might have appeared to others, and she, one was therefore to infer, was much more virtuous than others had thought.

However, even when celebrating his late wife as a model of those more traditional wifely virtues such as her special ability to endure all these hardships with grace, Ye Shaoyuan was also calling attention to the unfair treatment she was subjected to in the family. According to him, during the early years of their married life, many people thought they were a perfect couple to be envied, but they did not know that he hardly spent much time with her because his mother expected his full devotion to the preparation for the civil examinations. For many long periods of time he had to live away from home to study; even during those few days he did spend home, he had to sleep in the study. He could not spend a night in their own bedroom without his mother's permission.[19] His wife often had to stay up very late because his mother liked to do needlework deep into the night. Even in defending his mother for being strict and harsh by saying that she, as a widow with only one son, had to assume the traditional roles of a loving mother as well as a strict father at the same time (*ciwei jian fudao* 慈闈兼父道), Ye Shaoyuan acknowledged, not without bitterness, that his wife and he as a couple had to continue to live in this way (with little freedom to be intimate with each other) even after he had successfully passed the metropolitan examinations and had became an official.[20] His mother's continuing presence throughout their entire married life of thirty years (his mother and his wife died during the same year) had been a major factor in their being deprived of much of the time of intimacy the couple could otherwise have shared. Now in mourning his late wife, he was begging her for forgiveness and implicitly blaming his mother: "Was I so lacking in love that I appeared so cold to you? This was only because I did not dare to go against the instructions of my mother" (*wu qi wuqing, shuyue zhi ci, citing yifang, wang gan weili* 我豈無情, 疏越至此, 慈庭義方, 罔敢違戾).[21]

A great hobby for his wife, a talented poetess, was composing poems. However, her love for poetry incurred the displeasure of his mother, and she had to stop writing poems because the mother-in-law was concerned that her daughter-in-law's writing and exchanging poems with her son might distract the latter from his study for the examinations. Ye Shaoyuan even told us that his mother resorted to sending maids to spy on his wife to make sure the latter was not composing poems behind her back.[22] One could well imagine the miseries Shen Yixiu suffered given her deep love for poetry and its significance in their lives as a couple. Despite such protestations on the part of the grieving husband, the reader is also meant to conclude that his late wife was very much a virtuous daughter-in-law because she chose to endure the hardships rather than disobeying his mother.

When eulogizing their deceased wives, some literati husbands of earlier times, such as Luo Hongxian 羅洪先 (1504–1564), a neo-Confucian philosopher and scholar-official, had also mentioned with regret that, due to various reasons, such as travels or services as officials stationed in other areas, they could spend only little time with their wives.[23] Others were even more explicit in their praises of their wives for not complaining about the lack of bedroom pleasures due to their husbands' poor health or disinterest in sex. For example, the neo-Confucian thinker Wang Ji 王畿 (1498-1583) remembered his late wife this way:

> Knowing that I was not that interested in sex (*dan yu yu* 淡於慾), she gave up bedchamber pleasure (*ge chuangzi zhi ai* 割床第之愛). We tended to forget about this matter without bearing grudge against each other.[24]

The emphasis, however, was almost always on their wives' virtue of not complaining. Instead, Ye Shaoyuan's focus here is on the unfair treatment the family environment had imposed on his wife, while avoiding directly addressing the question of whether she complained.[25] Ye Shaoyuan rarely hesitated in showing his attachment to his wife and his desire to be alone with his wife in the boudoir, unlike some of the literati husbands who did not forget to assert their Confucian manhood by trying to convince us that bedroom pleasure was not something they were particularly interested in, as in the case of Wang Ji, even when they, as mourning husbands, were apologizing to their late wives for failing them in this regard.[26] Further, others might express regrets over their own Confucian moral prudence for not sharing enough time with their wives. However, such expressions of regret were also intended to enhance their own images as exemplary Confucians. For example, in a prose elegy on his late wife, when describing how little private time his wife and he had shared in their sixteen-year married life, Fang Bao expressed his regrets that he might have been too rigid in insisting on the Confucian principles (*zhiyi zhi guo* 執義之過) in dealing with his wife, sighing how difficult it was to cultivate one's moral nature and properly control one's personal feelings at the same time (*zhi xing yu qing zhi nan* 治性與情之難).[27] Very few grieving literati husbands before Ye Shaoyuan had gone as far as he did in expressing his frustrations over the hardships his late wife had suffered and in insisting on the importance of the intimate time a couple should be able to enjoy.

Overwhelmed by the loss of his beloved wife, and feeling guilty as a surviving husband, Ye Shaoyuan apparently was less discreet than he should have been, as expected of a filial son, when he presented his own mother as someone directly contributing to his wife's misery, albeit ever so politely. This sheer willingness to talk about the possible role of his mother in his wife's misery, which was quite rare at that time and which could have outraged some of his more conservative contemporaries during an age of absolute parental authority, was an eloquent testimony to his guilty feelings and despair as a despondent husband in mourning. Mourning and grieving seem to have granted him a rare license to say something he would normally not have said, even risking the accusation of being an unfilial son disrespectful to his own mother.

In underscoring the hardships his late wife had suffered and her capacity to endure them, Ye Shaoyuan did not directly challenge many aspects of the traditional notion of wifely virtue. However, the specific ways in which he tried to redeem himself by dwelling on his own sense of guilt and the possible role of his own mother in the suffering of his late wife compelled his readers to marvel how far he had departed from the biographical norms associated with a model wife. What is remarkable is probably not so much the particular image of a wife that he was able to reconstruct from his memories as the new portrait of a guilt-ridden husband he had painted for himself in the process of mourning and remembering.

Guilt looms even larger in the *daowang* writings of You Tong. Four months after bidding farewell to his wife, Caoshi, and heading for the capital in the north to participate in the special "Erudite Scholarship Examinations" sponsored by the imperial government, You Tong received news that his wife had passed away a month earlier. He asked for permission from the imperial court to return to attend his wife's funeral, but his request was denied. He could only send his eldest son back to his hometown, Changzhou (the modern city of Suzhou), a thousand miles away, to take care of the funeral. As he wrote in the biographical sketch (*xingshu* 行述) of his late wife not too many days after learning of her death, the fact that his wife died not long after his departure without his being at her bedside and his inability to go back home to attend her funeral made her death even more difficult to come to terms with, considerably deepening his feelings of guilt.[28]

In his shock, the grieving husband was still puzzled why his wife had died so suddenly, wondering what might have caused her sudden death. He blamed himself for not being there with her when she needed him most. According to him, the problems with his wife's health might have been caused by her having been in labor too many times (she gave birth to eight children and also suffered five miscarriages) and her insistence on breastfeeding her children despite her poor health.[29] Elsewhere, You Tong tells us that what made him feel most guilty was that she might not have died had he stayed home with her. He suspected that she had been prescribed the wrong medicine, something preventable if he had been home. Now he could not even bid her final farewell because the imperial court had denied his request to return home for the funeral. Smitten with a profound sense of guilt (*furu* 負汝: letting you down), he was convinced that his own career ambition had contributed to her tragedy.[30] You Tong imagined that his dying wife must have considered him a heartless husband (*boqing fu* 薄情夫) for being away at a moment when she needed him most.[31] Recalling how deeply his wife and he were in love, You Tong mentioned in particular the fact that he was a man of monogamy as proof of their deep conjugal attachment, a gesture quite significant among the male elite in a polygamous society at that time.[32] For You Tong, Caoshi was much more than a wife who took good care of his household and raised his children (conventional wifely virtues You Tong also duly mentioned). She was an intellectual companion as well, as he recalled elsewhere in a poem:

> In leisured daily life respectful you always were,
> You would blame me for being crazy when I was sometimes trying to be humorous.
> A friend in boudoir I have lost,
> Bereaved of my wife I also mourned the death of a soulmate.
> 閑居眉案整相莊, 偶語詼諧嗔我狂. 可惜閨房失良友, 斷絃真痛子期望.[33]

In the biographical sketch, You Tong tells us how at many important moments in his professional career Caoshi's decisive advices played a crucial role in helping him make the right decisions. For example, after passing the provincial civil examinations, You Tong was assigned to the post of *tuiguan* 推官 (official in charge of judicial matters) in the Yongping prefecture, east of the capital, a relatively poor area. Initially deciding against accepting the assignment, You Tong changed his mind and took the job only after his wife persuaded him that by becoming an official he could have a chance to bring glory to his parents. Once on the job, You Tong always tried to be lenient in judging cases because his wife urged him to go easy on people so that he could accumulate good merits in his next life for the sake of his own descendents. After being demoted for punishing the servant of a Manchu aristocrat without prior permission, he quit instead of contesting the decision by his superior thanks to his wife's reminder that it was time to return to their hometown now that his parents had become old. When he was recommended for the special "Erudite Scholarship Examination," he first was reluctant to go but eventually went after his wife advised him that he should not go against the order of the emperor. This, of course, led to irony, as her advice might have contributed to her death, if we are persuaded by You Tong that she might not have died if he had stayed home with her.[34] Thus, Caoshi's virtues, according to her grieving husband, were hardly confined to those expected of a submissive wife. Here the traditional roles of husband and wife were almost reversed: You Tong followed, while his wife led. Caoshi was fondly remembered by You Tong as a decisive woman of wisdom.

Another remarkable detail You Tong recalled about Caoshi was her quick temper—she could get upset easily. Frustrated by her husband's repeated career setbacks and exhausted by family chores, Caoshi would sometimes have outbursts, complaining that she did not marry him to become an old maid toiling in the kitchen and that she also wanted to enjoy comfort. Instead of getting upset, You Tong tried to comfort her by repeatedly apologizing and admitting there was really very little he could do to change the family's financial situation at the time.[35] This is hardly the image of an obedient wife that we have become accustomed to in many writings on exemplary wives produced at that time. In the eyes of his more conservative contemporary readers, this must have been an image of a shrew intimidating her hen-pecked husband, anything but a complimentary picture of a virtuous wife. Caoshi would indeed have appeared so if such detail had been mentioned by a commissioned epitaph writer or biographer, since his usual task was to emphasize only the exemplariness of the deceased. However, You Tong's mention of this in his biographical sketch did not undermine the sympathetic image of his late wife, largely because he, as a guilt-ridden husband, was trying to underscore how his own long frustrating career had brought hardships onto his late wife. Perhaps, the tremendous pains of bereavement You Tong was experiencing and the intense guilt at the moment of mourning had turned him into a husband more understanding or more indulging than many Confucian literati would have been in similar situations, complicating the representation of his wife's exemplariness. You Tong wrote not only to extol her virtues but also to redeem himself as a husband. This is certainly also true of Zhu Bangxian and Ye Shaoyuan, to various degrees.

Among the three mourning husbands discussed so far in this chapter, You Tong's claim of monogamy as a proof of his love for his wife is particularly interesting given the fact that polygamy was quite common among the elite at that time. Although Ye Shaoyuan might have taken concubines before,[36] he did not remarry despite the urging of his dying wife.[37] Zhu Bangxian remarried (probably pressured by his mother) when he already had quite a few sons. However, he felt that he had let down his deceased wife by remarrying. Many bereaved husbands deeply attached to their late wives often found themselves tormented by the question whether to remarry. Zhu Bangxian was not alone in feeling guilty about remarrying. Almost a century earlier, Wang Shunmin 汪舜民 (1453–1507), upon the death of his wife, declared in a sacrificial litany in her honor that there were four reasons why he should not remarry, one of them being that remarrying would be considered an act of betrayal to her. He eventually remarried, but he felt the need to write another litany to inform her of his decision, asking for her understanding.[38] Obviously, even when many men of the time took a widower's remarriage for granted, some of them did feel guilty doing so.

Before concluding this chapter on the implications of the guilt of a surviving husband for the ways he remembers and mourns his deceased wife, it should be noted that, overwhelmed by the grief of loss, a husband might also reveal certain aspects of his feelings toward her that he himself would have disapproved of on other occasions. As I have mentioned, Fang Bao when grieving for his late wife expressed his regrets that he might have been too strict with her when he tried to adhere to the Confucian ritual principles. His guilt was most likely related to his feeling that he might have wrongly blamed his late wife for what was apparently beyond her control. After the death of his younger brother, Fang Bao initially decided to postpone his marriage in order to follow the strict Confucian mourning rituals for his brother. However, he relented under the pressures of his future parents-in-law. Then he insisted on not consummating the marriage until the prescribed mourning period for his younger brother had passed, and yet again he relented after an uproar among the relatives and clansmen. This incident of "breaching the ritual rules for the sake of marriage" (*feili er chenghun* 廢禮而成婚) became something that haunted Fang Bao for a long time and likely also contributed to his unfair treatment of his wife.[39] Another factor might have been the conflicts between his wife and his sister-in-law (the wife of his elder brother, Fang Zhou 方舟) and the resultant dismay of his elder brother. According to Fang Bao, his elder brother was so upset about the frictions between Fang Bao's wife and his own wife that he insisted that he be buried with Fang Bao after they died rather than with his own wife.[40] In short, these were probably two important factors that might have contributed to what Fang Bao thought to be his unfair treatment of his late wife. It is interesting to note, however, that while as a grieving husband Fang Bao felt guilty toward his late wife, he demonstrated no such feelings when, years later, he wrote his "household instructions" for his nephew, where, rather than emphasizing treating one's wife fairly, he warned that the disharmony between brothers was often caused by the selfish attachment to their wives, echoing a familiar theme in traditional gentry household instructions.[41] Here we have two quite different images of Fang Bao, one of a grieving husband feeling guilty about treating his late wife unfairly, and the other of a patriarch warning against its male members being too willing to listen to their wives at the expense of the interests of a patrilineal family. Such inconsistencies on the part of a Confucian literatus are interesting, though by no means surprising (we will return to Fang Bao's writings on his sisters in chapter 8). Mourning and grieving could indeed be the "vulnerable" moments for a man, who was expected to keep constant Confucian vigilance against "selfish" conjugal attachment. They could constitute momentary moral "lapses" for a Confucian husband still in grief and tormented by personal guilt, when he was more likely to exhibit the kind of sympathetic understanding of his late wife that he would not have allowed himself to entertain on other occasions.

Despite these grieving husbands' different notions of what constituted female exemplariness, sympathetic and sometimes even new understanding of the deceased wife was made possible, to a large extent, by the fact that now the arbiter of her exemplariness happened to be her guilt-ridden surviving husband in his capability as her biographer. While none of these grieving husbands disputed the Confucian biographical imperative that the biographical narrative of a wife had to be presented in terms of her contribution to the "public" interests of a patrilineal family,[42] many of them also allowed, to varying degrees, their own private and personal feelings as grieving husbands to shape and complicate the images of their wives. Not always drastic, such deviations from the Confucian biographical norms of the exemplary are sometimes subtle and incremental, as demonstrated in the case of Zhu Bangxian's show of understanding of his wife's jealousy, the case of Ye Shaoayuan's emphasis on the hardships his late wife suffered in terms of the contributing role his own mother played, and in the case of You Tong's references to his late wife's bad temper and complaint of hardships in order to underscore his own guilt as a husband who failed his wife.

The preceding discussions point to a tendency on the part of these grieving authors to remember their late wives as unique individuals and their increasing attention to the private details in their lives. After all, a grieving husband had to legitimate his act of remembrances by emphasizing his status as a privileged biographer in terms of his unique knowledge about his female subject.[43] At the same time, it was also his unique and intimate knowledge that enhanced the likelihood of the Confucian biographical norms of the exemplary being complicated and even occasionally circumvented.

CHAPTER 3

HAGIOGRAPHICAL MEMORY

So far I have concentrated primarily on the secularizing trend in the memorial writings on women during the late imperial period. However, this period was also a time that witnessed the escalation of the chastity cult—a widespread endeavor among Confucian elites to celebrate widows who refused to remarry and, especially, women who committed suicide to protect their chastity or to vindicate their loyalty to their deceased husbands or even fiancés.[1]

The rise of this radical female exemplar discourse *lienü zhuan* 烈女傳 (biographies of female chastity martyrs), paradoxically, might have helped to expand the spaces within which the literati, when writing about the lives of women of the more ordinary kind, would feel less pressured to search for evidence of Confucian exemplariness in their female subjects. This was because there was now a special subgenre of biography reserved for such radical exemplars. In other words, an author would feel less constrained in talking about the aspects of the life of his female subject other than her Confucian exemplariness if her biography was not presented as a hagiography. This draws our attention to the simple fact that most women presented in memorial texts of the time were ordinary people since they were not perceived exemplary enough to merit a hagiography. They were being remembered simply as someone's mother, sister, daughter, or wife rather than a woman of extraordinary virtues. Unlike the biography for an average woman, a hagiography almost always had words or "generic tags," such as *lie* 烈 (martyrdom) or *jie* 節 (chastity), in its title, to clearly distinguish itself. Consequently, having decided not to have such a generic tag in the title of the biography of his female subject, the biographer was more likely to present her as an ordinary woman, although she might still be considered quite virtuous. This was probably why Fang Xiangying insisted that he did not want to attribute to his late mother all those glorious deeds of the famous historical figures lest the image he presented in the biography would become that of someone else rather than that of his own mother, emphasizing that his mother, though virtuous, was only an average woman. Another good example is Fang Bao's biography of his younger sister, where whether she should prepare to commit suicide to demonstrate her chastity when her husband was dying never comes up as an issue. Instead, she is said to move back to live with her natal family to seek financial and psychological support.[2] Despite his sister's failure in this regard, Fang Bao had no qualms insisting on her being a virtuous woman because he must have felt what he was writing was a biography rather than a hagiography and, therefore, the expectations and standards were different (more on this biography in chapter 8).

Here, in examining the relationship between biography and hagiography, Huang Zongxi's observation on women's biographical writings, already discussed in chapter 1, merits a closer look from a slightly different perspective:

> The rule of writing an epitaph is to focus on a few major events in the subject's life, while the small and trivial details in daily life are often left out. When it comes to the life of a woman, since it is made entirely of small and trivial details, there would be nothing else to talk about if one chooses to omit these details. Even in the case of [writing about] a woman of exemplary chastity, besides references to the notion of *jie* (chastity), the rest of the epitaph would still be on those small and trivial things in her life.[3]

Huang Zongxi is reminding people of the dilemma faced by a hagiographer of a chaste widow: while her action to maintain her chastity might be considered *the* central event in her life that carried public significance, just as a scholar-official's public career should be the focus of the biography of a man, her life was nevertheless composed mostly of insignificant deeds. This was why a hagiographer of women, meant to focus only on the important act of chastity, usually had to be very brief, and often even boring, because he had nothing else "significant" to talk about. This could also explain a tendency in hagiographical writings of female chastity martyrs during the late Ming and early Qing—to compensate for the lack of description of their daily lives, some hagiographers sought to "spice up" their narratives by emphasizing the unusual and graphic nature of the particular ways their female subjects chose to end their lives: such as the physical suffering of a prolonged process of suicide or the gruesome details of self-mutilation as a way of chastity vindication.[4]

What would become of the role of intimate or personal memory when a bereaved husband decided to mourn his late wife as a chastity martyr? A hagiographer tended to deliberately ignore "the small and trivial" in the life of his female subject lest the reader would be distracted from the hagiographical focus on the ultimate Confucian virtue of chastity and loyalty, while her uniqueness as an individual was his least concern. Likewise, in pursuing his hagiographical project on his late wife, a grieving husband often found himself being forced to deliberately refashion or even suppress his personal memory in order to present her as the ultimate exemplar of Confucian loyalty and chastity by focusing almost exclusively on the act of ultimate self-denial. In the rest of this chapter, I examine two cases in which a literati husband attempted to remember and commemorate his late wife as a chastity martyr. While personal (not necessarily always intimate) memory appears to have assumed some very different functions in these two cases, it considerably complicates the hagiographical process in both of them.

FROM BIOGRAPHY TO HAGIOGRAPHY

It was relatively rare that a hagiographer also happened to be the husband of his female hagiographical subject. This is largely because martyrdom of this kind often had the death of her husband as a precondition: a woman was honored as a chastity martyr thanks to her suicide upon the death of her husband. One rare but possible scenario: the husband had an opportunity to be the hagiographer of his own wife because he, expected to die (often due to seemingly incurable illness), somehow miraculously recovered, after his wife had already committed suicide under the belief that he was about to die.[5] We see such a case in the early Qing writer Zhang Zhen.

Zhang Zhen enjoyed quite a reputation as a prose writer in his hometown area in the Shandong region. Among his friends were such national figures as the famous poet and scholar-official Wang Shizhen, from the same region. Zhang Zhen was nominated in 1679 to participate in the special "Erudite Scholarship Examination" sponsored by the Qing imperial government, but he declined because he was still mourning his deceased mother at the time. When he was fifty-three, his wife of almost forty years, Lishi, died at the age of fifty-five (they were married when he was thirteen and she fifteen). Zhang Zhen was devastated by her sudden death, and he wrote quite a few memorial essays in her honor.

Zhang Zhen initially did not mourn his late wife as a chastity martyr. In a short epitaph he wrote for the burial of his wife, after briefly listing her virtues expected of a dutiful wife, he relates that his wife's health began to deteriorate due to the sadness and stresses she suffered as a result of the deaths of several of her children and grandchildren.[6] When Zhang himself became seriously ill, afraid that he might not recover, she no longer felt a reason to live. She did not eat for four days, and then died suddenly upon the news of the death of another of their grandchildren. Zhang Zhen did not present her death as a result of deliberate suicide or as an act of martyrdom.

Zhang Zhen later insisted that the brief epitaph he wrote in a rush could not do full justice to the life of his late wife. The main reason behind his failure to produce a better epitaph, he explained, was that he was so ill at the time of her burial that he had no time or energy to write something more elaborate. Apparently unhappy with his own hasty effort, Zhang Zhen later, after recovering from his illness, produced a much lengthier and very emotional biographical sketch of his wife with the hope that it could be the basis for someone else (a famous figure, he hoped) to write a much better epitaph for his late wife.[7]

The emotional and grief-stricken husband told us in this fairly detailed sketch that throughout their married life, whenever he was frustrated and whenever he felt he had no one to confide in, a brief conversation with his wife over a cup of tea immediately cheered him up. Although his wife did not read well, she always supported his artistic and intellectual pursuits by, for example, using her needlework to make a silk zither case for him or to decorate his collections of artifacts. Besides all the traditional virtues expected of an exemplary wife, as he carefully catalogued in the biographical sketch, what endeared his wife to him most was her devotion to him. He believed her eventual death was the ultimate expression of such devotion. Here Zhang Zhen was able to talk more about the context in which she died and his own deep grief: when she was led to believe there was no hope for her husband to recover from his illness, because several fellow villagers had already succumbed to a similar disease, she decided to end her own life. She refused food for four days and then died suddenly when she visited the house of their son to grieve after learning of the sudden death of their grandson. Zhang Zhen felt guilty because he, as a seriously ill person who was expected to die, miraculously survived, whereas his wife, seemingly healthy, died instead. He was convinced that his wife died for his sake.

However, at the same time, as this mourning biographer tries to convince us, her death was presented almost as something long anticipated by herself even before her husband got seriously ill: we are told that she had repeatedly indicated that she was quite content with what she already had in life and she did not fear death so long as her husband and her family were fine (thus there was no reason to commit suicide for the sake of her husband);[8] during the earthquake of 1668, he and his wife were buried under the rubble of their collapsed house. After they regained consciousness, his wife jokingly remarked that if she had died this way it would not have been so bad since everything happened so quickly and painlessly.[9] In short, she demonstrated an unusual calmness in facing the idea of death, an attitude of detachment characterized by what seemed a Buddhist transcendence.

Not too long after he finished his memoir/biography, with the help of one of his friends or relatives, Zhang Zhen succeeded in securing an epitaph for his late wife from the famous scholar Huang Zongxi.[10] However, compared to the biographical sketch Zhang himself wrote for his wife, Huang's epitaph was a dry summary of her virtuous deeds, lacking the emotional and dramatic power of the grieving husband's narrative. This was a not unexpected result when a biographical account written by grieving kin was shortened into an epitaph by someone who hardly knew the deceased. Especially for Zhang Zhen, this should have come as no surprise at all, since, when asked by one of his fellow villagers to write an epitaph for the latter's deceased wife, he himself explicitly acknowledged that, due to the generic conventions of an epitaph, he had to concentrate on the exemplariness of the wife (*fude fugong* 婦德婦功) while ignoring her grieving husband's emotional words (*qingyu* 情語) in the latter's biographical account of his late wife, on which Zhang Zhen based his commissioned epitaph.[11] Apparently, the epitaphic conventions dictated his approach and, more importantly, this time writing an epitaph for his friend's wife, he was only a detached biographer rather than a grieving husband/biographer himself.

If his own initial biographical account and Huang Zongxi's subsequent epitaph still left people with some doubt about his wife's death as a result of suicide (a deliberate act of martyrdom), and if these two biographical accounts contained too much information on the other aspects of her life to allow themselves to become a typical hagiography of "female chastity martyr," Zhang Zhen, seventeen years after her death, felt that she should have been extolled exactly as such and nothing less. He wrote a special essay (*qingci* 請辭) to plea with the famous to come up with a hagiography to celebrate his late wife's special virtue, so that *now* her carefully contemplated decision (*kuzhong* 苦衷) to follow her husband in death (*yisi xunfu* 以死殉夫) would not be forgotten in posterity.[12] In this passionate plea, Zhang Zhen for the first time tried to present his wife's death unequivocally as a result of *xunfu* (sacrificing her own life in order to follow her husband in death), something he hesitated to do in his lengthy biographical account nearly seventeen years earlier. Full of clichés frequently used to praise a typical good wife—"gentle, virtuous, affectionate, and submissive" (*rou zheng ci cong taoyu* 柔正慈從套語)—Huang Zongxi's epitaph proved a major disappointment to Zhang Zhen after all the years that had passed, especially after he had decided to commemorate her differently.[13] To make it worse, compared with his own biographical sketch, Huang's epitaph presented her death as even less likely a result of suicide:

> When Qiyuan (Zhang Zhen) was very sick, *ruren* (his ladyship) tended to him with medicine while herself not eating for four days. At that time, one of their grandsons died of small-pox and she died when she went over to mourn the death of that grandson. . . .[14]

Zhang Zhen now was specifically hoping someone could follow the conventional format of a hagiography of female chastity martyr by focusing exclusively on the significance of her act of suicide (*danti yishi zhi li* 单提一事之例) while omitting all the distracting minor details in her life (*lue qi suosui* 略其瑣碎), exactly what he himself had taken so much pains to describe in his earlier biographical sketch, this time in order to suit the image of a martyr of female chastity.[15] As mentioned earlier, Huang Zongxi had noted elsewhere that the focus on the small details in the life of a woman was actually what distinguished women's biographies from those of men—a gendered feature of life-writings on women. In fact, Zhang Zhen himself had praised profusely one of his friends, An Zhiyuan 安致遠 (1628–1701), for his ability to capture the virtues of his own wife in his writings by concentrating on the "small and trivial things" (*suoxie* 瑣屑) in her life.[16]

Of course, Zhang Zhen's present project was quite different: it was now a hagiography of chastity martyrdom, much more than a biography of an endearing wife. He now seemed to be particularly concerned that others might doubt his wife's intention of suicide, thus finding her image as a martyr less than fully convincing. To make it more difficult, he himself had already suggested in his own earlier biographical sketch that the direct cause of her death was her shock and despondence over the death of a grandson, not a deliberate intention to commit suicide for the sake of her husband by fasting. What is even more problematic is that, in his earlier biographical sketch, he had undermined his own case for his late wife to be celebrated as chastity martyr because he indicated that her health was already in clear decline due to the sorrows and stress she had suffered over the deaths of several of their children and grandchildren.[17] Even his mention of his wife's detached attitude toward death might have suggested that she was very different from a typical martyr of chastity, since the latter usually cared deeply about her own posthumous reputation. His late wife, however, as he had presented her, was so content with what she already had in her life that she was almost indifferent to death, a sort of detachment that Huang Zongxi, unfortunately (unfortunate, that is, for Zhan Zhen seventeen years later), seized upon in his epitaph by celebrating her as a woman of near Buddhist wisdom.[18]

However, after all these years, Zhang Zhen was now eager to offer additional direct evidence to bolster his wife's image as a faithful widow who had indeed committed suicide to die with her husband: in this "plea" essay, he recalled that his wife once explicitly spoke to him about her determination to commit suicide by fasting if he died before she did. He now insisted that her death was the result of a deliberate plan rather than something that happened by accident (*jinri zhi si, xiong you dingjian, fei chu ouran ye* 今日之死, 胸有定見, 非出偶然也),[19] as the deliberateness with which a woman chose her death was often an important "heroic" quality many hagiographers of female martyrs emphasized, as shown in Qian Chengzhi's hagiography of his late wife (to be discussed later). This belated presentation of such crucial direct evidence of her *xunfu* intention makes one wonder whether this was the result of this husband's own reinterpretation of the life of his late wife so many years after the fact. Time seems to have helped to bring about this gradual shift of a focus from the private attachment between them as husband and wife to the public image of a Confucian martyr of female chastity.

As evidence of the deep attachment between them, some grieving husbands might have indeed recalled the wishes once expressed by their wives to die with them. For example, in his biographical sketch of his late wife, You Tong also mentioned that his wife once wanted to end her life after she heard the rumor that her husband might have died in the chaotic days following the Manchu conquest. However, this was mentioned as an expression of her love for her husband rather than a case of a deliberate attempt to be a martyr of female loyalty and chastity.[20]

At a more personal level, Zhang Zhen, as a widower, must have had ambivalent feelings about such a rare opportunity of being at the receiving end of this ultimate act of devotion from his wife. He might have felt the need to extol such wifely devotion in the Confucian chastity rhetoric, presumably because this was the only acceptable way of publicly celebrating a wife's private devotion (otherwise it would invite criticism for its possible association with "indulgence"). However, earlier he had been somewhat hesitant about this approach in his biographical sketch of his wife. The act of private passion between husband and wife and the chastity martyrdom publicly celebrated by many of the Confucian ideological zealots indeed became difficult to distinguish given the fact that this would-be author of a hagiography of female chastity martyrdom was also the grieving husband of the woman being celebrated.

Zhang Zhen's case is particularly intriguing: almost seventeen years after he wrote an emotional biography/memoir of his late wife not long after her death, what interested him most was his wife's public image as a moral exemplar rather than the unique but "distracting minor details" associated with her life, exactly those private moments that only a grieving husband would cherish, a change on his part that could probably be attributed, at least in part, to the changing process from "mourning" to "commemorating." As time passed, the surviving husband's memory of his late wife became more distant, and probably less intimate. With the passage of time and the fading of memory, Zhang Zhen tended to re-remember his late wife more as an abstraction of the exemplary rather than an individual woman. He was concerned with his late wife's legacy in the collective memory of the public rather than what his late wife meant to him personally, as reflected in the private details captured in his earlier biographical sketch—precisely those details that the much-aged Zhang Zhen was asking her potential hagiographer to ignore in an attempt to better fit her image to the stereotype of an ultimate female exemplar. By celebrating his late wife as a chastity martyr, Zhang Zhen, now a commemorating husband, tried hard to rectify some of the deviations from the Confucian biographical norms of the exemplary he might have committed as a mourning husband in his earlier elegiac endeavors. Compared with a mourning husband, a commemorating husband, whose memory of his deceased wife was usually no longer that fresh and immediate, was more like a typical commissioned biographer or epitaph writer, who often did not personally know the biographical subject. Intimate knowledge was no longer that significant and, sometimes, the divulgence of such knowledge might even be detrimental to a public act of commemoration.[21]

The success of this new hagiographical project now depended on his deliberate "forgetfulness" as a commemorating husband. In a hagiography, intimate memory was irrelevant, even distracting, and had to be deliberately suppressed, as Zhang Zhen was apparently urging his wife's potential hagiographer to do. On the other hand, Zhang Zhen's case also points to the risks or vulnerability associated with the more private act of mourning on the part of a bereaved husband when the memories of the deceased wife and the guilty feelings as a surviving spouse were still fresh enough to render him susceptible to the sway of those sentiments that might have made his late wife appear less than fully exemplary, as he had shown in his earlier biographical sketch.

FROM HAGIOGRAPHY TO HISTORIOGRAPHY

Qian Chengzhi was a well-known Ming loyalist poet and scholar in the early Qing. Unlike Zhang Zhen's wife, who fasted and eventually died because she was thought to have intended to die with her dying husband, Qian Chengzhi's wife committed suicide by drowning herself in order to avoid being raped by soldiers/bandits.[22] Qian himself was not the direct reason why his wife committed suicide. Consequently, personal guilt was not something looming particularly large on his mind when Qian wrote about his late wife. Besides, Qian's biographical sketch (*xinglue* 行略) of his wife was written quite a few decades after her death. As he was becoming old, he was increasingly concerned that the facts of his wife's martyrdom would fail to be transmitted to posterity if he did not write them down. Thus the sketch was written for the sake of public commemoration rather than private mourning, as it was meant to be the basis for others to come up with a formal hagiography or other commemorative writings, most likely to be collected into the local history.

Qian had apparently tried hard to have his wife's heroic deeds recorded in local histories before but was very upset when he learned that the county magistrate of his hometown, because of a personal grudge against him, instructed the compilers of the local gazetteer to leave out the entry on his wife (more on this later).[23] The main purpose of the biographical sketch of his wife was to preserve these first-hand "facts" for future historians to keep alive the memory of his wife's heroic act.

While the fact he was the husband of his own female biographical subject remained an important factor in shaping this hagiographical project, it appears that Qian was quite deliberate in producing this biography as a conscientious Confucian historian carrying out his solemn *public* duty to record the heroic deeds of a martyr of female chastity rather than producing a personal memoir of his own late wife.

Reading through this relatively long biographical sketch, the reader is given the impression what concerned the author most were the perceived "factual" basis of his hagiographical narrative and the need to maintain his narrative authority as someone uniquely privy to the details in the life of his female biographical subject: being her husband and having lived with her for so many years granted him the special privilege as a "witness" to the heroic and virtuous deeds of this heroic martyr. In short, not diminishing in any way the objectivity of his narrative, the fact that the biographer was also the husband of the female biographical subject was emphasized to enhance his narrative persuasiveness by virtue of the firsthand, privileged information he possessed.

At the beginning of this biographical sketch of his wife, Fangshi, however, it is the image of his mother-in-law, Wang ruren, that dominates. When his future wife's father was seriously ill, Wang ruren sliced off a piece of flesh from her arm to make medicinal soup for him, a familiar radical act of *gegu* 割股 usually associated with a filial son or daughter in Confucian exemplar discourse, but here recorded to underscore her wifely virtue. Upon his death, she shaved her head and defaced herself in order to demonstrate her determination to remain a chaste widow, actions that won profuse praise from Qian's own father. At thirty, before she died, holding Qian's hands, this would-be mother-in-law pleaded to him that he should study hard and take good care of her daughter because, after all, it was she who had chosen him to be her future son-in-law.[24]

This "mini biography," or rather "mini-hagiography," of the mother-in-law at the beginning of the biography of his wife not only points to the "chastity" tradition associated with his wife's family (it was in his wife's genes, so to speak) but is also intended to explain part of the motivation behind his wife's ultimate act of chastity martyrdom. She herself had repeatedly expressed the hope that her mother should be honored by the government and the public as a chaste widow, whereas such honor, by inference, was also what she herself wished to receive by virtue of her own actions. His wife was quite happy that her husband began to achieve some fame as a man of letters because she believed that he would thus be in a good position to apply to the government for the award of a chaste widow to honor her mother. When chaos broke out after the Ming monarchy was toppled, she expressed her bitter disappointment and insisted that her wishes regarding her husband's fame were not for her own sake but for the sake of increasing the possibility of her mother receiving honorable mention by the government; when Qian was caught in the factional fighting of the Southern Ming politics and found himself on the run, she deplored his loss of ambition and felt that the facts of her mother's chastity would over time remain unknown to people.[25] Such desire to have her mother's chastity publicly celebrated on his wife's part in turn anticipated Qian's desire as the author of this hagiographical project to have his wife publicly commemorated as a chastity martyr. It was her duty as a daughter to have her mother's virtuous deeds glorified, just as it was Qian's duty as a husband and an educated Confucian man to make sure through his writings that his wife be remembered in posterity as a chastity martyr.

In the biographical sketch, his wife's act of martyrdom was the obvious focus, but Qian also devoted attention to her more "common" wifely virtues as proof of her overall exemplariness as a model wife, such as her household management skills, something she acquired only after their marriage. At the beginning, indulging in reading and writing poetry, she knew very little about household matters, but she learned quickly once she began to devote herself to such duties after deliberately deciding to put aside her writing brush and inkstone.[26] This certainly forms an interesting contrast to the image of *guixiu* 閨秀 (an educated woman in boudoir) wife in those accounts of companionate marriages discussed in Dorothy Ko's study of women in seventeenth-century China (Shen Yixiu, Ye Shaoyuan's wife, discussed in chapter 2, was just such a *guixiu* wife). Although her literacy and literary ability might be related to her knowledge of various Confucian teachings on women, she never considered reading and writing that important when it came to the duties of a wife, a gesture sometimes emphasized in hagiographical celebration of chastity martyrdom if the woman happened to be educated.[27] He also mentioned, as evidence of his wife's practical wisdom, her decisiveness when it came to the burial of his deceased father, as they managed to bury him before the bandits could wreak havoc in their hometown.[28]

However, the central story in this hagiographical project is his wife's act of martyrdom, a crucial event, which, our author himself, however, did not witness. Nevertheless, one could not help but be impressed by the dramatic manner in which Qian Chengzhi was able to reconstruct the events associated with her death, as if he had actually witnessed the suicide himself, and such dramatic intensity of his narrative was meant to enhance its historical authenticity:

> That night, the moon and the stars shined brightly and then the clouds gathered. Rain began to pour down. As dawn approached, the rain became even heavier. I took my son and went to look for her body. The river's water level almost reached as high as that of the banks with many dead bodies floating everywhere but there were not any women's bodies. Turning back to take a look at the river bank, I saw near where we stood a body covered with a reed mat and several feet of hair stretching from that person's head. With the rain making everything murky, at first we could not recognize who that person was. After observing carefully for a while, my son cried: "That's mother. In the boat, mother sewed together all the pieces of the clothing she was wearing [that day] and told me 'I will drown myself if I run cross soldiers. This way they cannot remove my clothing and expose my body.'" I checked her clothing and indeed all the pieces were tightly stitched together.[29]

With no eyewitness account as to what exactly happened during that fateful moment, the reader is expected to infer, based on the son's account, that

Qian's wife must have decided to commit suicide as soon as she saw or heard the approaching soldiers, before any of them could get close to her. His wife's clothing remaining intact was a fact Qian Chengzhi repeatedly emphasized in the biographical sketch and elsewhere in his other writings concerning his wife. Qian recalled that his late wife's face still looked fresh, as if she were alive, and all the pieces of clothing stitched together over her body remained intact when she was encoffined and buried a long time after being recovered from the bank of the river.[30] Of course, the fact that they could recognize her body only by the clothing she was wearing that day was a key point whose significance one should not miss: rather than a wife or a mother, she, now for the public, was first of all a martyr of chastity: her intact clothing became the ultimate emblem of her inviolable chaste body, which she had apparently sacrificed her life to protect.

Particularly interesting about this biographical sketch are its dramatic qualities, as captured in the passage quoted above, including Qian's reliance on his son as a witness to testify to what his wife must have done, although no one had actually witnessed her death, as well as his meticulous attention to, for example, the changing weather conditions of that morning when they were trying to locate her body, specifics he was able to recall from his memory several decades later. All this was meant to enhance the persuasiveness of his narrative as historically accurate. Here personal memories also mattered, but not for the reason of demonstrating the intimate attachment between husband and wife or mother and son, but to authenticate a historical record of Confucian chastity martyrdom.

There was another important ingredient in the making of the typical image of chastity martyr that Qian did not forget to emphasize in the biography: the deliberateness with which a chastity martyr prepared for and planned her suicide. Elsewhere, in a correspondence with one of his friends, who was compiling a book in honor of heroic martyrs in the aftermath of the collapse of the Ming, Qian Chengzhi apparently had his own late wife on his mind when he tried to drive home the importance of distinguishing among many different kinds of death:

> To die is not easy, and yet to transmit the story of death is not easy either. Some of those who died were fortunate and some not. However, those who were fortunate to have their stories recorded are not all the same. There were those who died because they intended to commit suicide and there were also those who died but who did not intend to die. In the past when the bandits began to roam around, there were several thousands of women in my

hometown who got drowned in the water when they suddenly found themselves unable to escape from the bandits. In fact, seventy percent of those died [by walking into the water] out of fear of being killed whereas thirty percent chose death out of fear of being violated. Among [the thirty percent] some were prepared to commit suicide all along and some were wearing clothing with all the pieces stitched together as people found out later when their bodies were recovered; some, after being captured, shouted insults at the bandits and then were violently butchered. Consequently, they all died and yet they died quite different deaths. How could people fail to differentiate among these deaths?[31]

In this biographical sketch, he tells us that ever since the chaos and fighting broke out after the fall of the Ming, his late wife swore on many occasions that she was ready to die:

When some women in the village came back alive from the bandits, she yelled at them, demanding to know how they managed to stay alive. When they replied that they had tried to commit suicide but failed, she laughed: "That was because you did not prepare to die. In such an age of disorder, which day could not be a day of death and which place could not be a place where one could die? How could one fail to die if one was always ready to die?" Many fellow villagers still mentioned with admiration this remark of hers up to the present day.[32]

Her suicide in the Zhenze Lake area was something she had long prepared for:

Before reaching the Zhenze Lake, when our boat was moored on the Fen Lake, my wife became concerned. Knowing we were in danger, she tried hard to persuade me to run far away and suggested that we allowed the two sons to take the Buddhist order, while she would drown herself with the daughter in her arms. However, I did not consent.[33]

Thus, this was not the first time his wife had entertained the idea of committing suicide for the sake of martyrdom; she was in fact always ready to take her own life whenever there was the possibility of encountering a dangerous situation. This time Qian did not approve rather out of commonsense, as the danger was not imminent at all. Of course, such extreme acts were often not based on commonsense. Nevertheless, this shows how eagerly his wife longed to be a martyr, something Qian did not approve of this time but still admired tremendously.

Soon his wife got her real chance to achieve martyrdom. This time she was able to sew into his son's clothing a piece of paper with a suicide poem written on it because she wanted to make sure that her husband was fully aware of her honorable intent after she died. This was meant to show that she had planned her suicide long ago and executed it with the kind of deliberateness only a determined martyr such as she was capable of.[34] Further, unlike Zhang Zhen's wife, Qian's wife cared deeply about her posthumous reputation, as she had repeatedly shown her eagerness to see that her own mother would receive posthumous recognition as a chaste widow from the imperial court.

Readers were likely struck by the absence of expression of husband–wife attachment, as one would expect in a biography written by a grieving husband. Qian must have been extra cautious in not allowing any such expression to undermine the "objectivity" of his hagiography of his wife, probably a sign of his anxiety over the possible accusation that he could be biased in choosing to glorify his own deceased wife as a martyr. Such anxiety on his part was quite likely, since he himself, during the violent Ming-Qing transition, had insisted that one should be very cautious in believing the words of relatives and friends of the deceased in deciding whether to honor that person as a martyr of loyalty or chastity when compiling historical books.[35]

Both Qian Chengzhi and the later Zhang Zhen were "commemorating" husbands. So many years after the deaths of their respective wives, their primary concerns became the public or historical significance of their wives' "martyrdom" rather than their own personal memories of a shared private married life. Both of them also felt an obligation to their wives to spread their good names, although personal guilt was still an important factor behind Zhang Zhen's hagiographical endeavor. However, Qian Chengzhi had a much larger concern. A Ming loyalist himself, he was very conscious of the need to preserve memories of all those who had attempted to vindicate with their own lives their loyalties to the former dynasty. He was the author of *Suozhi lu* 所知錄 (*A Record Based on What I Know*), a chronologically arranged history of the Southern Ming. The book's title was meant to underscore Qian's own self-consciousness as a historian who insisted that he would record only what he knew (i.e., not relying on unreliable sources that he could not verify). He showed tremendous interest in collecting and preserving materials on those loyalists who had died or committed suicide for the sake of the fallen Ming dynasty.[36] His biographical sketch of his wife was intended to be read in the context of his overall effort regarding the collective memory of a lost nation as well as those who had sacrificed their lives in the chaotic process. Like many Ming loyalists, Qian was obsessed with the different ways a person died or committed suicide in dynastic transition, despite or because of the fact that he himself did not commit suicide. Zhang Zhen's intention was slightly different in part because he felt that public celebration of his wife as the ultimate exemplar of Confucian chastity was the best reward she could receive for her extraordinary act of devotion. His feelings were related to his personal guilt as a surviving husband, the recipient of such devotion.

When Zhang Zhen wrote the earlier biographical sketch of his late wife, he apparently did not intend it to be the material for a future hagiography, as Huang Zongxi's epitaph, which was based on his sketch, seems to have confirmed. This is also partly why the biographical sketch was full of *qingyu* (emotional words), to use Zhang's own term, and other "trivial" details of their happy marriage. While wifely virtues are indeed carefully listed, Zhang Zhen also emphasized the attachment between them as husband and wife, and her refusal of food and her desire to die with her seriously sick husband were presented as evidence of such attachment between them, rather than as proof of abstract Confucian virtue—chastity and loyalty. It was an act of passion more than anything else. Seventeen years later, when Zhang Zhen tried to launch his hagiographical project, he had to resort to suppressing his intimate memories of these "trivial" details, as he urged her would-be hagiographer to simply ignore all those distracting minor details in his biographical sketch and focus on her heroic act of chastity martyrdom, as Huang Zongxi had apparently failed to do in his epitaph. The case of Zhang Zhen best illustrates the important differences between the biographical and the hagiographical by allowing us to see how the commemorating husband tried to reduce the life of his late wife to a hagiographical sketch, with personal memories being deliberately suppressed. The case has much to tell us about the process through which a biography could be turned into a hagiography, although Zhang Zhen's hagiographical project did not succeed in the end because he could find no one to write a hagiography for his wife.

If there was such a change of mind on Zhang Zhen's part from being a grieving husband in mourning to a public promoter of his wife's supposed female martyrdom, there was never hesitation on the part of Qian Chenghzi, who tried hard to celebrate his late wife as a martyr ever since her suicide. In a poem in honor of her on the day of the first anniversary of her death, Qian wrote:

With one word from the Grand Scribe her fragrant soul could be comforted;
When is the time her biography would be written into history?
太常一字芳魂慰，列傳何時付史編[37]

He obviously understood well what his late wife wanted most—her name being recorded in history, while he himself duly assumed the role of Grand Scribe by producing this biographical sketch. Indeed, so many years after her death, Qian wrote about his late wife as a historian, while trying to maintain a historical distance between himself as an objective historian and his late wife as a distant historical figure. In this regard, he was apparently helped by the several decades that had elapsed between her death and the time of his decision to pick up the brush to write this biographical sketch.

Almost from the beginning, Qian Chengzhi had tried to see the death of his wife in the large context of the fall of the Ming dynasty, as many men and women had committed suicide in different circumstances, but all for the reason of wanting to vindicate their loyalty or chastity. After all, the Zhenze Lake where his wife drowned herself was also the place where one of his loyalist friends met his death.[38] For him, it was the place that witnessed the collective heroic deeds of many loyal subjects and chaste women (*zhongchen liefu chenshi di* 忠臣烈婦沉屍地).[39]

In Qian Chengzhi's case, personal memory was appropriated to reconstruct the public image of his wife as a chastity martyr. The personal meanings of his memory of his late wife were not important as far as he, as historian, was concerned. They served only to authenticate public implications—how his wife was worthy of the honor of an ultimate exemplar of Confucian chastity. His wife drowned herself because, we are told, she had to defend her chastity; it had nothing to do with her personal feelings for her husband. Qian Chengzhi wrote this biographical sketch mainly out of his sense as a conscientious Confucian historian expected to record only what was publicly significant. Unlike Zhang Zhen, Qian eventually succeeded in having his late wife recorded in history. Quite different from his response to Zhang Zhen's similar plea, Huang Zongxi, a Ming loyalist himself, accepted Qian's request for an epitaph with enthusiasm.[40] Huang's epitaph might have played a role in the biography of Qian's wife being eventually included in the section of female martyrs in the Ming History,[41] the national history of the Ming dynasty compiled by the Qing imperial court, due to his reputation and probably the fact that some of his friends and disciples were directly involved in the Ming history project at that time.

In contrast, Zhang Zhen's case illustrates the long way women's biographical writings in general had come in becoming more secular and the important role intimate memories played in the process. He had to suppress much of his intimate memory in order to reduce her biography to a hagiography. On the other hand, Qian Chengzhi's biographical sketch demonstrates that even in writing a hagiography for a Confucian chastity martyr, personal memories, or, at least, those highly selective personal memories, could also help enable the story of a chastity martyr to be presented from a different, sometimes less dogmatic, angle. Ironically, Qian Chengzhi's "historical record" sometimes reads very much like a work of *xiaoshuo* (fiction). This could probably be attributed to personal memory, which injected an unusual dramatic quality into an otherwise quite somber hagiography. Here personal memory was relevant only when it became not so "personal" and when deployed for the sake of enhancing the verisimilitude of the Confucian virtue of female chastity. Compared with Zhang Zhen, a "failed" hagiographer, whose hagiographical project was nevertheless rooted in his deep personal guilt over being the cause of his wife's death, Qian Chengzhi ultimately triumphed as a Confucian historian: his late wife was presented as a historical figure, a female martyr of Confucian chastity worthy of being recorded in the national history. In contrast, Zhang Zhen remained a bereaved husband in perpetual private grieving despite his effort to have his late wife remembered as a public figure—a Confucian female exemplar. Zhang Zhen failed in his hagiographical attempt precisely because he could not forget or, more specifically, he could not forget those distracting trivial things in the life of his late wife, which might have "diluted" or compromised her image as a chastity martyr.

The cases of Zhang Zhen and Qian Chengzhi have certainly helped to complicate our understanding of the secularization process of memorial writings in late imperial China, especially the diverse roles assumed by personal and intimate memories. As examined in detail in chapter 8, in his litany and biography in honor of his younger sister, the famous eighteenth-century poet Yuan Mei insisted that her tragedy was the direct result of her having read too much and too literally these hagiographies of female exemplars of chastity. Yuan Mei made it very clear that he had no interest in presenting his sister as a hagiographical subject. On the contrary, she was presented as a victim of that very hagiographical tradition. This is yet another example of how a man's close relationship to his female biographical subject conditioned his view of the issue—only this time the biographer happened to be her grieving brother. However, in the next chapter, we turn our attention to Shen Fu's *Six Records*, an unprecedented work of *daowang* narrative, in which intimate memory has found its ultimate triumph in its most secular form—personal memoir focusing on the deep attachment between a married couple.

CHAPTER 4

WOUNDED MANHOOD

Before examining in detail Shen Fu's *Six Records*, arguably the most sophisticated *daowang* work in premodern China, a quick look at the immediate literary context within which it was produced is in order. If we consider the seventeenth century a golden age of Chinese elegiac prose writing, as represented by works produced by writers such as Ye Shaoyuan, Mao Xiang, and You Tong, then the turn of the nineteenth century saw the emergence of a group of *daowang* authors who broke even more new ground.

As mentioned earlier, traditionally it was relatively rare, for various reasons, for a grieving husband to commission a formal biography (*zhuan*) for his deceased spouse, not to mention authoring one himself. This began to change when Ye Shaoyuan and Chen Que wrote moving biographies for their late wives and when the Qing poet Wang Shizhen had biographies commissioned for two of his deceased spouses. By the eighteenth century, such biographies became even more common. The essayist Chen Zhi wrote a biography for his wife even while she was still alive. The writer Jin Zhaoyan 金兆燕 (1718–1789) authored a biography of his late wife, claiming he did this for the sake of his children, even though he acknowledged that she had not done anything extraordinary in her life. One quality both Chen Zhi and Jin Zhaoyan admired about their late wives was their practical wisdom and down-to-earth approaches to life. Jin claimed that his late wife was his best friend, whose advice had benefited him throughout their married life.[1]

The poet and minor official Chen Wenshu was an even more innovative biographer of his female relatives. Known for his gallant endeavors to promote women poets, he wrote two extraordinarily long biographies to mourn his wife and his more famous daughter-in-law, Wang Duan, both of whom were well educated. Reading his long biography of his daughter-in-law, a poetess and widely admired scholar, one is struck by the father-in-law's deep respect for her intellect.² He wrote the biography as if his female subject were his own equal, or even his mentor, rather than his daughter-in-law, displaying tremendous admiration for her literary talent, scholarship and, not least, religious wisdom. Conventional womanly virtues were not its focus at all, given that Wang Duan was by no means an exemplary daughter-in-law, as she devoted herself to writing and scholarship without taking on any serious household responsibilities, often with the consent of her father-in-law.

Equally long and even more significant for the discussion of this chapter is the biography Chen Wenshu wrote for his late wife, Gong Yucheng. It is particularly significant in that it offers a detailed account as to how his wife became an alcoholic and how she remained addicted to heavy drinking for almost thirty years. According to him, after the sudden death of their younger son, despondent, Gong fell very sick and stopped eating food. Their elder son, Chen Peizhi, went to pray in the temple of the god of medicine and received the instruction that his mother could have thirty more years to live if she practiced the art of *bigu* 辟穀 (a Daoist practice of trying to achieve good health and longevity by avoiding rice and similar foods) and that she could take wine and *e'jiao* 阿膠 (colla corri asini: donkey-hide gelatin) in place of food. Initially, Gong Yucheng drank wine only as a way to treat her illness, but gradually she began to enjoy the pleasure of drinking. Not long after, she became a heavy drinker. Soon, cups were replaced with big mugs. Each day, she started drinking as soon as she completed her morning toilet and would sip wine until noon; then after a nap, as darkness fell, she would resume drinking and not stop until well past midnight. She consumed on average four flagons of wine a day. When young family members gathered in her room, and whenever she felt happy, she would pick up a wine mug; her face would burst into a big smile if a relative visited her and brought her a big jar of wine; she would acknowledge happily when her grandchildren called her "a drunken immortal" (*jiuxian* 酒仙).³ This made Chen Wenshu wonder:

> In the ancient times, Liu Ling and Ruan Ji were known for their love of wine, but they both had suffered many frustrations in their careers. Late in their lives, they turned to alcohol to relieve themselves of their anxieties and as a way to conceal their talents and political views from being noticed in order to avoid trouble. They were quite unlike my wife, who was born in a time of peace and who had a harmonious family. She was also quite content and felt fairly complete in her relationship with her husband. Perhaps "drunken immortal" might indeed be a fitting name for her.⁴

Due to her addiction, Gong Yucheng was no longer able to run the household effectively. She had to formally ask Chen's concubine, Guan Jingchu, to manage daily affairs, acknowledging that she had been neglecting her duties as a daughter-in-law due to her illness and addiction to drinking (*shijiu duobing* 嗜酒多病).[5] Although Chen Wenshu was very careful in presenting his wife's drinking problem, even sometimes defending it as necessary for treating her illness or maintaining her health, the reader could still sense his frustrations:

> My wife was a person who could be quite strict and demanding. Old and suffering from illness and drinking heavily, she easily threw temper tantrums whenever she was upset, often keeping other people on edge. However, she tended to forget things quickly and usually did not dwell too long over something that had already happened. . . ."[6]

Despite his frustrations, he insisted that Gong Yucheng had been a good wife. Even with her illness and alcoholic addiction, she demonstrated wisdom and courage in making important decisions. For example, she had a way to deliver bad news to his mother (such as the death of his younger brother) when they could not hide it from her anymore, without causing too much harm to the old lady's health. She had been a very tolerant and understanding mother-in-law in her dealing with their daughter-in-law, Wang Duan, who, because of her illness and devotion to literary scholarship, did not help much with the management of the household. When Wang Duan began to devote herself to the practice of Daoist/Buddhist self-cultivation and would not show up to pay respects to her mother-in-law for several days or even more than a month, his wife never showed displeasure. She treated her daughter-in-law with respect, as if she were a guest (*binke* 賓客).[7]

There is little doubt that Chen Wenshu grieved deeply over the death of his wife of almost fifty years, and remembered her fondly despite her flaws. As a mourner, Chen Wenshu showed a surprisingly "liberal" attitude toward his wife and his daughter-in-law when he wrote about them, suggesting almost a new pattern of gender relationships in this family, although a palpable sense of family tension pervades his biography of his wife. Chen's biography of his wife should be remembered, among other things, for its surprisingly detailed portrayal of an alcoholic woman, an image quite unprecedented in the history of Chinese *daowang* literature.

Family tension continued to receive exposure in the literati's *daowang* writings in the first half of the nineteenth century. The official and philologist

Long Qirui 龍啟瑞 (1814–1858), in his memorial writings on his late wife, did not shy away from this topic. In fact, he attributed the cause of his wife's death to family frictions. Like Ye Shaoyuan of the late Ming, Long deeply regretted that he could not spend much intimate time with his wife early in their marriage because his mother was very strict and his father insisted on his total devotion to preparing for the civil examinations. In the epitaph, which was more formal, Long mentioned only that his wife died of tuberculosis.[8] In the sacrificial litany, however, he revealed that she had disputes with someone in the family and that he was surprised to learn that her eventual death was directly related to such disputes (*yishen xun zhi* 以身殉之: died for the sake of this), although he did not go into specific details as to whom she had disputes with and how such disputes led to her death.[9]

Indeed, by the first half of the nineteenth century, family tensions had become an issue grieving husbands were less likely to shun when writing about their late spouses. Still, most remained reluctant to provide specifics. Chen Wenshu's contemporary Shen Fu's *Six Records* is a particularly significant work in this regard because of its candid manner in confronting this issue. Further, writers such as Chen Wenshu appear to have pushed to the limit in terms of how long and detailed a work of traditional *daowang* genres, such as biography, could be. Ignoring many conventions associated with various traditional *daowang* genres, Shen Fu's *Six Records* is truly revolutionary in terms of how and what one could write when one mourned one's late wife. In the remainder of this chapter, I focus on this remarkable work, whose innovativeness and complexities merit a close examination.

AN AUTOBIOGRAPHICAL MEMOIR

Considered by many to be a work in the style of *yiyu ti* (words of remembrance), named after Mao Xiang's famous memoir *Plum Shadow* and probably influenced by it, Shen Fu's *Six Records* is a much more innovative work than the term *yitu ti* could suggest, due to its unprecedentedly complex narrative structure and persistent insistence on placing a grieving husband's memories of his late wife in the full context of the tensions within an extended family and its frank focus on the intimate details of his married life. Unlike other memorial writings examined in this study, *Six Records* is what I would call an autobiographical memoir. Despite its possible redundancy, this term probably best captures its generic hybridity: it is at once both Shen Fu's own autobiography and his memoir of his late wife, Yun. His reflections on his own life are closely intertwined with his memories of his late wife. It is also the first work in the long history of Chinese *daowang* literature lengthy enough to require being divided into chapters. Among the four extant chapters, the first three contain primarily memories of married life; still, in the fourth chapter, relating his travels around the country, his wife's presence, though limited, remains. What makes *Six Records* so different from all other elegiac texts we have looked at so far in this study is that, besides its sheer length and the abundant details of daily life it covers, the grieving author's memories of his late wife are carefully embedded in his musings on his own past—his own frustrations and failures in life and career as an educated man. It is this focus on his marriage and his late wife that distinguishes the work from all other Chinese autobiographies produced up to that time,[10] and yet its simultaneous explicit and complex autobiographical agenda also sets it apart from most of the *daowang* works we have examined thus far.

The way *Six Records* begins is indicative of its generic hybridity and innovativeness: "I was born in the winter of the 27th year of the reign of the Emperor Qianlong, on the second and twentieth day of the eleventh month" (67; 25).[11] This opening sentence signals that this is the author's self-narrative—his autobiography. Yet, instead of proceeding with an account of his ancestors or his childhood, the narrator starts to tell the reader how he married his wife Yun, thus suggesting that what follows might not be a typical autobiography. Presenting Yun as the focus of his narrative, Shen Fu, however, is apologetic enough to feel the need to appeal to the authority of the Confucian classic *The Book Odes* for justification: "The very first of the three hundred songs of the *Book of Odes* concerns husbands and wives, so I will write other matters in their turn" (67; 25). He argues that given the many important things in his life to talk about, he would follow the precedent set in this Confucian classic by beginning with an account of his wife, thus pointing to Yun's central place in his life and the possibility that what followed would indeed be a memoir of his late wife, thus largely a *daowang* narrative.

Since marriages were usually pre-arranged by parents in traditional China, and very few men had the chance to see or meet their future wife until the wedding day, courtship before marriage was relatively rare, and recalling one's courtship when remembering one's late wife was even rarer (Mao Xiang's *Plum Shadow* is an exception because his concubine Dong Xiaowan was once a courtesan). Because Shen Fu's mother was Yun's aunt (her father's sister), the two had opportunities to see each other whenever his mother visited her natal family. In fact, it was the thirteen-year-old Shen Fu who, having fallen in love with his cousin, pleaded to his mother to arrange the marriage with her. Fortunately, his mother consented, a rare case in which a young man was able to have an almost decisive say in choosing whom he was going to marry, preparing the reader for this story about a couple deeply in love.

Yun could read and compose poetry, a quality that attracted Shen Fu early on. However, this would also later cause her troubles: Shen Fu, the narrator, prepares the reader from hindsight, in this way: "Then as a joke I wrote on her manuscript, 'The Embroidered Bag of Beautiful Verses.' I did not then realize that the signs of her early death were already there" (68; 27).[12] By giving her manuscript the title "The Embroidered Bag of Beautiful Verses," Shen Fu might have unwittingly brought a curse upon his future wife, as it was well known that the gifted Tang poet Li He 李賀 (790–816), who died at the age of twenty-seven, had the habit of placing completed poems in an embroidered bag. As the reader will soon learn, Yun's ability to write would be one of the reasons for strained relations between her and Shen Fu's parents. That Yun's talent contributed to her early death was an important argument the narrator makes in *Six Records*, a view not unrelated to his explanation for his own frustrations in life—his own talent and his aspirations to be independent might have similarly caused him many troubles. Here, *daowang* (mourning the female other) and grieving for one's own misfortune (the male self) became virtually inseparable (more on this later).

Throughout the first two chapters, which are about the happy days the couple shared, the narrative is often punctuated or interrupted with subtle signs and comments from hindsight by the narrator that ominously foreshadow the events to be described later. These are premonitions the subtle implications of which only Shen Fu, the narrator (the narrating "I" or the remembering "I") can fully appreciate, while Shen Fu, the "character" (the Shen Fu or "I" that is being remembered or written about) apparently could not. This injects a sense of foreboding to his memories of otherwise happy moments in their lives. It also dramatizes the distance and the differences between the Shen Fu who is remembering and the Shen Fu being remembered. For example, earlier, when Shen Fu met Yun for the first time, he recalls, "I had a chance to read her poems that day, and though I sighed at her brilliance I privately feared that her future life was not going to be too happy" (*fuze bushen* 福澤不深) (67; 26).[13] This is a description of a feeling of the teenaged Shen Fu, apparently colored by the older Shen Fu's hindsight on what would later happen. As it is doubtful a thirteen-year-old boy would have such a presentiment, this description is rather an interpretation of the later Shen Fu's feelings written many years after his wife had tragically passed away.

Very few grieving husbands wrote of the appearances of their late wives, although some were more likely to do so in the case of their late concubines.

One of the very few exceptions was the case of Ye Shaoyuan, discussed in chapter 2, but his praise of Shen Yixiu's beauty tends to emphasize its spiritual appeal (comparing her to a pine tree, etc.). Thus what Shen Fu proceeds to do in this regard is quite unprecedented, as he specifically describes his wife's physical charms:

> Yun had delicate shoulders and a stately neck, and her figure was slim. Her brows arched over beautiful, lively eyes. Her only blemish was two slightly protruding front teeth, the sign of the lack of good fortune. But her manner was altogether charming, and she captivated all who saw her. (68; 27)

Likewise, the physiognomic observation that her front teeth were a sign of her lack of good fortune must have been a reflection from hindsight by the older Shen Fu rather than the observation of a thirteen-year-old boy—another example of how time had profoundly shaped the representations of the past, as memory is inherently revisionist.

Shen Fu married Yun when he was seventeen, and the narrator does not refrain from describing in detail the happy and often intimate time they shared as a newlywed couple. This is how Shen Fu recalls these intimate moments:

> We sat up making jokes, like two close friends meeting after a long separation. I playfully felt her breasts and found her heart was beating as fast as mine. I pulled her to me and whispered in her ear, "Why is your heart beating so fast?" She answered with a bewitching smile that made me feel a love so endless it shook my soul. I held her close as I parted the curtains and let her into bed. We never noticed what time the sun rose in the morning. (69; 29)

Very few Chinese men had described the intimate time they spent with their wives in such a frank manner as Shen Fu does here. He then recalls how they as a newlywed couple tried to navigate their ways in the hierarchical and sometimes "treacherous" environment of an extended family:

> Whenever we would meet one another in a darkened room or a narrow hallway of the house, we would hold hands and ask, "Where are you going?" We felt furtive, as if we were afraid others would see us. In fact, at first we even avoided being seen walking or sitting together, though after a while we thought nothing of it. If Yun were sitting and talking with someone and saw me come in, she would stand up and move over to me and I would sit down beside her. Neither of us thought about this and it seemed quite natural; and

though at first we felt embarrassed about it, we gradually grew accustomed to doing it. The strangest thing to me then was how old couples seem to treat one another like enemies. I did not understand why. Yet people said, "Otherwise, how could they grow old together?" Could this be true? I wondered. (72–73; 33)

Here Shen Fu remembers how they first had to behave furtively as a couple within an extended family but gradually they began to be more free with their expressions of affection for each other, hinting that their loving behavior, no matter how discreet in the eyes of a modern reader, might have alienated themselves from some in the family, a suggestion that seems be reinforced in chapter 3, when, after recalling how his wife passed away, he acknowledges this was because they loved each other too much (*guoyu qing du* 過於情篤). Despite his reference to the saying that "an affectionate couple could not grow old together," a sort of fatalistic but vague rationale he appeals to, Shen Fu's specific reference to "their loving each other too much" as the reason for her early death might suggest something more specific: they showed too much affection for each other "in public," as "being too affectionate" was repeatedly cautioned against in traditional Confucian discourses regulating husband–wife relations (as discussed in chapter 1). Here, once again, the account of happy moments in their married life is overshadowed by a sense of inevitable tragedy.

Their honeymoon was soon interrupted when his father instructed that he should leave home to study with a tutor in another place, leaving his bride behind. Departing from the conventions of traditional life-narrative (including both biography and autobiography) that information on one's ancestors and father is usually provided at the beginning since these male figures of older generations were typically the defining factors in shaping a man's Confucian identity, Shen Fu instead tells of his late wife first and does not mention his father until well into the narrative. When he does introduce his father, he presents him as the one who disrupts their honeymoon by ordering him to leave to study with a distant tutor. In fact, as Shen Fu remembers, his father turns out to be a major cause of their miseries.

FATHER'S OPPRESSIVE PRESENCE

According to Shen Fu, Yun was a bride constantly worrying about fitting into the new environment of her husband's family: "As a new bride, Yun was very quiet. She never got angry, and when anyone spoke to her she always replied with a smile. She was respectful to her elders and amiable to everyone else. Everything she did was orderly, and was done properly" (69; 19). This reads like the routine praise of a daughter-in-law one often encounters in a typical biography of a woman or an elegiac narrative by her relative or husband.[14] However, Shen Fu's intention here is to show how, despite her best behavior, Yun was nevertheless forced into a hopeless predicament in her relationships with her parents-in-law.

Since Yun was literate, Shen Fu's father asked her to write to him on behalf of her mother-in-law when he was working away from home. Yun soon had to stop, however, when Shen Fu's mother began to suspect she had written something improper in the letters, as there was gossip at home. This upset the father, who complained to Shen Fu that "your wife will not condescend to write letters for your mother." Later, Yun really infuriated the father when the latter happened to open and read one of her letters to Shen Fu, who was working with him at that time, which arrived after her husband had left:

> Yun wrote of my younger brother's borrowing from the neighbor, and also said, "Your mother thinks the old man's illness is all because of the Yao girl. When he is a bit better, you should secretly order Yao to write to her parents saying she is homesick. I will tell her parents to go to Yangzhou to fetch her home. This way, both sides can disclaim responsibility for her departure." (75; 97)

Here, the Yao girl was the concubine Shen Fu's father took under the arrangement of Yun. Working away from home, his father insisted on finding himself a girl from his hometown to be his concubine to "take care of" him. Shen Fu wrote to Yun, asking her to find his father such a concubine after a friend related his father's wishes to him. Yun lied to her mother-in-law about the girl to cover up the matter, but when the truth was revealed she incurred resentment from the latter. Now, after learning of the father's recent illness, Shen Fu's mother began to blame the concubine for having depleted his health. This is why Yun tried to have the girl sent back, in order to appease the upset mother-in-law. All this made his father furious, especially after Shen Fu's younger brother claimed he knew nothing about the loan, which he had actually taken from a neighbor, with Yun serving as the guarantor. Now his father began to accuse Yun of borrowing money behind Shen Fu's back and that she had demonstrated disrespect to the elders by calling her mother-in-law "your mother" and the father-in-law "the old man" (here, in fact, Yun was just quoting her mother-in-law, as the latter had said "the old man").

The father even sent a messenger home to try to have Yun expelled. Shen Fu could only apologize to his father and then rushed home, in fear that Yun might commit suicide. Eventually Shen Fu and his wife had to move out of the family to live somewhere else.

Though later his father invited them back after learning what had really transpired, he soon had them expelled again due to his displeasure after learning of Yun's swearing sisterhood with a sing-song girl:

> Your wife does not behave as a woman should, swearing sisterhood with a sing-song girl. Nor do you think to learn how to improve yourself [by associating with good people]. Instead, you befriended with petty people. I cannot bear to put you to death. Make plans to leave home, and make them quickly. If you take longer, I would send you to the court, accusing you of being unfilial. (78; 99)[15]

The reader can well imagine the wrath of his father and its consequences in a time when a father enjoyed absolute authority over his son and when being unfilial was one of the most serious sins or crimes a man could be accused of.

Yun's falling out of favor with his parents was only one of the many factors contributing to Shen Fu's strained relationship with his father. Throughout his life, Shen Fu's father appears to be the cause of many of his miseries. This is the way Shen Fu describes how he began to study to become a *muyou* 幕友 (a secretary on the personal staff of an official):

> During the summer of 1781, in the eighth month, my father fell sick with malaria and returned home. When he was cold he wanted a fire, and when he was hot he wanted ice. I advised him against this but he did not listen, and so his illness eventually turned into typhoid fever and grew worse daily. I waited on him with soup and medicine, never closing my eyes day or night for almost a month. My wife Yun also became very ill, and was confined to her bed. I was quite depressed and there is no way to describe it.
>
> One day my father called me to him and said, "I am afraid I will not recover. You have studied a few books, but ultimately this will not help you to make a living. I am going to entrust you to my sworn younger brother Jiang Siqi, so that you can continue in my profession." . . . It was from this time that I began studying to work in government offices. Why record these unhappy events here? I reply, I record them because it was from this time that I abandoned my study and began my wandering. (*paoshu langyou zhishi* 拋書浪游之始; 115–116; 105)

Obviously, to become a *muyou* was not a career choice Shen Fu himself made but one made for him by his father, whose illness at that time, we are told by the son, got much worse because he refused to listen to his son's advice and who, therefore, brought sheer miseries to both the son and the daughter-in-law. Note the sentence "it was from this time that I abandoned my study and began my wandering": here "study" most likely refers to his preparation for the civil examinations, the respected traditional path to career success almost every educated male at that time aspired to. Shen Fu was never given a chance because his father did not think he could succeed in the examinations.[16] Basically, Shen Fu is implicitly blaming his father for sending him onto this miserable career path that would condemn him to lifelong poverty. Further, Shen Fu appears to suggest that his father contributed to his poverty in many other ways:

> My father, the honorable Jiafu, was the most generous gentleman, anxious to help those in trouble, to assist anyone in need, to marry off other people's daughters and to bring up their sons. There are countless examples. He spent money like dirt, most of it for other people. (96; 73)

Knowing the kind of poverty Shen Fu suffered in his life, as he has carefully detailed in the *Six Records*, the reader could detect signs of deep bitterness, even when Shen Fu appears to be praising his father's generosity.

Shen Fu feels that both his wife and himself were treated unfairly by other members in his family in addition to his parents. His wife was subjected to disrespect by many in the family:

> Although I was the eldest son in the family, I was the third child, and so at first everyone called Yun "third lady." Later, however, they suddenly started to call her "third wife" (*san taitai*; implying she was a concubine). It began as a joke, but then became usual practice, so that everyone from the elders to the servants was calling her "third wife." I wonder, was this the beginning of the disagreement in our family. (96; 73)

Shen Fu seems to be suggesting that some in the family conspired against them.

Another source of tension is his strained relationship with his younger brother, Qitang, who, Shen Fu points out earlier, borrowed money from someone else, with Yun serving as the guarantor, but who later denied to their father that he ever did, getting her into trouble. To inherit more properties from their father, Qitang tricked Shen Fu into staying away from his sick father until it was too late for him to bid farewell to the dying father. Qitang even arranged some debtors to collect debts from Shen Fu soon after the death of the father. Claiming that he did not want to fight with his brother for his father's property, Shen Fu had to leave the family.

Never before had a Chinese man had so much to say about how he and his late wife had to suffer as a result of their strained relationships with other family members and how unfairly they had been treated by others in the family, especially by his own father and younger brother. One is often struck how Shen Fu (especially the remembering Shen Fu) always sided with his wife in defending her.

EMASCULATED AND TRAPPED IN THE FEMININE WORLD

The entire second chapter of the *Six Records* is devoted to the account of how Shen Fu and his wife managed to construct a small private world of their own, filled with various small but aesthetically refined constructs such as miniature hills or dwarfed trees. At the very beginning of the chapter, Shen Fu traces his love for "small things" to his childhood obsession with small insects and many other tiny objects. As a child, he had a special knack for imagining these small things into something quite big: for example, in his imagination, grasses could become forests, mosquitoes could become cranes flying in clouds, and so on. However, a traumatic incident happened:

> One day while I was absorbed in my imaginary world, my egg was bitten by an earthworm (in Suzhou we call the male organs eggs), so that it swelled up and I could not urinate. The servants caught a duck, and were forcing it to open its mouth over the wound, when suddenly one of them let go of the bird. The duck stretched out its neck as if to bite me there, and I screamed with fright. This became a family joke. (86; 56)

Why does Shen Fu here recall his becoming a "family joke" as a child? This reminds the reader how Yun was called "third wife" by everyone in the family. Both of them appear to have suffered disrespect in a rather unfriendly family environment. However, there are much subtler implications: this chapter is about the trauma of "symbolic castration" and its consequences. As we see later, his love for "small things" was closely related to his experience of emasculation.

The remainder of chapter 2 focuses on how the adult Shen Fu managed to find various ingenious ways to enjoy little leisurely pleasures with his wife in the confined spaces of their small residence due to his inability as a man to afford the "big spaces" of a large house.[17] In other words, making do with small spaces was now primarily a harsh economic necessity rather than an aesthetic choice. A point Shen Fu repeatedly emphasizes is that their hardships were caused by his being a *pinshi* (a poor scholar) with very limited means, or that he was a man of career failures:

> Poor scholars (*pinshi*) who live in small crowded houses should rearrange their rooms in imitation of the sterns of the Taiping boats of my home county, the steps of which can be made into three beds by extending them at front and back. Each bed is then separated from its neighbor by a board covered with paper. Looking at them when they are laid out is like walking a long road—you do not have a confined feeling at all. When Yun and I were living in Yangzhou we arranged our house in this fashion. . . . Yun had laughed about our handiwork, saying "The layout is fine, but it still does not quite have the feel of a rich home." I had to admit she was right! (90; 61)

Despite his bragging about his unique ability to find pleasures in the confined domestic spaces and to create the illusionary feeling of spaciousness out of such a confined space, there was always a vague sense of lack, reminding him of the actual big spaces he could not afford as a *pinshi*. Elsewhere in this chapter Shen Fu is more direct about this point when he explains the reason that he raised flowers in vases rather than pots is not that "I did not enjoy looking at them in pots, but because our house had no garden I could grow them in pots myself" (87; 57).

Even when he and his wife seemed to be enjoying the pleasures of their miniature world in their confined spaces, something unexpected would always happen to expose the ephemeral nature of their carefully constructed illusions. Shen Fu raised a pot of orchids—his favorite flower—but one day it suddenly dried up and died. "Only later did I learn that someone who had asked for a cutting and been refused had poured boiling water over it and killed it" (87; 56). A similar incident occurred later, after Shen Fu and his wife had built a landscape in a pot with miniature hills, a pavilion, and a river in it: "We were as excited about it as if we were actually going to move to those imaginary hills and vales. But one night some miserable cats fighting over something to eat fell over the eaves, smashing the pot in an instant" (91; 62).

The imaginary world of big spaces Shen Fu and his wife managed to construct in their crowded tiny residence proved to be as fragile and vulnerable as his childhood imaginary world of small insects was easily destroyed by a "giant"—a not-so-big toad—an episode Shen Fu has recalled at the beginning of this chapter, where his childhood memory seems to have been dominated by the traumatic incident of his penis being bitten by an earthworm and later nearly bitten by a duck. Small spaces and the obsession with trying to imagine various small things into big things seem to be intimately associated with his damaged manhood—his injured penis as a child and his bruised male ego as an adult *pinshi*. Because of their poverty or his failure to provide for the family, Shen Fu and his wife had to do their utmost to find "pleasures of leisure" in their crowded residence by constructing a world of miniature hills and bonsai (*pengzai* 盆栽) that would enable them to sustain the illusion that their crowded living space was not that small. The feminine nature of these small domestic spaces is emphasized when Shen Fu tells us how his wife was often better at these projects.

The emasculating implications of these confined domestic spaces that dominate chapter 2 become all the more pronounced when contrasted with the "real" big spaces that characterize chapter 4, "The Delights of Roaming Afar," which is about our narrator's seemingly manly activities: his visits to many famous places around the country. But before we delve into a detailed discussion of chapter 4, a brief look at the structure of this autobiographical memoir is in order.

As its title suggests, *Six Records of a Floating Life* originally contained six chapters. However, as we have it now, the work contains only four chapters, with the last two chapters missing. Among the extant four chapters, chapter 1, "A Record of the Joy of the Boudoir" counters chapter 3, "A Record of the Sorrows of the Misfortunes" in terms of contrasting joy and sorrow. If their joy is confined mainly within the feminine space of the boudoir, then sorrow takes places whenever the outside world begins to intrude. In turn, chapter 2, "A Record of the Pleasures of Leisure," counters chapter 4, "A Record of the Delight of Roaming Afar," as the former focuses on the confined feminine domestic spaces, and the latter the expansive spaces beyond the domestic, the masculine domain in which a man could find fulfillment of his manhood. Consequently, readers could fully appreciate the gender implications of the confined domestic spaces of chapter 2 only in relation to the masculine spaces that define chapter 4.

It is in chapter 1, on the "joys" of the boudoir, where the reader is introduced to the gender implications of the spaces: the confining nature of the domestic feminine space and the masculine world beyond the family compound. After hearing Shen Fu's raving about a local festival, Yun expresses her wishes to go, but worries it might be improper for her since she is a woman. Under the encouragement of Shen Fu, she decides to cross-dress as a man so that she can join him on the outing. Here the fact that Yun must masquerade as a man in order to travel beyond the feminine space of the boudoir is certainly a poignant reminder of the symbolic boundary between the domestic space of the feminine and the masculine space of the outside world. Travel, especially traveling afar, were the important gender privileges only a man could enjoy at that time. Travel was a badge of a man's masculinity, as Shen Fu once explained to his wife:

> It's a pity that you are a woman and have to remain hidden away at home. If only you could become a man we could visit famous mountain and search our magnificent ruins. We could travel the whole world together. Wouldn't that be wonderful? (77; 40)

If chapter 2 is about how Shen Fu must come to grips with his emasculation in the confined domestic spaces as a frustrated and poor scholar, then chapter 4 is about his desperate attempts to regain his manhood by presenting himself as a man who has traveled widely, someone able to roam in those big "manly" spaces around the country, conforming to the Confucian image of a manly gentleman, as celebrated in the common saying: "A true man has lofty ambitions that reach the four corners of the earth" (*zhangfu zhi zai sifang* 丈夫志在四方).[18] In chapter 4, he need not pretend that the small spaces where he found himself trapped were not that confining, as he has tried so hard to do in chapter 2, because here he is seen to be enjoying the delights of traveling afar as only a man could do.

ROAMING/WANDERING IN MASCULINE SPACES

Chapter 4, "The Delights of Roaming Afar," in fact, begins on a not-so-delightful note:

> I have traveled about working in government offices for thirty years now, and the only places in the world I have never been to are Sichuan, Guizhou and

Yunan. The pity is that wheel and hoof have followed one another in such quick succession. Everywhere I have gone I have been accompanying others, so that while beautiful mountains and rivers have passed before my eyes like drifting clouds and I have been able to form some rough idea of what they are like, I have never been able to search out and explore secluded places on my own. (113; 101)

Here the feeling is at least mixed: Shen Fu is boasting of having traveled to many places around the country, yet because most of these trips were undertaken while he was serving as a *muyou* or having to accompany his employers, he did not have an opportunity to explore secluded places on his own, suggesting his dependency on others might have undermined his experience as a traveler. All these frustrations are related to his aspirations to be a true man of independence.

Indeed, Gong Weizhai 龔未齋, Shen Fu's contemporary, who was also a lifelong *muyou*, attributed his inability to be a true man to his career as a private secretary for officials:

> A true man should be able to stand on his own feet (*zhangfu dang zili* 丈夫當自立) and he should not rely on the pity of others.... A failure throughout my life, I really feel ashamed of myself for not being able to stand on my own feet.[19]

For many in the profession of *muyou*, one of the most emasculating aspects of their experience was their inability to stand on their own (*zili*). As a private secretary on the personal staff of an official, a *muyou* totally depended on the whims of his employer, partly because their relationship was not institutionally guaranteed by the imperial bureaucratic system at all. Working for the official, he was being paid by that official rather than the imperial government, and their relationship was completely private.[20] In the words of Gong Weizhai, "though often presented as a guest or a friend, he is actually treated no differently than a retainer."[21] It is the ambiguities associated with the identity of *muyou*, which, as the term itself suggests, underscore his dual status as an advisor/secretary (*mu* 幕) as well as a guest/friend (*you* 友); more often, the fact that he could also be reduced to being a retainer or, even worse, a servant, also made the actual experience humiliating and emasculating. The treatment as a retainer is all the more humiliating precisely because of the expectation to be respected as a friend. Indeed, *zili* is the very notion Shen Fu clang to when he tried to vindicate his manhood by insisting that he did not care for fighting with his brother over the inheritance after his father had died, as he declared in very similar wording: "A true man cherishes his ability to be able to stand on his own feet (*da zhangfu gui fu zili* 大丈夫貴乎自立). (93; 110) Being unable to "stand on his own feet" was certainly the predicament in which Shen Fu often found himself as a *muyou*.

In chapter 4, right after the paragraph on his unhappy dependency on others as a traveler, Shen Fu tries to reassert his intellectual independence (*zili*):

> I like to have my own opinion about things and not pay attention to other people's approval or disapproval. In talking about poetry or painting, I am always ready to ignore what others value and to take some interest in what others ignore. And so it was with the beauty of famous scenery, which lies in any case entirely in what one feels about it oneself. Thus there are famous scenic spots which I do not feel anything extraordinary, and there are unknown places that I think are quite wonderful. (113; 101).

Of course, the harsh reality is that his intellectual independence was often severely undercut by his economic dependency, as repeatedly mentioned in the chapter. Throughout this chapter, supposedly about his attempts to reassert his manly image by emphasizing how widely he traveled, there is a subtle tension between his total dependency on others as a *muyou*, who was able to travel around the country only because he was accompanying his employers to travel to the latter's different official posts, and his aspirations to feel like a man of independence (*zili*), at least when he was traveling.

In sharp contrast to the image of dwarfed trees and miniature hills in chapter 2, here the dominant images are all those of grand landscape: "From there West Lake looked like a mirror, while the city of Hangzhou was as small as a ball and Qiantang River looked like a belt. We could see for hundreds of *li*, quite the most wonderful vista I have ever seen" (115; 104). And: "The view from the pavilion was boundless, but all that could be seen were angry waves reaching to the horizon" (121; 113). These are "real" grand vistas rather than the artificial bonsai and miniature hills he and his wife constructed in the confining spaces of their home. They are truly "masculine" spaces in part because a woman with her bound feet, such as his wife, could only dream of visiting these places, even if she cross-dressed herself as a man as Yun is said to have done in chapter 1.

On the other hand, to show that he was and still is a man of independent views, Shen Fu often chooses to differentiate himself from others in offering his own opinions on certain popular tourist spots:

> The most famous place in Suzhou itself, Lion Forest, was supposedly created in the style of paintings by Yunlin with splendid rocks and many old trees, but to me it looks like a pile of coal dust covered with moss and ant hills, without the least suggestion of the atmosphere of mountains and forests (*quanwu shanlin qishi* 全無山林氣勢). In my humble opinion, there is nothing particularly wonderful about it. (136; 136)

Note Shen Fu is here faulting Lion Forest for its artificiality and lack of naturalness, while artificiality is a quality that certainly characterizes all those miniature mountains or bonsai trees he had cherished so much in chapter 2. In fact, miniature hills and bonsai trees are all about "taming" nature within the domestic space. The reader is here reminded only more poignantly how desperately Shen Fu had tried to escape from the confined domestic space (in spite of the illusion of big space he and his wife were able to construct) to assert his stance as a manly traveler who embraced and enjoyed "real" nature.

Unfortunately, many times, as Shen Fu tells us, he could not visit a scenic place he really wanted to see because the official for whom he was working at the time had to move or was appointed to a different post:

> In the second month of winter that year we reached Qingzhou. There Zhuotang received the letter promoting him to be the Inspectorate of the Dongguan Circuit, and left me behind at Qingzhou. I was disappointed at being denied this opportunity to see the mountains and rivers of Sichuan. (138; 139)

And later, in the autumn of 1807, "Zhuotang was dismissed from office and appointed to the Hanlin academy, and I accompanied him to the capital. I never got to see the so-called mirage of Dengzhou after all." (141; 144). Like its beginning, chapter 4, which is about the "delights" of "roaming afar," ends on a rather unhappy note, reminding the reader that his effort to vindicate his manliness via emphasizing his intellectual independence was often compromised by his status as a *muyou* and the fact that his ability to travel as a man was totally dependent on the emasculating profession that he disliked so much. Here, Zhuotang 琢堂 was the style name of Shi Yunyu 石韞玉 (1756–1837), his childhood friend, who later became a famous and prolific writer as well as a high government official and who hired Shen Fu to work for him as a *muyou*. Working for someone who was his childhood friend and who, in contrast to him, was a great achiever in life (achieving phenomenal examination successes by taking first place in the metropolitan exams and becoming a high official), while in every way he himself a failure, must not have been easy for Shen Fu.[22] Although he does mention how Zhuotang helped him (he even gave him a girl as his concubine after the death of his wife), Shen Fu never expresses the kind of strong warm feelings about this friend that he has reserved for several other friends in the *Six Records*. The fact that Shen Fu insists on referring to him simply by his style name, Zhuotang, rather than using his official titles indicates that he considers him his equal instead of his superior or employer, underscoring, not without irony, the ambiguities inherent in the relationship between this *muyou* and his employer.

This leads us to the meaning of the word *langyou* 浪游 (here it is translated by Pratt and Chen as "roaming afar" in their translation of the title of chapter 4). Shen Fu uses this very same word to refer to the "wandering" life of a *muyou* when he mentions that ever since his father had ordered him to take up the profession of *muyou*, he had to give up his "study" and begin his "wandering," as quoted before: "Why record these unhappy events here? I reply, I record them because it was from that I abandoned my study and began my wandering" (116; 105). Here *langyou* refers to the frustrating life of wandering he had to endure in order to make a living. Consequently, *langyou* could be a happy masculine act of free roaming, but could also be unhappy "wandering," which was often emasculating and confining, even in big spaces, just as he had experienced in the crowded domestic spaces in chapter 2.[23] Indeed, chapters 2 and 4, despite the apparent contrasts between them in terms of the different gender ramifications of spaces, are actually about two aspects of the same issue—Shen Fu's attempts to come to grips with his own gender anxiety as a *muyou*, someone who could not stand on his own feet.

THE MANHOOD OF A LOVING HUSBAND

Among the long trips Shen Fu mentions in chapter 4, there is one to Guangdong, which, however, was not a trip that he took to accompany his employer as a member of his personal staff, but rather a "business trip" he undertook with the husband of his younger cousin to do business in the south. His account of this trip does not focus on sightseeing or their business activities but rather his adventures in the pleasure quarters. Patronizing prostitutes was certainly a male privilege, and thus might have been presented to help enhance his self-image as a true man, the main agenda of the chapter. We are told that he chose a sing-song girl named Xiu'er as his companion, largely because she looked like his wife, Yun, and he even wished that his wife could be there. Shen Fu seems to be insisting that even while he was having a sexual relationship with another woman he remained loyal to his wife, since he chose to sleep with Xiu'er because she resembled his wife, and, further, he was convinced that his wife would appreciate this and she would be perfectly happy in joining them, as he has told us before that Yun was anxious to have another sing-song girl to become his concubine. Shen Fu even demonstrated loyalty to Xi'er the prostitute because, unlike many patrons, throughout his sojourn in Guangdong, he contends he was monogamous (that is, he never slept with other prostitutes as most other patrons did there). While trying to vindicate his manhood as a patron of the pleasure quarters, he, Shen Fu is insisting, was different from other men, especially when it came to relationships with women: he was more sensitive to women and more loyal to those of them he had relationships with, even though he did not disavow the male privileges afforded by this patriarchic society.

Much has been said about Shen Fu being a loving husband. Indeed, it was not common for a man at that time to openly side with his wife in disputes between her and his parents in showing how she was wronged by his family and especially his father, an attitude quite remarkable given the traditional Confucian emphasis on a son's obligations to his parents and the strong suspicion toward a wife as a family outsider. It is even more remarkable that he has described in such detail the unfair treatment of his wife at the hands of his parents and his own frustrations over such treatment. Such remarkable sensitivity and empathy on Shen Fu's part, I would like to contend, might be related to his own marginalized position as a *pinshi* and his unhappy experience as a son. We have looked at how Shen Fu must have felt his manliness undermined due to the oppressive presence of his father, who once even threatened to put him to death, which might have contributed to his own repeated career failures. Ironically, it was precisely his marginality and his feeling of emasculation that placed him in a unique position in which he could better empathize with his wife, who had suffered so much unfair treatment due in large part to her even more marginalized position as a woman and daughter-in-law. By the same token, it was his own frustration in his inability to be an independent traveler that made him so understanding of his wife's desire to venture beyond the confines of boudoir to see more of the outside world. He even urged her to cross-dress as a man in order to break free from the gender restrictions imposed on her as a woman.

A common wish a loving couple often expressed in those times was that they could continue to be husband and wife in the next life because they loved each other so much in this life. However, here we are given an interesting twist: Shen Fu proposed that in the next life Yun should be reborn a man and husband and he himself a woman and wife (78; 40). That is, he wished they could switch their gender identities and reverse their roles as husband and wife in the next life. This is quite interesting, as a popular belief, influenced by the Buddhist concept of karma, was that when a man committed a sin he would be reborn as a woman in his next life as punishment, while a woman would be reborn as an animal in her next life as punishment for her sin. Here, Shen Fu apparently did not mind being reborn as a woman in the next life, because he had such a good understanding of Yun and such an empathy with her for her plight as a woman. It was much easier for him to identify with a woman. The context in which Shen Fu made this proposal of gender switch between him and his wife in their next lives reinforces this impression of Shen Fu as a man who could easily identify with a woman. They were talking about Yun's wishes to travel the country together when they became old because it was more difficult for a young woman to venture far beyond the confines of her home. Sun Fu commented that they would become too old to travel. Then Yun said: "Then if we can't do it in this life, I hope we can do it in the next" (78; 40). Yun's remark led Shen Fu to propose their gender switch in the next life. Precisely because he had experienced so poignantly the confining feeling of the crowded spaces of the domestic, as he so desperately tries to come to grips with in chapter 2, as well as his dependency on others as a *muyou*, which enabled him to travel extensively and yet which, at the same time, severely undercut his freedom and independence as a man, as described in chapter 4, Shen Fu could fully appreciate his wife's aspiration to travel the country.

Citing not without sarcasm the conventional saying "Lack of talent in a woman is a virtue," Shen Fu attributes the suffering and tragedy of his wife to her being too talented, because it is her literacy, her ability to write, that got her into trouble in the first place after his father asked her to write the letter for the mother and all the problems ensued. However, there is a deeper implication: understanding the reasons behind the special enthusiasm on the part of many marginalized literati for this notion of talent causing tragedy, we should not find it difficult to see how Shen Fu is identifying himself with Yun in their shared fate of a talented person being mistreated by others or neglected by their times (*sheng bu fengshi* 生不逢時), a common theme in literati literature. Despite their shared positionality in this symbolic gender order, Shen Fu cherished his wife, Yun, precisely because she, as a woman relegated to a much more marginalized position, was able to make her husband feel more manly about himself. Shen Fu's special appreciation of Yun in this regard can be seen from the way he detailed her persistent endeavor trying to find him a concubine. It was an indication of her virtue as an unjealous wife and a reaffirmation of Shen Fu's status as a man and as a husband. This kind of polygamous privilege and Yun's embrace of such privilege on the part of her husband were supposed to enhance Shen Fu's manly image. Here, Shen Fu's sense of his own manliness was apparently not being threatened by the potentially lesbian implications in Yun's professed love for Hanyuan, while the latter was the same girl whom she wanted Shen Fu to take as a concubine. Shen Fu and Yun even jokingly made reference to the *Lianxiang ban* (*The Fragrant Companion*), the play by the seventeenth-century playwright, Li Yu, in which a wife, who has fallen in love with another girl, arranges the latter to become her husband's concubine so that the two could live together forever (51).[24] In fact, Yun was heartbroken after learning that Hanyuan was taken by a rich man and became the latter's concubine. Here, strangely enough, such potentially lesbian attachment among the spouses of a polygamous man could in fact enhance, rather than undermine, his manliness—at least this is what Shen Fu is suggesting. Unfortunately for Shen Fu, he was eventually denied such an opportunity of polygamous bliss, partly because he was merely a poor literatus (*pinshi*).

It appears there were special qualities about Yun that made Shen Fu feel better about himself as a man. For example, Shen Fu had a lot to say about his wife's literary talent, but he makes sure his readers know that she was not well educated enough to challenge his status as a man of Confucian education. She was just at the right level for him to feel that he was still far superior. This is the way Shen Fu describes how he tried to cultivate his wife: "When we were first married Yun was very quiet, and enjoyed listening to my discussing things. But I drew her out, as a man will use a blade of grass to encourage a cricket to chirp, and she gradually began to express herself" (76; 38). Despite all his love and his professed respect for her intellect, enjoying a special sense of superiority, Shen Fu could be quite condescending to her. More importantly, Yun never complained about Shen Fu's career failures or his incompetence being the root cause of their poverty. Instead, she was quite capable of consoling him:

> "One day we should build a cottage here and buy ten mou of land to make a garden around it," said Yun happily, "We could have servants plant melons and vegetables that would be enough to live on. What with your painting and my embroidery, it would give us enough to drink wine and compose poetry [with our friends]. We could live quite happily wearing cotton clothes and eating nothing but rice. [You] don't have to worry about the need to travel far away [to find a job]." (79; 43)

What Yun offered here is, on the surface, a utopian picture of the life of a hermit, shielded from worldly worries. Of course, this was in sharp contrast with the reality they were facing. First, due to her husband's career setbacks, they would never have enough money to build even a cottage, much less buy ten *mou* of land. Consequently, they would have no land that their servant could farm and from which they could produce enough for them to live on. In fact, her suggestion that what they could earn from Shen Fu's painting and her embroidery would be just enough to cover the cost of entertaining friends pointed to the meagerness of their actual total income and its inadequacy.

Elsewhere in *Six Records*, Shen Fu describes how Yun helped him entertain his friends with the conventional phrase "selling her hairpin to buy wine" (*bachai gujiu* 拔钗沽酒) (93; 64), an allusion to the poetic line from one of the most famous *daowang* poems by the Tang poet Yuan Zhen (discussed in chapter 2), when the latter praised his late wife for helping defray the cost of entertaining his friends with the money she got for selling her hairpin. However, what is deeply ironic here is that now Yun was suggesting that they had to combine their earnings (from the sale of his paintings and her embroidery works) just to cover the cost of entertaining friends (selling her hairpin would be only a one-off act, which could not ensure a sustainable income in the long run). In other words, all Shen Fu was earning from selling his paintings would not be enough even to cover the cost of entertaining friends, while he had originally planned to sell paintings as a way of supporting the family. Shen Fu opened a shop selling paintings, but he soon discovered it did not make business sense.

Despite the unintended irony in Yun's expressed wishes, she did show that she was not a wife who would complain about her husband's incompetence. Here we are reminded of the Ming writer Gui Youguang's deep appreciation of his late wife precisely for the same reason: she consoled Gui Youguang that they could lead the life of a reclusive couple now after he returned home, having failed to pass the provincial examination once again, as he recalled after she had passed away.[25] For a Confucian literatus suffering repeated career setbacks, his wife's understanding was particularly appreciated. Shen Fu's deep love for Yun must be related to her unique capacity to caress his injured male ego. This is why he insists that the boudoir of their home, though very small, was a place where he could find "joys" and "pleasures," despite its ultimate fragile and illusionary nature; it was a place where he could pretend he was a man of *zili*.

Yun thus played a dual role in Shen Fu's struggle to come to terms with his gender identity as a marginalized man who felt emasculated: she was an integral part of the small and confined world of the feminine in which Shen Fu could feel shielded from the harsh reality of the outside masculine world; yet, at the same time, as an understanding and subservient wife, she also served to help nurse his bruised male ego, making him feel better about himself as a man. This is probably what has made *Six Records* such a complex text, where the autobiographical (his memories of his own past selves) and the biographical (his mourning and memories of his late wife) converge to constitute arguably the most intriguing *daowang* work in Chinese literary history: Shen Fu is grieving his late wife as well as his own "self," insisting that both had been treated unfairly by fate:

> Why are there misfortunes in life? They are usually the retributions for one own sins, but this was not so with me! I always have been friendly, frank, and open, and kept my word to others, but these qualities only became the reasons for my troubles. (96; 73)

In a way, *Six Records* could be read as its author's protest against the unfairness of the world he and his wife lived in, a world constituted by many unsympathetic and sometimes unkind people, even including some of his own family members. Shen Fu was not the first husband to reveal tension between his late wife and other important members in his family, such as his parents. As we have examined, Zhu Bangxian, Ye Shaoyuan, Long Qirui, and others have touched on this issue, but they were relatively brief and furtive. It is the special length Shen Fu goes to in defending his late wife's innocence and in emphasizing his own helplessness in trying to shield her, as well as his insistence on his being also the victim of such family tension, that set him apart from other mourning husbands. Whereas many grieving husbands had referred to hardships and even unfair treatment their late wives were subjected to, Shen Fu was probably the first to explicitly identify himself with his late wife in terms of both being the victims of the mistreatment by family members and society. It is this strong identification that renders his *daowang* so compelling. Here we have a quite new image of a grieving husband: his mourning of his late wife was closely tied to his grieving over his own failures in life—*daowang* is being turned into an act of double grieving: he grieved not only over the death of his wife but also his helplessness as a husband and perceived failures as a man.

CHAPTER 5

FRAGMENTS OF ANXIETY

If Shen Fu's *Six Records* is unprecedented in its detailed exposure of family tension in his married life, this is, at least on the surface, the very topic that Jiang Tan tries to avoid in his memoir *Fragments*. Jiang Tan and his wife Guan Ying (1822–1857) were considered a perfect match, a pair of "golden boy and jade girl" (*jintong yunü* 金童玉女).[1] Both were steeped in the literary tradition and shared a fervent love for poetry and other intellectual pursuits.

Compared with Shen Fu and his wife, Yun, both Jiang Tan and especially Guan Ying were better educated, and probably more deeply steeped in the literati cultural traditions. They appear to have been more compatible with each other intellectually. Guan Ying's high intellect played a significant role in their married life and is celebrated with much fanfare in Jiang Tan's memoir. Here we do not see the kind of patronizing attitude Shen Fu occasionally exhibited toward his wife in *Six Records*. Instead, Jiang Tan adored—even nearly felt awed by—Guan Ying's intellectual acumen. He wrote this memoir to record many of the cherished moments the two shared; however, a strong feeling of foreboding permeates the text, a feature shared by Shen Fu's *Six Records*. But in contrast to the image of Yun that Shen Fu has reconstructed for us, the image of Guan Ying we are able to derive from the writings by both Jiang Tan and herself is that of a quite independent wife with much greater social mobility as a woman. Such independence and mobility are evidenced in her friendships and literary exchanges with many other educated women. Compared with Yun, Guan Ying apparently enjoyed a much wider social circle, which included many well-educated women who shared her literary interests, as reflected in many of her poems and the prefaces she composed for the collections of poems authored by some of these friends.[2] In *Fragments*, Jiang Tan mentions many trips they undertook together, visiting gardens, hills, temples and even the examination hall in the provincial capital. Guan Ying seems to have enjoyed much more freedom of mobility than Yun. We may recall that Yun had to cross-dress herself as a man in order to make certain trips with her husband, but this was not much of an issue for Guan Ying, probably pointing to the increased mobility a significant number of Chinese women were enjoying by the mid–nineteenth century.³ However, it is the trips Guan Ying undertook without her husband's company that are most significant for our discussion in this chapter. Her mobility and frequent absence from home caused much anxiety in her husband.

Many decades after it was first published, *Fragments* gained much wider readership when it was republished in the early twentieth century, and especially since its reprint in the popular series *Meihua wenxue mingzhu congkan* 美化文學名著叢刊 (the Literature of Aestheticized Life Series) published by the Guoxue zhengli she in 1935, which also includes, among other titles, memoirs such as Mao Xiang's *Plum Shadow*, Shengfu's *Six Records*, and Chen Peizhi's *Fragrant Garden*.⁴ These four memoirs have been republished together countless times ever since, although *Fragments* has remained the least read among the four. It has also received the least amount of critical attention. Such oversight might be related to the fact that, in contrast to the other three works, *Fragments* reads more like a collection of random notes. It does not offer a coherent narrative of the couple's life, while the relative lack of information on the author and his wife seems to have also discouraged readers from trying to fill in the many gaps in this fragmented narrative to make it a more meaningful and substantive memoir. However, the recent rediscovery and consequent accessibility of the couple's other extant works should allow us to take another look at this unique memoir from a new perspective.⁵

Controversy has surrounded *Fragments* as to whether the memoir is elegiac in nature. Some of Jiang Tan's contemporaries, such as the historian Chen Jicong 陳繼聰 (d. 1882), testified that it was. Chen claimed that in 1859 it was Jiang Tan himself who left him with copies of his wife's collected poems and the memoir *Fragments*, asking him to write a biography of her.⁶ However, Zhu Jianmang 朱劍芒, the editor of the popular *Meihua wenxue mingzhu congkan* series, and other modern scholars have contended that this could not have been the case because the preface to *Fragments* was dated the second year of the Xianfeng reign (1852), while there was evidence that Guan Ying was still alive in the fourth year of the Xianfeng reign (1854): for instance, her preface to her own collection of *ci* poetry was dated 1854.⁷ More recently, Li Huiqun has called attention to the date of Guan Ying's death, the twenty-first of the first month of the *dingsi* year (1857), mentioned by Jiang Tan himself in his preface to the collection of his elegiac poems, *Chouluan ji* 愁鸞集 (*Collection of the Sorrows of A Love Bird*) dedicated to her memory. Jiang Tan published this collection of mourning poems as an appendix to Guan Ying's own collection of poems *Sanshi liu Furong guan shicun* 三十六芙蓉館詩存 (*Poems from the Studio of Thirty-Six Hibiscuses*). Li also points out that *Fragments* itself actually contains a reference to an event that must have happened after Guan Ying had passed away (more on this later) and she thus concludes that the original preface to *Fragments* must have been written for its earlier version and that, most likely, Jiang Tan later revised and expanded it after the death of Guan Ying.[8] Consequently, the extant *Fragments*, as we have it now, is a collection of writings he committed to paper *both* before and after her death.

Different from the elegiac memoirs by others, such as the *Plum Shadow* by Mao Xiang, who might have influenced Jiang Tan, this memoir, as suggested by the phrase *suoyi* (literally, miscellaneous remembrances) in its original Chinese title, is made up of fragments of memory that defy chronological ordering. It begins with the author's wedding night in 1843 (*guimao* 癸卯). The following is the order in which many other specific years are mentioned in the memoir: 1844 (*jiachen* 甲辰), 1847 (*dingwei* 丁未), 1845 (*yisi* 乙巳), 1827 (*dinghai* 丁亥), 1832 (*renchen* 壬辰), 1844 again, 1848 (*wushen* 戊申), 1844 once more, 1846 (*bingwu* 丙午), and finally 1849 (*jiyou* 己酉). In other words, the narrative shifts back and forth, following no particular order, contributing to the reader's impression that this is a collection of random and fragmentary memories. What further deepens this impression is that hardly any transitions among the paragraphs recall other events in the memoir. If this is Jiang Tan's memoir about his wife, the reconstruction of her "life history" is apparently not his main purpose. Instead, it is a collection of "moments" in their shared life, framed by no particular teleology except for occasional premonitions that his wife would not live long in this world.

The word *yi* (remembering, recalling) appears altogether more than twenty times in this relatively short memoir. Sometimes Jiang Tan tells the reader a particular event he is recalling took place certain years ago, thus enabling the reader to infer the time at which this act of remembering/writing took place. For example, the narrator tells us that he and his wife were engaged in 1827 when they were around the age of four or five, and they did not get married until fifteen years later. He recalls how, due to customs regarding engaged couples, during the fifteen-year period between the engagement and wedding, the two were always carefully separated and could not talk to each other, although several times they found themselves in each other's presence. The narrator then sighs that they have been married for ten years now, thus placing this particular memory in 1853. In another paragraph, the narrator tries to recall the content of a long poem he sent to his wife in the autumn of 1848. He then explains that he has been trying to find the lost manuscript for almost ten years, thus implying that this act of recalling took place in late 1857 (if 1848 counted as one of the ten years). Unlike many other paragraphs in the memoir, these two contain specific "time markers" to inform readers that these two events were being recalled at two different times, one in 1853 and the other in 1857, suggesting that different parts of the memoir were written by the author at different times.

Here, the specific time during which he recalled sending the poem (i.e., 1857) is significant because it tells us that Jiang Tan must have recalled and written down the account of this episode after the death of his wife, as elsewhere he mentions that she died in early 1857. Despite the fact that most of *Fragments* was written while Guan Ying was still alive, it was later intended by the author, after revision and additions, to be read as a part of this grieving husband's *daowang* project in memory of her. This is why it was appended, together with his own elegiac poems, to the collection of Guan Ying's own poems, *Sanshi liu Furong guan shicun*, which he published about eight months after her death, in the eighth month of the seventh year of the Xianfeng reign (1857),[9] to commemorate her.

Fragments as a memoir is as much about what the couple did together, such as visiting a certain place, as about his memories of the literary texts they have composed together or individually on such occasions. Often the focus of his memory is a literary text or a poem rather than the event that occasioned the writing of such a literary text. Occasionally, he would deplore his inability to recall the exact content of a poem, as if the event itself was not as important. For example, he mentions that the two prayed to the Jade emperor for forty-nine days in the hope that his father's illness could be cured, and Guan Ying composed a prayer essay in the form of parallel prose, which, according to Jiang, was a splendid piece of erudition (*ciyi aoyan* 辭義奧艷).[10] He deeply regretted that he could not reproduce it based on memory, as the original manuscript had been lost; otherwise the reader might have had an opportunity to really appreciate his wife's literary talent. Here their praying for his father's recovery from illness does not seem to be as important as Guan Ying's essay of parallel prose.

It seems that, without the aid of poems or other forms of literature, most of what the two did together would remain "meaningless" or simply not worth remembering. The reader is made to feel that it is often poetry itself that is worth remembering, not the event that occasioned it. This is probably why the most important thing worth recording about their wedding night, Jiang Tan seems to suggest, is the poetic lines they composed in the little poetry contest they held that night. The wedding night poetry contest was the first event recorded in the memoir, a beginning that has irked quite a few modern readers because they have found it rather farfetched, and it pales considerably compared to Shen Fu's account of his wedding night in *Six Records*.[11] To these readers, the memoir is too obsessed with seemingly trivial memories to shed light on the couple's daily life.

To better appreciate this memoir, we must read it in close juxtaposition to the numerous elegiac poems Jiang Tan wrote after Guan Ying's death. Here, the mourning poet was much less constrained in revealing what was truly on his mind, as if Guan Ying's death and the literary medium of poetry had "liberated" him, and, as a result, he had fewer qualms about revealing those not so happy moments in their married life. Reading through the poems Jiang Tan wrote to mourn Guan Ying, one is struck by his explicit insistence: his grief as a bereaved husband was made much worse by his recent memory that his then sick wife was separated from him for quite a long time during the last several months of her life, after she returned to her natal family at the request of her mother, and that she eventually died there rather than at their own residence. This is something not touched on at all in the memoir *Fragments*.

In the preface to his collection of *daowang* poems to honor his deceased wife, Jiang Tan states:

> My mother-in-law came to take her back to stay with her natal family. She had her clothing washed and ready. At that time, it was raining and leaves were falling from the trees, while the cicadas were signing sorrowful autumn songs. She was quite sad stepping onto the carriage, trying to wipe away her tears. I thought at that time our separation was only temporary and she should not cry. Who could have expected that she would die in a few months?[12]

There is no explicit complaint yet about his mother-in-law, though his unhappiness is palpable. The tone, however, is dramatically different when this same event is recalled in the long elegiac poetic series "Daowang bashi shou" 悼亡八十首 (Eighty Mourning Poems):

> While already a bird to leave she was, on two separate cold branches we
>   were now forced to perch.
> 此身已是將離鳥，猶使寒枝兩處栖.

The agony of separation is obvious here. Lest the reader fails to fully appreciate what is being suggested by these two lines, the grieving poet provides a note: "On the fifteenth day of the ninth month, her mother came to take her. She was already very sick. I tried to stop her but did not succeed."[13] She was taken from him.

In another poem, Jiang Tan goes so far as to directly accuse his mother-in-law of failing to give his wife timely medical care while the latter was staying with her, at a time when her illness had yet to deteriorate so precipitously, implying his wife might have been still alive if she had been under his care at their own home. He even bitterly complains that his mother-in-law looked down on him and accused her of acting very unreasonably when she suddenly decided to take Guan Ying back to her natal family:

> Though not that important I might be, quite unreasonable after all her action was
> 我固不足重，終恐非人情。[14]

A poem in another set of elegiac poems reads:

> Ever since hurried onto carriage she was, like floating dust the willow catkins were flying all above her house.
> Writing and composing poems she had stopped, and worsening her illness was as the medicine failed to work.
> With books piling up like a pillow in bed, into the medicine stove more firewood had to be fed.
> A couple of deep attachment we had been all our married life, and yet not allowed I was to cool your body with my own like Mr. Xun.
> 一自催歸陌上輪，謝家飛絮滿輕塵。箋筒不用詩先廢，丹餌無靈病太真。禪榻半堆書作枕，藥爐惟借葉添薪。平生相敬如賓友，不許荀郎暫熨身。[15]

Of particular interest is the last couplet, where he complains bitterly how he was denied the opportunity to nurse his sick wife. Here Jiang Tan refers to the legend of Xun Fengqian 荀奉倩 from the Sixty-Dynasty period (222–589). Mr. Xun was said to have stayed outside naked in the freezing weather in order to cool his own body, with which he would later cool the body of his wife, who was running a high fever.[16] Because Guan Ying's mother had her brought back to her natal home, he was, Jiang Tan now claims, prevented from taking care of his sick wife in a way only a loving husband could. There is a sense that the intimacy between them as husband and wife was somehow also violated. Here we are reminded of the famous late Ming *daowang* poet Wang Cihui's poem employing this similar allusion:

> Priggish and Prudish all her life, she would not allow Mr. Xun to cool her body with that of his own.

平生守禮自謙畏，不受荀郎熨體寒。[17]

Of course, different from Jiang, Wang is complaining that his wife was somewhat too conservative, while Jiang Tan is here blaming his mother-in-law for denying him the opportunity to be with his wife during the last days of her life.

However, such resentment toward his in-laws, so pronounced and persistent in his *daowang* poems, is largely invisible in the memoir *Fragments*, which is meant to focus mostly on those cherished moments he shared with his wife, even though not all of them could be characterized as happy. One possible reason is that most of this memoir was written before the long traumatic separation prior to her death that had completely soured his relationship with his mother-in-law. However, reading his *daowang* poems should make us realize that there are subtle signs in the memoir that already suggest the crises in their fifteen-year marriage, many of which were related to the role of her natal family. As mentioned earlier, there is a curious episode in the memoir in which Jiang Tan refers to the disharmony in their relationship. He is recalling a long poem he composed ten years before, the only act of remembrance in this memoir, which, we can be certain, took place after Guan Ying had passed away. Jiang Tan tells us that in the autumn of 1848, he sent Guan Ying a long poem that contained many euphemistic references to their strained relationship and painful separation(s). The poem begins this way:

> Stuck on the cold screen were the dead dragon flies, and under the lamp the fallen flower petals had turned purple in the cold air of the autumn.
> Sleepless in bed with rain and wind blowing outside, to cut the candle stick he sat up during the middle of the night.
> The cold autumn rain and wind the jade pillow knew best, and the most lovesick were the mirror and hairpins.
> Heart-broken I am thinking about the lady in the boudoir, imagining this must be the time when she tidied up her hair under the fading lamp.
> 乾螢冷貼屏風死，秋逼蘭釭落花紫．滿床風雨不成眠，有人剪燭中宵起．風雨秋涼玉簟知，鏡台釵股最相思．傷心獨憶閨中婦，應是殘燈擁髻時．

This is a painful picture of separation and loneliness. He apparently missed his wife terribly. Then the poem mentions the possible cause of this separation:

> Out of blue you asked for money from me, then the next day you decided to visit your natal family.
> The day when you left the green lotus leaves just began to curl up, and packing clothes you were as I remember.

> With the autumn wind starting to blow during that time of the year,
>   blocked again was the ferry boat as it sailed back.
> Like a piece of silk I was easy to be discarded; weather you have brought
>   enough clothing is still a concern on my mind.
> 無端乞我賣薪錢, 明朝便決歸寧去. 去日青荷初卷葉, 羅衣曾記箱中疊. 一年容
>   易到秋風, 渡江又阻歸來楫. 我似齊紈易棄捐, 懷中冷暖仗人憐.

The poem concludes with a couplet in which he is imagining that he eventually went to visit his wife at the residence of her natal family:

> Walking by the residence of her natal family tomorrow, the steps of a pair
>   of embroidered shoes I will be hearing before entering the house.
> 明日謝家堂下過, 入門預想繡鞋聲.[18]

The images of autumn, the season often associated with melancholy in Chinese poetic tradition, dominate here, reinforcing the implications of autumn in the title of the memoir—"Fragments of Memories under the Autumn Lamp." Autumn is also the time Guan Ying would be taken away from him, as she would eventually die at the residence of her natal family the following winter. What is particularly interesting here is that the conventional image of a lonely woman pining away in the boudoir on a sad autumn day for the sake of her beloved, who failed to return or who might have already abandoned her, is now replaced with the image of a lonely husband pining away at home, feeling abandoned, after his wife had returned to stay with her natal family. The gender roles have been reversed.

In fact, this is the only place in *Fragments* where disharmony between the two is explicit, although such reference, significantly, takes the form of a poem. Jiang Tan's decision to quote this lengthy poem focusing on their conjugal disharmony, as he, now already a bereaved husband, was revising his memoir from hindsight, must be understood, at least in part, as a result of his deteriorating relationship with his wife's natal family during the last several months of her life. In this relatively long poem, although we can also find expressions of regret and guilt at his own fault, its main focus is on the frustrations and loneliness of separation. Having told us that the poem was composed and sent to his wife in the autumn of 1848, now after quoting the poem, Jiang Tan specifically informs us of the time when he was trying to recall and when he tried to jot it down so that he would not forget it again in the future: "I have not been able to find the manuscript for ten years. I suddenly recalled this poem while lying in bed. I grabbed a brush and wrote it down as if I were in a dream."[19] Thus we know his memory of this poem must have been shaped or even colored by his bitter experience of the long separation from his wife after she returned to stay with her natal family to spend the last few months of her life. To insert this long poem about their marriage problem into the memoir, most of which he might have originally written to celebrate the cherished moments in their married life while his wife was still alive, must have reflected more the new mindset of the now bereaved husband ten years later.

Guan Ying's repeated long visits to her natal family (*guining* 歸寧) proved to be a constant source of frustrations and anxieties for Jiang Tan. It was likely that she would return to stay with her natal family for a considerably long time whenever the two had issues with each other. A reading of his *daowang* poems compels us to reinterpret the memoir from a slightly different perspective.

Early in *Fragments*, right after the account of their happy wedding night, Jiang Tan recalls how lonely he was and how much he missed Guan Ying after she returned to her natal family, though no specific reason for her *guining* was provided this time. He composed two poems describing his lonely feelings, reminding himself and readers that his wife had yet to return after she left to stay with her natal family exactly thirty-five days earlier. He was literally counting the days on fingers, longing for the quick return of his wife.[20] Here, once again, he felt lonely and almost "abandoned."

Besides conjugal disputes, another possible reason for Guan Ying returning to stay with her natal family was her poor health—it appears that she often chose to stay with her natal family (or her mother would ask her to return to her natal home) whenever she was sick, as if she felt her natal family could give her better care. This is probably the reason his sick wife never returned after she went back to her natal family during the final several months of her life. In *Fragments*, Jiang Tan once recalls that Guan Ying was sick and stayed with her natal family for more than sixty days. He had to go there quite a few times whenever she, in her illness, became worried that she might have to leave the world without bidding him a final farewell.[21] In the writings by both Jiang Tan and Guan Ying, the latter's illness was a frequent topic.

Jiang Tan complained in one of his *daowang* poems how her illness and her frequent *guining* visits might have contributed to the loss of the kind of physical intimacy he cherished:

> Floating over the meditation bed was the steaming smoke of the medicine pot, and throughout the spring she spent the night with candle lit.
> Adding to the loneliness was the buzzing of flying insects; two years it has been since we stopped sharing the quilt.

禪榻霜絲裊藥煙,一春長自背燈眠.蟲飛聲起添惆悵,不共蘭衾已二年.²²

In her discussion of the topos of illness in late imperial Chinese women's poems, Grace Fong argues that illness might help create an alternative space for these women, where they, exempt from the common household chores and daily routine, tended to become more conscious of their own bodies and emotions.²³ In Guan Ying's case, her illness often gave her an excuse to go back to stay with her natal family, a "feminine" sphere where her husband sometimes must have been made to feel like an outsider.

In that feminine sphere were Guan Ying's two sisters, to whom she was very close. In fact, her younger sister Peiqi's death (two years before her own), according to Jiang Tan, was the direct cause of the rapid deterioration of her own health,²⁴ while another younger sister Lüqiong was often the caretaker when she was ill and returned to stay with her natal family. Of course, Lüqiong was also the editor of her collection of poetry, as indicated in the *Sanshi liu furong guan shicun*.²⁵ The bond among these sisters might also have been strengthened by their shared pursuit of religious transcendence, from which Jiang Tan might have felt somewhat excluded. In a poem describing a religious experience shared with her sister Lüqiong, Guan Ying envisioned the two of them would achieve Buddhist enlightenment together:

> For achieving enlightenment the Buddha has the lotus raft ready; beyond
>   the river of desires you and I will sail together.
> 聞道覺王有蓮筏,與君同出愛河津.²⁶

It is said that Guan Ying was a devout Buddhist believer, and Jiang Tan tried to follow her.²⁷ Her collection of poems actually begins with a set of ten poems on the topic "Taochan" (Finding Salvation in Chan Buddhism).²⁸ In many ways, her frequent illness might have also deepened her belief in Buddhism, as she indicated in a poem titled "Wobing" 臥病 (Bedridden with Illness):

> Not thirty yet I am, and at a withered face I am surprised to stare.
> The snare of the red dust I shall flee, and the broom I will let go.
> Others I want to urge: do not fight over trivial matters.
> Whether I really believe you may ask: just read the Sutra of Perfect
>   Enlightenment.
> 我年未三十,皺面恆自驚.行將謝塵鞅,放手苕帚行.勉矣後來者,慎莫蝸角爭.
>   謂我信不信,請讀圓覺經.²⁹

Her constant illness and poor health seem to have made her even more eager to embrace the ultimate escape promised by the other world.

On the other hand, Guan Ying might have also felt that her effort at religious transcendence was somehow being compromised by her obligations as a wife. She actually urged Jiang to take a concubine so that she could devote herself more completely to Buddha. She set up a different room for prayer and meditation, where she would often start reciting sutras very early in the morning every day.[30] Here one is reminded of another more famous couple, who had also received the compliment as being a pair of "golden boy and jade girl," the well-known scholar and poet Wang Duan and her husband Chen Peizhi. As we explore in more detail in chapter 6, Chen Peizhi took concubine Wang Zhixiang at the encouragement of Wang Duan because the latter felt she herself was too occupied with her intellectual pursuit and religious devotion to properly fulfill her role as a wife. Jiang Tan and Guan Ying must have known about Wang Duan, who also happened to be from their hometown area, as it is specifically mentioned in *Fragments* that the two of them visited a local temple to see the artifacts left by Wang (she died in 1839).[31]

However, having a concubine to share wifely duties was apparently not enough of a relief for Guan Ying as she was trying to achieve religious transcendence. She once managed to blame specifically her husband's influence for her inability to completely disentangle herself from the attachment to literary writing:

> I have pursued the Way for ten years and I had already sworn that I would never fall again into the trap of literary writing. However, led astray by my husband, I fell into my old habit again after marriage.... As for writing poems, my husband should give it up and join me on the journey together.[32]

On the other hand, Jiang Tan appears to have had great admiration for his wife's religious wisdom, and even followed her lead. He became quite religious himself. He adored and nearly worshipped her, believing she was much smarter than he was and at a much higher level in terms of religious enlightenment. Jiang Tan was even convinced that Guan Ying was indeed the reincarnation of the famous late Ming female visionary Tanyangzi 曇陽子 (1557–1580).[33] Sometimes, for Jiang Tan, his wife was a female immortal, whose otherworldliness pointed to a spiritual sphere somehow beyond his reach. At the same time, this sense of distance, whether physical or spiritual, might have bothered Jiang Tan.

Consequently, *Fragments* can almost be read as an attempt on his part to shorten the distance between himself and his wife by constructing an aesthetic realm of other-worldliness the two of them shared:

> The autumn moon was so beautiful. Qiufu [Guan Ying] had the maid carry the lute and they went boating among the lotuses on the twin lakes. At that time, I was just coming back from Xici. By the time when I reached home, they were already gone. Following the instructions given on the rind, I was able to track them and eventually met them under the second bridge of Suti. On the boat, Qiufu played on the lute the music of "The Autumn Sorrows of the Han Palace." I put a coat over her while listening to her playing. The surrounding hills were completely cloaked in the fog, with the moon and stars reflected in the water. The lute music was like many pieces of jade clinking, making one wonder whether it was the clinking of the ear rings and bracelets of an immortal or the sound of Heaven. Before the music ended, the boat already reached the southern bank of the Qi garden. We disembarked from the boat and knocked at the gate of the White Cloud Nunnery. The abbess was an old acquaintance of ours and she invited us to sit down. She had people gather the seeds from the lotus pond and prepared for us lotus seeds soup. The soup smelled so good and tasted so refreshing that we felt as if our whole bodies were cleansed. This was especially heavenly compared with the smell of the dusty world outside. We boated back and got onto the land at the Duanjia Bridge. Once on land, we laid a bamboo rug on the ground and talked to each other for a while but the noise of the town's madding crowd was really hurting our ears, as if we were surrounded by buzzing flies.[34]

This is the reclusive world of religious detachment both Guan Ying and Jiang Tan aspired to but often found difficult to sustain. However, Jiang Tan had an uneasy feeling that his wife might also cling to a uniquely feminine sphere that was beyond his reach. She frequently visited and stayed with her natal family whose members prided themselves on its own rich female literary tradition, while leaving him home alone for long periods of time. Her natal family and her periodical sojourns there pointed to a world his wife liked to dwell in but from which he felt excluded. The more he felt excluded, the more anxious he felt about such exclusion.

Finally, Jiang Tan became so desperate that he was willing to do anything to be accepted into the world of Guan Ying's natal family. He confessed in a note to one of his elegiac poems that the day before her death he even dreamt of marrying Guan Ying as an uxorilocal husband.[35] The long separation from her during the last few months of her life when she was staying with her natal family had made him so eager to be reunited with her or to be part of that "exclusive" world that he was willing to reconcile with his mother-in-law, whom he resented so much, and live as part of their family through an uxorilocal marriage. This confession is particularly significant because the last few months of his wife's life were also the time when his relationship with her natal family probably reached its lowest point: "Cherished relatives in the past we were, and now kin who despise each other we have become" (昔以黃金親, 今乃骨肉賤).[36]

What also contributed to the strained relationship was his own sense of inferiority. His repeated failures in the civil-service examinations might have been a factor. As mentioned earlier, he felt his mother-in-law looked down on him. In one of his *daowang* poems, he mentioned that he and Guan Ying once visited together the examination hall where the booth he had sat for examinations was located. During the visit, Guan Ying pretended to be an examinee herself, sitting in the very examination booth where her husband had once sat, and she sighed: "What a pity that I am not a man. Otherwise I could wage the battle together with you men!"[37] Given Jiang Tan's poor examination performance, one could not help wondering if Guan Ying was suggesting that she could have done better than her husband if she had been granted a chance to take the examinations as a man. Elsewhere in *Fragments*, Jiang Tan confessed that his wife was ten times smarter than he was when it came to debating skills and quick wit.[38]

Whereas he repeatedly expressed his admiration for the literary talents of Guan Ying and her sisters, he might also have felt somewhat intimidated by both Guan Ying and the other female members of her natal family. Guan Ying had always been very proud of the rich female literary tradition of her natal family and considered herself the proud representative of that tradition, as she reflected in a poem she wrote on her thirtieth birthday:

> The oldest among the six siblings I am, and the inheritor of the family's
>   literary tradition of three generations I have become.
> 弟妹六人惟我長, 詩書三世愧家承.

In a note to this poem, Guan Ying pointed out with apparent great pride that both her great grandmother and grandmother had their collected works published.[39] Her grandmother was the person who had tutored her when she was young. She felt so attached to her grandmother that she once cut flesh off her arm to make medicinal soup in the hope it would help to heal her when she was very sick. She often showed the scar on her arm to her husband.[40] Jiang Tan also wondered about the literary talents of her precocious younger sister, Peiqi, whose religious spirituality and transcendental beauty appear to have mystified him so much. Once she even thoroughly put him to shame by proving him to be no match for this younger sister-in-law when it came to the game of go.[41] In short, her natal family's rich intellectual and religious traditions might have worsened Jiang Tan's inferiority complex. This is probably why despite his repeated expressions of admiration for her natal family's literary tradition, he would also take opportunity to take a jab at it at the same time:

> While rather mediocre are the family's other children, the only one worthy of the family tradition is you.
> 景升諸子皆豚犬, 不愧門楣僅有卿。[42]

This appears to contradict his praises of her sisters elsewhere. One possibility is that by "other children" here he meant her male siblings. In any case, his anxiety over appearing inferior in the eyes of his in-laws seems clear.

Compared with *Fragments*, most of which was written while Guan Ying was still alive, Jiang Tan's *daowang* poems demonstrate concerns that were much more this-worldly, as if her departure to the other world had compelled him to remember her now more as a wifely woman than she had been made to appear in the memoir. Now that she had departed for another world, what he remembered and missed most about her was her this-worldly qualities as his wife, a sentiment that dominated his *daowang* poems. Many of these poems are also characterized by a more keenly felt sense of frustration at being excluded from her "alternative space," which was often associated with her natal family, as he recalled the painful separations resulting from her frequent trips of *guining*.

In contrast to his fragmentary memoir, Jiang Tan's *daowang* poems are much more narrative orientated in that they tend to offer a more coherent and complete picture of their married life with all its ups and downs. Here Jiang Tan is far more frank and detailed in airing his grievances against his in-laws. It is indeed very rare for a grieving husband to focus so much in his elegiac poems in memory of his deceased wife on the tension between himself and his mother-in-law and the latter's alleged role in their marriage problems. As we have discussed in the preceding chapters, family tension as a topic began to receive more exposure in grieving husbands' elegiac writings beginning from the late Ming. What is new in the case of Jiang Tan, however, is his different deployment of these two important elegiac genres. Ever since *daowang* poetry gained popularity during the Tang dynasty almost one thousand years earlier, it had always been known for its lyrical intensity. A new trend in the development of the *daowang* poetry in late imperial China was its shift toward narrativity—it was becoming less lyrical but more narrative oriented: some grieving poets began to write ever larger sets of poems in order to maximize their narrative potential to chronicle their marriage or the life-history of the deceased. In this regard, Jiang Tan's large set of poems "Daowang bashi shou" (Eighty Elegiac Poems) fits this pattern well. These eighty poems carefully chronicle the ups and downs of their fifteen-year marriage, her bouts of illness, even the moments of his vigil as she lay in her coffin, and of course his loneliness as the bereaved. Significantly, we have learned so much more about their married life from his *daowang* poems than from the prose memoir.

Another aspect of the new trend in the development of late imperial *daowang* poetry is its fascination with those topics traditionally assumed not so poetic or not so suitable for poetry, such as the images of a spouse in her deteriorating health while she was still alive or even her death image as she lay in a coffin, as we found in the works of the late Ming poet Wang Cihui:

> To have a portrait made of her I lifted the cover, but after looking at the face several times I could hardly believe it was her.
> A portrait of her in smile the painter was asked to paint, but regrettably only too often she cried when alive.
> 屍堂揭白寫形模，幾遍端詳未是他。欲倩畫工追笑靨，可堪連歲泣時多[43]

Likewise, this is the way Jiang Tan recalled bidding farewell to Guan Ying's body lying in the coffin:

> Difficult it was to capture her grace in a portrait, with lotus petals just put on her hair after she died.
> Not to forget her grace in the past, so hard I tried to observe her appearance while holding onto the coffin.
> 小影驚鴻寫亦難，臨行更換藕花冠。異時肥瘦休忘了，仔細憑棺一痛看。[44]

Both Wang and Jiang were trying to capture the last images of their deceased wives as they bade final farewell to their bodies, images not often encountered in typical *daowang* poems before the Ming.

Ultimately, what has made Jiang Tan stand out as a mid-nineteenth-century *daowang* poet is the detailed poetic exposure he gave to his uneasy relationship with his in-laws and to the family tension, and, to a more subtle extent, his own anxiety and inferiority complex as a husband and son-in-law. In our discussion of Shen Fu's *Six Records*, we have examined how the author tries to come to terms with his own bruised male ego. Jiang Tan, however, approaches this same issue from a different angle: he reveals how his wife's superior intelligence and her natal family's sense of superiority contributed to his anxieties as a man. At the same time, Jiang Tan also, perhaps inadvertently, draws our attention to the complicated implications of the close relationships many late imperial married women maintained with their natal families in a society otherwise dominated by its predominantly patriarchal value system. This is an interesting issue to be explored in more detail in chapter 8, where I look at it from the perspective of a male member of the natal family in the context of how deceased married women were mourned and remembered by their grieving brothers.

As discussed in preceding chapters, while revealing family tension in elegiac works of prose, such as biographical sketch, litany, memoir and even epitaph, was becoming more common, or at least, less uncommon during the late imperial period, such topics were still very rare in *daowang* poetry during that same period. Jiang Tan, however, appears to have been much more comfortable dwelling on the problematic aspects of his marriage in poetry, perhaps due to poetry's propensity toward euphemism and conciseness. Furthermore, what Jiang Tan did was almost an inversion of the generic role of *daowang* poetry: he chose to construct a fragmentary aestheticized world of conjugal harmony in his prose memoir, which was quite lyrical and even poetic, while leaving rather unpoetic topics such as marital tension and conflicts with his in-laws to be explored in his *daowang* poems, helping blur the conventional distinctions between these two elegiac genres, one poetic and the other prosaic, a testament to the more general phenomenon of a gradual and partial convergence of the different elegiac genres discussed in chapter 1.

CHAPTER 6

REMEMBERING CONCUBINES

Compared with a wife, a concubine was usually less likely to become the subject of her surviving husband's eulogy after she died.[1] However, during the late imperial period, with the increasing acknowledgment of concubinage in social life,[2] its gradual integration into the structure of a family, and the elevation of the status of a concubine,[3] more grieving literati husbands resorted to writing to mourn their deceased concubines,[4] and some of them even wrote elegiac essays for these concubines that were significantly longer than those for their deceased wives, ignoring the longstanding Confucian insistence that the hierarchical distinctions between the two must be maintained. This chapter is a look at how differently, in comparison with deceased wives, deceased concubines were mourned and remembered by their husbands and what such differences could tell us about the male mourners as polygamous husbands.

FROM THE BIOGRAPHICAL TO THE AUTOBIOGRAPHICAL

When one writes a biography of someone to whom one is closely related, autobiographical implications are often inescapable. This was certainly true in the case of writing a biography of one's own wife in late imperial China. However, the range of possibilities for the autobiographical became much wider when it came to writing about one's concubine, due in part to the fact that a grieving husband might feel less constrained as a result of her ambiguous status in a polygamous family. A concubine often straddled the roles of spouse, maid, and sometimes even entertainer.[5] This afforded a biographer much more freedom with which a concubine's image could be constructed, even manipulated, for sometimes vastly different autobiographical agendas.

That said, I begin my discussion with a case that is not so autobiographical but very illustrative of the wife–concubine distinctions a grieving polygamous husband was expected to rigorously maintain in mourning his different spouses. In an epitaph for his deceased concubine, Xie Bitao, the Ming scholar-official Sun Cheng'en did his best to emphasize how duly aware Xie was of her own humble status as a concubine within the familial hierarchy and how accordingly and appropriately she behaved. Sun gave several examples to illustrate this point. Due to his quick temper, Sun often scolded Xie harshly whenever he was slightly upset, but she never complained and always remained absolutely submissive. His principal wife, Lady Wu, was quite strict and could be intolerant, but Xie persisted in being respectful and subservient. During hot summer days, Xie would stand next to Lady Wu, fanning her to keep her cool when she was using the toilet.[6]

Besides her concubinary virtues of humbleness and submissiveness, another point Sun Cheng'en dwelt on in the epitaph was what he perceived to be a serious flaw in his concubine, namely, her lack of wisdom. Xie gave birth to two daughters and three sons, but none survived beyond infancy. As a result, she was deeply depressed. Feeling sympathetic for her, Lady Wu arranged to have Xie adopt Kemao, her own nephew (the son of Lady Wu's younger brother). Xie cherished and loved the child as if he were her own biological son. Unfortunately, Kemao turned out to be rather lazy. Resistant to the supervision of adults, he often neglected his study. When given a position in the central government in the capital, Sun Cheng'en planned to take Kemao along with him in order to keep a close eye on his studies. However, Xie asked Kemao to be left home so that she herself could supervise his studies, since, according to her, burdened by his official duties, Sun would be too busy to oversee the son. He first wondered in laughter: "How could you, a woman, control him, when he has remained stubbornly lazy even though I tried to flog him [into good behavior]?"[7] Initially reluctant, Sun eventually relented at the insistence of Xie, mistakenly thinking that Kemao might be more willing to listen to his adoptive mother. However, without Sun's strict discipline, Kemao now became even more difficult to control. Xie could do nothing but cry. Then things got worse, and before long she died brokenhearted:

> Now I am already quite old and Xie was not too young either [when she died]. How could I still be so attached to her [so that I wrote this epitaph]? This is only because she was a diligent woman who liked to worry a lot. . . . She wanted to have her son educated and yet she ended up dying for him. She did not understand her son well enough to know that he was very difficult

to educate and yet she tried so hard nevertheless. This led to her early death. She could be considered unwise (*yu* 愚) but nevertheless deserving sympathy. This is why I feel so sad.⁸

Rarely do we encounter a case in which a grieving husband so directly criticized his deceased spouse for being unwise in the very epitaph he wrote to honor her, since an epitaph was supposed to be always eulogistic. Here Xie being his concubine was certainly a factor. Sun Cheng'en considered her to be a fairly average woman, implying that as a biographical subject, a concubine did not need to demonstrate extraordinary wifely virtues in her life to merit an epitaph after her death, unlike the case of a formal wife, who was usually held to a higher wifely standard. To better appreciate this point, we should read Xie's epitaph next to the one Sun wrote for his formal wife, Lady Wu, who died years earlier than Xie.

Sun's wife, Lady Wu, as he presented in a more elaborate epitaph, was just the opposite of concubine Xie despite their shared devotion to their common husband. In sharp contrast to Xie, Lady Wu was said to be a woman of great wisdom and decisiveness, whose opinions her husband deeply respected. Early in their marriage, it was Lady Wu who constantly pushed her husband to study hard, an influence especially crucial to his examination successes given that he lost his father when he was quite young. Here Lady Wu was presented to have almost assumed the place of his deceased father in terms of keeping him focused on his study; after he passed the civil examinations and became an official, it was again his wife who constantly reminded him of the need to control his quick temper in dealing with his subordinates. A point Sun emphasized in the epitaph is the great loss he felt as a result of the death of his wife because he could no longer rely on her wise counsel. In sharp contrast to his condescending attitude toward his concubine, Sun Cheng'en presented his wife almost as his equal; her intellect and wisdom were what he respected and missed most.⁹ Reading these two epitaphs side by side illustrates that a grieving husband was likely to feel less pressure to rely on evidence of "wifely exemplariness" to legitimate his elegiac endeavor in the case of a concubine, partly because of the different expectations of a wife and a concubine. Sometimes this difference in expectations appears to have given a grieving husband more freedom or latitude in what he could divulge in remembering and writing about his deceased concubine.

Sun Cheng'en's contemporary, Nie Bao 聶豹 (1487–1563), the neo-Confucian thinker and scholar-official, is another case in point. Though more constrained than Sun in extolling his late wife in the epitaph he wrote for her,

Nie Bao was still quite profuse in praising her household management skills, detailing how unselfishly she helped raise several children of his kinsmen. Following Li Mengyang's famous line on how it took the death of his wife for him to really appreciate her, Nie sighed that he did not begin to truly appreciate the value and worthiness of his wife until she had passed away.[10]

Nie's epitaph of his late wife forms an interesting contrast to a much briefer one he wrote for his deceased concubine. At the very beginning of that epitaph, Nie made the point that the status of this concubine was much elevated due to her giving birth to a son (*yi zi gui ye* 以子貴也), as if he was suggesting that he probably would not have honored her with an epitaph had she not had a son. After giving a brief account of her humble family origin, he went out of his way to explain the symbolic meaning of her name, Taoxiang 桃香 (peach blossom fragrance). She was so named because her family hoped that she would be as "fruitful" or as "productive" as the peach blossom tree outside their family gate.[11] Consequently, she as a person in her role as a concubine was mainly identified in terms of her reproductive capability. However, most of the epitaph is devoted to the chronicling of Nie Bao's own career successes, such as the military campaign he led to pacify the border areas. In what basically amounts to a self-chronicle, he only briefly mentions his concubine Taoxiang because her giving birth to his son was thought to have brought a blessing to the military campaign.

For Nie Bao, the life of this humble concubine was significant or worth being remembered mainly because she had given him a son and because her life served as a nice footnote to his great career success. Writing an epitaph for her was largely an excuse for celebrating his own spectacular triumphs in realms both public and private: victories on the battlefield and success in perpetuating his family's patriline. Here, the biography of a concubine became a self-congratulatory autobiography, something Nie Bao might have felt much more hesitant to attempt in an epitaph on his formal wife. Nie Bao's autobiographical agenda was certainly aided by the fact that his biographical subject was his concubine, who was meaningful to him mainly as the birth mother of one of his sons.

Entering the seventeenth century, we find some grieving husbands were more innovative in turning the mourning of the death of a concubine into an occasion for self-celebration, or even self-invention. The dramatist and writer Li Yu 李漁 (1610–1680) raised to a new level of audacity the act of self-aggrandizement in the form of a biography of his concubinary "others," highlighting the range of possibilities afforded to a bereaved husband by the occasion of spousal mourning due to the ambiguous status of a concubine.

Li Yu wrote a so-called combined biography (*hezhuan* 合傳) for two of his deceased concubines.[12] Different from those mourned by Sun Cheng'en and Nie Bao, these two concubines were, at the same time, entertainers in his private family theater troupe. That is to say, besides serving as his concubines in the inner chamber, they also performed functions outside his household. They traveled and performed for the rich and the powerful, as Li Yu and his family theater troupe toured different regions, while serving as his concubines/maids at the same time. Because of their dual roles as concubines (functioning in the realm of *nei*, the inner, where women were typically confined) and entertainers who sometimes performed in semi-public spaces for people other than his own family members,[13] Li Yu appears to have felt that he had free license to reveal more private aspects of their relationships.

Just as what Nie Bao has done with his epitaph of his concubine, Li Yu begins his biography with an act of "naming." He tells us that neither of these concubines had ever been given their first names when they were alive (a sign of their humble origins) and people simply addressed them as Jinjie 晉姐 (the sister from the area of Jin) and Lanjie 蘭姐 (the sister from the area of Lan). Now that they were both dead, to commemorate them, Li Yu decided to name them respectively as Fusheng (resurrection) 復生 and Zailai 再來 (returning) as an expression of his grief over their deaths and his wishes that they could come back to this world again. This act of naming performed at the beginning of their biography serves as a reminder of Li Yu's own multiple roles as the husband, master, and biographer in defining the meanings of the lives of these two otherwise nameless female slaves. It was him, the husband/master/biographer, who had owned them when they were alive and who had the ultimate authority to define and finalize the meanings of their lives now that they were dead.

The first half of the biography is about how Fusheng came to become both Li Yu's concubine and an actress in his family theater troupe. He spent a lot of ink detailing her uncanny gift for opera singing and performance despite the fact that she was from northern China, while the kind of opera they were performing was based on the southern tradition. She repeatedly surprised him and others with her performing talents and her ability to understand and capture the meaning of a play or an aria. Unfortunately, Fusheng died not long after giving birth to a daughter. Before she died, she told others that she felt no regret now that she had been given a chance to serve a talented man such as Li Yu. She only wished that she could be able to serve him again in her next life. To enhance his credibility as a biographer, who is telling us how much his biographical subject admired him, Li Yu went out of his way to note that she said this without his being present and asked others not to tell him what she had said. He learned of this from others only after she had passed away.

The focus on the second concubine Zailai is, however, not her talent as an actress but her spousal loyalty, though Li Yu did not forget to tell us how pretty she was. She was particularly handsome when she cross-dressed herself as a young man: "Those who do not really know her only regard her as an actress/entertainer [*geji* 歌姬,] but she was really my handsome friend [*yunyou* 韻友]."[14] Here the vocabularies of the heterosexual and homosexual became almost indistinguishable. However, the central theme in this portrait of Zailai is still about her loyalty to the biographer and her aspirations to join the ranks of his concubines as the bearer of a son. Once she mistook that her master would let go all the concubines/actresses after Li Yu sent away one of them because the latter was quarrelsome and easily jealous. Zailai insisted that she would die rather than leave. This caused the wife and other concubines to tease her:

> My wife pretended to suggest: "The master is now old. It is best for you to find someone you really want when you are still young." Zailai replied: "The master is indeed old, but among the mistresses [*zhumu* 主母; referring to Li Yu's other concubines who did not perform as actresses and whose status were higher], there are quite a few young ones. If they have chosen to remain, how could I alone fail to stay?" The concubines said: "We all have sons. If you fail to produce any son, whom are you going to rely on in the future?" She replied: "The mistresses rely on their sons. I would rely on whoever they rely on." My Wife and concubines were all moved to tears. One of the concubines, who had three sons, was so touched that she would offer one of them to Zailai for her adoption. Zailai said, "Please wait a few more years. If I fail to give birth to a son, then please arrange this."[15]

This reconstructed conversation among his wife and concubines not only illustrates Zailai's attachment and loyalty to Li Yu, but also, more significantly, hints at the perfect harmony within his household despite the fact that the husband had so many concubines.[16] Li Yu would not miss this opportunity to remind his readers of his polygamous success in having numerous sons (early in the biography, he justified his taking concubines by saying he had no sons, now the proof of his polygamous success).

A masterful fiction writer and playwright, Li Yu injected into this biography of his concubines a special dramatic flavor, as demonstrated in the quoted conversation above. What is even more remarkable is the conclusion of the biography:

> Alas, who am I? Once I wondered in my mind: I don't have the talents possessed by geniuses such as Sima Xiangru, Bai Letian, Su Dongpo, nor do I have the wealth of Shi Jilun or the power of Li Mi and Zhang Jianfeng. Yet the beauty of these two girls was not far below that of Wenjun, Fansu, Zhaoyun, Luzhu, Xue'er and Guan Panpan. Why? If the Creator had already given them to me, why did he have to take them away from me? If I deserve them, then taking them away is wrong; if taking them away can be justified, then they should not have been given to me in the first place. I am further puzzled: women usually care a lot about two things about their spouses: appearance and age. How about my appearance? I dare not compare myself to Anren or Shubao. Even standing next to Wan Can, Zuo Si, I would feel ashamed about my own homeliness. If we follow the rules of seniority, even Qiying and Zhenshuai would concede the seat of honor to me. [How can I be compared with] all those youthful people? If this is indeed the case, then they should have been busy finding someone who could provide them with the security of livelihood. Why should they instead seek to be associated with someone who might bring them hardships in life, willing to be broken in a coarse pot? Someone might say, if one seeks deeper reasons, it has to be due to their appreciation of talent after all. For the moment, we don't have to be concerned with the question whether I have talent or how much talent I have. Even if I do have talent, it takes a talent to appreciate another talent. They were not well educated and yet they knew what talent really was and showed true appreciation. From the ancient time to the present, this is indeed the most puzzling thing to decipher. What I could do is to provide this sketch of their lives to merely show that I will not forget them. If I truly deserved these two concubines/actresses, then people can judge for themselves. Whom am I going to deceive?[17]

Those familiar with the witty style of Li Yu's writings should not be surprised by the unabashedly smug tone of this passage,[18] though they might still be amazed to find such straight-faced self-celebration in a biography he had supposedly written for his two concubines.

Of course, recognizing/appreciating talent is expected to be mutual. In the preface to a set of elegiac poems dedicated to Fusheng, Li Yu once again declares:

All my friends who had watched her performance, after learning of her death, composed poems to honor her and all these poems are very sad and touching to read. However, they honored her for her skills rather than her talents, her beauty rather than her virtue. Skill is something one could perfect through study and practice, and beauty is something that could be acquired with superb makeup, while her natural ability to recognize the intention and the talent of an author [the playwright—namely, Li Yu himself] and her graceful deeds of virtue are something difficult to fully appreciate if one does not possess special acumen.[19]

According to the husband, while Fusheng and Zailai demonstrated their appreciation of his talent by being willing to be his concubines, it was also he who showed ultimate appreciation of their talents and virtue by producing this biography. Here the theme of *hongyan zhiji* 紅顏知己 (a beauty recognizing and appreciating a talented man) made familiar in the scholar-beauty romances extremely popular during that time is being reworked by Li Yu into his own autobiography in the form of a biography of his concubines. Only this time, the usual dashing and handsome young scholar (*caizi* 才子) is being replaced with the elderly and homely "self" of our biographer,

SELF-VINDICATION AND A NEW AESTHETIC OF CONCUBINAGE

Li Yu's contemporary Mao Xiang, much more serious about his memories of his deceased concubine, was in many ways more innovative and more elaborate in writing about her. After his concubine, Dong Xiaowan, a former courtesan, died at the age of twenty-seven, Mao Xiang first wrote a long eulogy in verse titled "Wangji Dong Xiaowan aici" 亡姬董小宛哀辭 (In Mourning of My Deceased Concubine Dong Xiaowan) to commemorate her, in which he explicitly argued that he married Dong Xiaowan, the former courtesan, for her virtue rather than her sexual appeal, and he was definitely not a lecherous man, or in his own pleading words, "The reader of this eulogy should know that Mr. Dengtu is not a lecherous man" (*shi zhi du chi zhe, dang zhi Dengtu zi fei haose zhe ye* 世之讀此者，當知登徒子非好色者也.[20] Made famous in "Dengtu zi haose fu" 登徒子好色賦 (Rhapsody on Mr. Dengtu's Lecherousness), attributed to the writer Song Yu 宋玉 (ca. 229–ca. 222 BC), the figure of Mr. Dengtu had become almost synonymous with a lecher in classical literature. In this rhapsody, to defend himself against the accusation made by Mr. Dengtu that he was a lecherous man, who might seduce the palace ladies of the King of the Chu, Song Yu questioned Mr. Dengtu's own moral character by saying that the latter had five children with his wife despite her utter ugliness.[21] However, Mao Xiang seems to have argued against the grain by implying that despite the traditional association of Mr. Dengtu with lecherousness (a figure Li Yu had readily compared himself to in the previously discussed biography for his love for young and pretty women when he was offered his future concubine Fusheng),[22] he was actually a man of moral integrity. The reader is invited to question Song Yu's somewhat farfetched moral logic that Mr. Dengtu was a lecherous man because his sexual desire was so strong that he slept with his wife despite her ugliness (they had five children together). On the contrary, Mr. Dengtu was not lecherous precisely because he properly fulfilled his role as a husband despite his wife being so unattractive. By the same token, marrying a famous courtesan, such as Dong Xiaowan, an act that had caused people to compare him to Mr. Dengtu, by no means indicated that Mao Xiang was a lecherous man because he married her for her virtue rather than her sexual appeal, just as Mr. Dengtu still loved his wife even though she was quite ugly. Mao Xiang seems to suggest that he was misunderstood as "lecherous," just as Mr. Dengtu had been for almost two thousand years; thus, there was a more urgent need for self-vindication in an even lengthier memoir, this time in the form of prose, which should afford him much more space to make his case.

Mao Xiang starts his long memoir with an important disclaimer: at the age of forty, this grieving husband would never imitate those dissipated youths to write an amorous tale to harm the reputation of his deceased concubine, who happened to be a former courtesan. Obviously, this apologetic rhetoric had more to do with the desired self-image of the mourner than that of the mourned, an important factor to consider when reading this memoir. His immediate goal is to rectify the misperception that Dong was merely a sexy courtesan: she should be remembered as an exemplary concubine rather than a courtesan known for her sexual appeal.

This mourning project of vindication was such that Mao Xiang found all the existing forms of traditional elegiac genres inadequate for his purpose. He had to literally invent a new elegiac form on his own—*yiyu* 憶語 (words of remembrance). He titled this memoir *The Remembrances of the Convent of the Plum Shadow* after the name of the convent where Dong was buried. It was designed to give him flexibility in terms of length and format. Instead of an elegiac essay of several pages, the memoir became a work long enough to be a volume by itself (*yizhi* 一帙).[23] In terms of the details of private life it contains and its sheer length, this memoir was indeed unprecedented in the history of the Chinese *daowang* tradition. The innovative nature of *Plum Shadow* is closely related to its biographical subject. Writing about his concubine, who was once a renowned courtesan, in this form offered him opportunities to dwell at length on elements that an essay in the traditional elegiac genre—usually reserved for "proper" women—could not, freeing him from the constraints of elegiac conventions. For example, Mao Xiang devotes almost one-fourth of this lengthy memoir to the depiction of their courtship before she was married into his family, something quite rare in elegiac writings, in part because they had ample opportunities to mingle with each other due to her being a courtesan, while this would be virtually impossible in the case of a wife since formal marriage was almost always pre-arranged by the parents among the elite. In other words, premarital courtship became a topic in Mao Xiang's elegiac memoir of Dong Xiaowan partly because she was once a courtesan and partly because this was a memoir about a concubine rather than a wife. Thus, an argument can be made that this work of significant innovation in the history of Chinese *daowang* tradition was made possible in part by the fact that its elegiac subject was a former courtesan/concubine.

During the three years of on-and-off courtship, surprisingly, the person who did most of the courting was Dong Xiaowan, rather than Mao Xiang. This role reversal would be less a surprise if Dong's position as a courtesan was taken into consideration. Even then, however, there was more to Mao Xiang's passivity as a lover. The grieving husband took great pains to show that throughout the courtship he was a participant, not only passive but even often reluctant. In fact, several times when pushed too hard by Dong, Mao Xiang was almost ready to end their relationship in fear of its negative impact on his family.

What is even more surprising is his account of his infatuation with another woman during his very courtship of Dong Xiaowan. Not long after meeting Dong, Mao Xiang was introduced to another famous courtesan, Chen Yuanyuan, and immediately fell for her. He pledged to meet her again when he returned from a trip. Later, he was so happy to see Chen again, after learning that the rumor she had been abducted by someone related to the royal family turned out to be inaccurate because she managed to hide herself in a safe place. However, when pressed by the desperate Chen to marry her:

> I smiled, replying: "There is no such easy thing in this world. Besides, my father is now stranded in the war-ridden area. I plan to go back [to rescue my father], even ready to discard my wife and children. True, I have visited

you twice but this has been something I did out of boredom after I had been blocked on my route to elsewhere. Your unexpected words really shocked me. If you insist on this, I have to refuse while plugging my ears so that I won't harm you in the end." Adopting a mild tone, she said, "If you promise you won't desert me in the end, I swear I am willing to wait until your father has safely returned." "If this is the case," I replied, "I promise to see you again." Surprised and happy, she said many words but I can't recall what she said specifically. I left her with eight poems I just improvised.²⁴

Next year he indeed returned, but it was too late. Ten days earlier, Chen Yuanyuan had been abducted by that powerful man. Although deeply disappointed, Mao Xiang insisted that he felt no regret about his decision to ask her to wait since he had had to help his endangered father, even if it meant he had to let down a woman he loved (*rang yi ji yanqin huan'nan, fu yi nüzi wuhan ye* 然以急嚴親患難, 負一女子無憾也).²⁵ After all these years, Mao Xiang wanted his readers to have no doubt about his conviction that filial duty took absolute priority over his obligations to a courtesan he happened to take a fancy for out of boredom. The casualness of his relationship with Chen was emphasized by the narrator Mao Xiang himself when he made the point to tell us that he could not recall specifically what she said to him just before leaving her for the last time or he was now too impatient to recall her exact words. However, he did not forget to recall that he left her with eight improvised poems, reminding the reader their courtship was nevertheless still an exercise of the cultured rites a romantic literatus and a courtesan were supposed to go through. One's memory becomes selective not without reason.

Why did Mao Xiang have to take the trouble to mention in detail in his elegiac memoir dedicated to his concubine Dong Xiaowan, a former courtesan, that he almost married another courtesan? This brief episode of his involvement with Chen Yuanyuan amidst his courtship of Dao Xiaowan was presented as a prelude to what later would transpire between him and Dong. In their relationships to Mao Xiang, Dong was a repetition as well as a continuation of Chen, both being courtesans eager to marry into a respectable family despite a lukewarm lover. The similarities in terms of these two women's significance in Mao Xiang's life were underscored by the fact that he immediately turned to Dong after Chen became unavailable, as if the two were completely interchangeable, similar to a patron visiting brothels—two different stops along an amorous journey undertaken by a brothel frequenter, an experience that Mao Xiang, the memoir writer, could not help bragging about despite his disclaimer that he was no lecher.

Despondent now that Chen Yuanyuan was taken by another man, Mao Xiang suddenly recalled his earlier encounter with another courtesan, Dong Xiaowan. He decided to visit her, only to find that she was suffering from nearly the same fate: being taken advantage of by a powerful family. Their relationship was soon reignited. However, when pressed by Dong Xiaowan, Mao Xiang repeatedly postponed the moment of decision by using various excuses, such as the need to focus on preparing for the examinations, the situation of his father, and his lack of money. Even when his friends arranged everything and had Dong Xiaowan delivered to his home—ironically, with the assistance of his wife Sushi—Dong had to be hidden away somewhere for a long time before he dared to inform his father. In fact, it was his wife who took the initiative to find a proper place for her husband's new concubine to live, a fact Mao Xiang mentioned with gratitude as evidence of his wife's virtue.[26] However, it also suggests that throughout the courtship, Mao Xiang was a passive, hesitant, and reluctant lover. It seems that Mao Xiang was pushed every step of the way by others into his union with Dong Xiaowan—either by Dong herself, by his own friends, and even by his wife.

Mao Xiang's carefully constructed self-image as a casual and reluctant lover remained fairly consistent throughout the early part of the memoir. The implied message is that the author could be a romantic type, patronizing brothels, but he would never overstep the limits of proprieties when it came to the Confucian duties of a filial son. This is probably what Mao Xiang meant when he insisted at the end of his verse eulogy in honor of Dong that he was no lecher. Further, the fact that both of these attractive courtesans were so eager to offer themselves to him as his concubines also enhances his image as a romantic literatus despite, or, precisely because of, his being a reluctant lover. Now he could have it both ways: he was a romantic *caizi* whom famous courtesans sought after and yet, at the same time, he was also a man of Confucian integrity.

Once Dong Xiaowan was married into the family, Mao Xiang wanted his readers to believe, she turned out to be even more conscientious about her Confucian duties as a concubine in a polygamous family than anyone could ever expect. Now that she was reborn as an exemplary concubine, she immediately gave up everything that could associate her with her past. She stopped wearing makeup, put away all the music instruments, and stopped wearing pretty dresses. Instead, she turned all her energies to what a proper woman was expected to do: needlework. Even her past training as a courtesan—her literacy—was now "transformed" into a special skill associated with wifely virtue; she could now serve as her husband's able secretary, rendering assistance in his various literary and scholarly endeavors. She was so careful in attending to the needs of other family members, we are told, that she behaved even more respectfully than the family maids. Another telling example of her virtue as concubine was her willingness to part with her husband so that he could take better care of his parents and his wife when they were trying to escape the fighting raging in Mao Xiang's hometown. When Mao Xiang proposed to her that she go with one of his friends instead of his family, Dong Xiaowan's reply spoke volumes of her perfect understanding of her humble status as a concubine in the family: "Your parents and children are one hundred times more important than me."[27]

It was this reformed woman, an exemplary concubine, rather the famed courtesan, that Mao Xiang tried to reconstruct in his memoir, for himself as well as for his readers. In the end, despite her upbringing and her past as a courtesan, Dong Xiaowan died an exemplary woman. Here, mourning is a redeeming process for the mourned, a former courtesan, and the mourner's remembrance is a ritual act of reconstructing a "proper" woman out of the deceased, whose earlier life as a prostitute deviated from the Confucian norms of the exemplary.

At the same time, the bereaved, by virtue of this mourning process, was also able to vindicate himself by proving he was not a lecher since the woman he married was a virtuous concubine rather than a sexy, morally questionable courtesan. The more exemplary a concubine Dong Xiaowan was presented in his "words of remembrance," the more persuasive he would sound in his assertion that he was not a lecher. Mao Xiang's friend, Zhang Mingbi 張明弼 (1584–1652) apparently felt that this memoir had effectively achieved its goal in this regard:

> Hunger for sex/beauty is just like hunger for food. The person who suffers from hunger, once filled, wouldn't want to eat anymore even if he is presented with the most delicious food. After nine years Mao Xiang still had not enough of her. Why? Because what he has been after is virtue rather than her sexual appeal (*jide fei jise ye* 飢德非飢色也)![28]

According to Zhang, after nine years of marriage, Mao Xiang was still "hungry" for his concubine, and he continued to desire her in his memories while her physical body had already perished. Never to be satisfied, this kind of hunger, perpetuated by memory, had to be a longing at the highest level—the desire for virtue.

This is indeed one of the central agendas of Mao Xiang's elegiac project on his concubine, with its emphasis on her virtue rather than the sexual appeal of this former courtesan. That is why at the very beginning of his memoir, Mao Xiang went out of his way to warn his readers that they were to be disappointed if they expected his memoir on this famed former courtesan to be a sensual story full of "embellishments" (*shi* 飾); this is also why Mao Xiang wanted to convey the impression that he was a dutiful husband to her even if, or precisely because, he had been a reluctant lover at the beginning when she was still a courtesan. Consequently, the mourning of Dong Xiaowan was also an occasion for the mourner's self-redemption—to redeem his own image as a lecher and to vindicate his own virtue as a dutiful husband, just as Dong Xiaowan was shown in his memoir to have been able to redeem herself by becoming an exemplary concubine. Memory, especially ritualized memory as re-enacted in the process of mourning, has a special redeeming quality. An integral part of the mourning process, for this polygamous husband, remembering is redeeming as well as self-vindicating.

Plum Shadow as "words of remembrance" also highlights the complicated function of memory. Mao Xiang took great pains to call his readers' attention to the significance of the word *yi* 憶 (recalling, remembrance) in the title of his memoir. This was also the word that headed the oracular verse he received when he drew a lot in the Guandi temple before they were married:

> Recalling the breaking of the hairpin into halves in the orchid chamber in the past,
> she wonders why he suddenly failed to send her any words.
> Hoping in vain for a union like the intertwined branches,
> who would expect that it won't work out in the end?[29]
> 憶昔蘭房分半釵, 如今忽把音信乖.
> 痴心指望成連理, 到底誰知事不諧?

Surprisingly, this was also the ominous oracular verse Dong Xiaowan drew when she sought predictions about her future. Now that Dong Xiaowan had passed away, Mao Xiang was convinced that the word *yi* was meant to predict that his concubine would die young, thus later becoming only accessible to him through memory. After only nine years of marriage, he was condemned to being a perpetual mourner living only with her memory for the rest of his life.

To better illustrate the special redeeming function of remembering on the part of a bereaved polygamist, we may digress for a quick look at a very telling episode in chapters 58 and 59 of the famous eighteenth-century novel *Honglou meng* 紅樓夢 (*Dream of the Red Mansion*; also known in English as *The Story of the Stone*). The actress/maid Ouguan was caught burning spirit money in the garden, but she was saved by the male protagonist Jia Baoyu from getting punished by the old maid. Later Baoyu learned that Ouguan, who used to play the leading male role on stage, fell in love with another actress Diguan, who often played the female role. After Diguan died, Ouguan was quite sad, but before long she fell in love with another actress, Ruiguan, who now played the leading male in place of Diguan. When others accused Ouguan of forgetting her old love after getting her new one, she insisted that she had not forgotten Diguan. She argued that this was just like the case of a man: he could not be accused of being unfaithful to his first wife if he remarried, as long as he kept her memory fresh. No wonder this argument touched Baoyu so deeply, who is known for his promiscuous (though not necessarily always sexual) love for so many girls, since this lesbian love affair reinforced the polygamous privileges of a man in heterosexual relationships. A man could feel attached to many different women, as Baoyu apparently does in the novel, as long as he does not forget his "old love." Burning spirit money or other acts of mourning could accomplish the redemptive function of allowing a polygamous man to claim that he was a devoted husband or lover despite his polygamous relationships with many women, so long as he was able to show that he kept the deceased in memory, whereas a similar redeeming strategy, of course, is out of the question for a woman in a polygamous society.

Thus, *daowang* ritual was capable of helping a man to redeem himself for being a polygamous man in terms of not only his past monogamous failures when his spouse was still alive but also in his continual failures after her death. While claiming Dong Xiaowan was always in his memory, Mao Xiang must have had fewer qualms in taking other concubines after she passed away, just as many years earlier he turned to Dong herself soon after another courtesan (Chen Yuanyuan) became unavailable.[30] This polygamous privilege was a man's entitlement, and such entitlement should not have prevented him from claiming he was a faithful lover and a devoted husband, as long as he did not "forget." Ironically, precisely because so many men took polygamous privilege for granted, monogamy or, at least, pledge of monogamy could sometimes become a powerful rhetoric for love on the part of a man, as we have encountered in the case of You Tong.

Many years later, after his principal wife, Madam Su, died, Mao Xiang's commemoration of her took the form of a more conventional *jiwen* (sacrificial litany). Apparently, the much lengthier *yiyu* (memoir), the new elegiac form he invented for remembering his deceased concubine, he must have felt was less suitable for his wife, presumably because of its unconventional nature. In this litany, the grieving husband fondly remembered how kindly his formal wife Madam Su had treated Dong Xiaowan. He further reminded us that it was his wife who arranged everything for Dong after she first arrived. It was interesting to note that the virtue of not being jealous was something a bereaved polygamous husband often would like to extol in remembering his deceased wife, but in the case of a concubine, this virtue was mentioned with much less frequency. Perhaps because of her humble status, a concubine was not so much in position to show jealousy in a polygamous family. In other words, for a polygamous husband, his wife's jealousy was a much more serious problem. Therefore, this virtue of lack of jealousy on the part of a wife merits even more praise.

Furthermore, unlike the long memoir he wrote for Dong, Mao Xiang's litany for his wife focuses on the central role of the deceased in the family and her relationships with many different family members.[31] Madam Su's married life was presented to be closely tied with the ups and downs of the Mao family. This becomes especially significant in comparison with the way Dong Xiaowen was remembered. If Madam Su was celebrated as a virtuous wife, whose role was essential to the well-being of his extended family (including Mao's parents, and his brothers and other relatives), then Dong as a concubine was remembered in large part as someone whose significance was appreciated mainly in terms of her relationship with the husband himself. In the memoir, Mao Xiang spent considerable amount of ink in detailing the cultured, leisured life Dong and he shared: how she assisted him in his various literary and scholarly endeavors, the special food or refined tea they shared together, and so on—in other words, how she had enriched his personal life rather than how she had directly contributed to the patrilineal interests of the family, as his wife Madam Su was extolled for in the litany.

Indeed, a concubine, because of her ambiguous status within a polygamous family, was often judged by a different set of standards. The image of a reformed former courtesan Mao Xiang carefully constructed in the memoir emphasizes that Dong was a woman of tranquility (*qingnü* 靜女), a quality not typically associated with a courtesan, therefore more proof of her as a woman of exquisite taste. Her aesthetic sensitivity (her love for flowers and the moon, etc.) and special culinary tastes are closely associated with the self-image the grieved husband tried to project for himself—instead of a lecher, he was a gentleman of refined taste and cultural sophistication, as demonstrated in his appreciation of a woman such as Dong, an aspect of himself that had little chance to manifest in his relationship with his formal wife, Madam Su. This memoir about his concubine, unlike his litany for his wife, was more about a spouse's role in this husband's own "private" life rather than that in the "public" spaces of an extended patrilineal family. The fact that there is no mention in the memoir of whether Dong Xiaowan gave birth to a child, or whether she was ever pregnant, a topic so important in Li Yu's biography of his concubines, might have added to this impression that she as a concubine was remembered for her cultural sophistication rather than the typical wifely contributions such as progeny, the usual Confucian justification for concubinage.

Mao Xiang was able to construct from his memories of Dong Xiaowan the image of a new model concubine who was mainly admired for her unique ability to enrich the personal life of her polygamous husband, an aspect of concubinage that had seldom received active sanction in Confucian discourse on wifely duties. Mao Xiang was probably the first literati husband who offered such a detailed and intimate account of an aesthetics of concubinage that only a man of high cultural taste such as he could offer. This is another important aspect of Mao Xiang's self-vindication agenda—what he appreciated most in Dong Xiaowan was not the vulgar sexual appeal average folks expected in a romance with a prostitute, but her unique aesthetic sensibility as a former courtesan in addition to many of her more traditional Confucian virtues.

MOURNING CONCUBINE AS WIFE

Thus far, we have focused primarily on how differently a concubine was mourned by her polygamous husband. However, the distinctions between wife and concubine could be complicated in certain circumstances. In the accounts of deceased concubines that we have discussed so far, the bereaved husbands seldom mentioned their household management ability, which was, however, a crucial quality in an exemplary wife. This silence can probably be attributed to the fact that a concubine, given her relatively low status in the family, was usually not given this important wifely task. However, this might change if the wife died or became unable to carry out this duty, in which case a concubine was likely to be asked to manage the household, contributing to the blurring of distinctions between wife and concubine.

Here, the case of the nineteenth-century scholar-official Fang Junyi 方浚頤 (1815–1869) is illuminating. Fang's wife, Madam Zhou, died at the age of forty-seven, and his concubine, Xie, died at the age twenty-eight. He wrote a biographical sketch for both of them, and yet, interestingly enough, the one for his concubine is significantly longer than the one for his wife.[32] This subtle inversion of the hierarchical order of wife and concubine became even more pronounced since the grieving husband chose to write a "biographical sketch" for both of them, unlike the case of Mao Xiang, who wrote a memoir for his deceased concubine and a sacrificial litany for his deceased wife. In the latter case, the much longer length of the memoir was not so significant since it was an elegiac form invented by Mao Xiang himself, without any existing conventions to define its significance in terms of its hierarchical implications. Reading these two biographical sketches in juxtaposition, one regarding Fang's wife and the other his concubine, should tell us much about their author as a polygamous literatus.

One important difference between these two biographical sketches is the sense of guilt that filled the author's memory of his concubine, which, however, was conspicuously absent from his biographical sketch of his wife. Fang always believed that he might have inadvertently contributed to his concubine's early death when he failed to take the advice of a doctor when she was seriously ill. What made him feel even guiltier was that a few years earlier she had saved his life when he was suffering from a near-fatal illness; she had chosen the right medicine for him, while all other doctors' prescriptions failed to work.

It was his wife, Madam Zhou, who herself selected Xie and arranged to have her husband take her as a concubine and, according to him, she took a liking for her from the very beginning, believing that the concubine was a girl of good luck, because as soon as she was brought into their family, the husband received a major promotion in the imperial government. A year later, before she died, Madam Zhou told her husband to treat Xie well and that the concubine could be a good "assistant inside the household" (*neizhu* 內助) despite her young age, suggesting that she could take up the task of running the household in her place (if he did not plan to marry another wife). Later Xie indeed proved to be a very competent household manager and, according to the husband, she performed splendidly the duties of a wife. In a way, the concubine Xie's admirable wifely performance later was also presented as a vindication of his wife's insight.

In recalling Madam Zhou's life, Fang mentioned that he had great respect for her because she often cautioned him against excessive drinking and partying. In his biographical sketch for the concubine, he expressed regret that he continued to behave in such a way after the death of his wife. Yet his concubine's approach was said to have been rather different. Whenever Fang went out partying deep into the night, Xie always stayed up late, waiting for him to return, for which he felt quite guilty. However, he did not mention she ever criticized him as his late wife had done, suggesting that as a concubine Xie was much more discreet in reproaching her husband. Unlike a wife, instead of direct reproach, the best the concubine could do was to use her silent deeds to subtly admonish. Given her lower status, Xie was certainly an exemplary Confucian concubine in this regard.

Just like his virtuous wife, who had arranged her husband to take Xie as concubine, Xie now performed this same "wifely" deed: she arranged to have Fang take another girl, Zhu, as his concubine/maid, and later treated the latter's child as her own. She was just as unjealous as her predecessor, Madam Zhou, another sign of her qualities as a potential wife. Zhu felt so attached to Xie that she cut off a piece of her own flesh to make medicinal soup for Xie three times when the latter was seriously ill. This, according to Fang, reminded him of what his eldest daughter had done when Madam Zhou was gravely ill. By comparing Zhu's act of *gegu* to that of the filial act on the part of his own daughter, Fang seems to be reaffirming the hierarchical distinctions between a concubine and a wife, as well as those among different concubines. In her relationship to Xie, the maid Zhu acted as a filial daughter would act—Zhu respected Xie as a mother figure, as prescribed in the Confucian ritual discourses, even though Xie was never formally promoted to be his formal wife after the death of Madam Zhou. However, as far as Zhu was concerned, Xie occupied the position of the principal wife.

This was probably why Fang felt so gratified that, after Xie died, some of his nephews and nieces insisted on mourning Xie as his formal wife rather than concubine by observing the one-year mourning period prescribed for a deceased aunt. When asked whether such apparent violation of the traditional mourning ritual codes was appropriate, Fang offered a spirited defense:

> The sages established rituals on the basis of feelings/emotions. When one's feelings are sincere, even if they are beyond what is considered moderate, the sages would not forbid their expressions. This is "the rituals that have not been codified into the ritual prescriptions" (*wangyu li zhi li* 亡於禮之禮).[33]

Fang felt especially gratified because his nephews and nieces had apparently done what he might have qualms doing himself: explicitly honoring Xie as a wife rather than a concubine.

Fang Junyi's biography of the concubine Xie highlights the ambiguities and fluidity associated with a concubine in terms of her status within a polygamous family, even though his basic biographical rhetoric is also designed to reaffirm the wife–concubine distinctions at the same time. The fact that she gave birth to a son might have enhanced such fluidity, although this does not appear to be a factor that Fang tried to highlight in the biographical sketch (he mentioned the birth only in passing).[34] One would be tempted to speculate that one of the reasons that she was not formally promoted to be his wife was her humble family origin, about which Fang remained conspicuously silent in the biographical sketch. The gap between her family background and that of Fang was probably just too big to allow him to formally honor her as a wife.

However, what has made this case particularly interesting is how mourning rituals could be manipulated to give Xie the kind of recognition her husband could not give her when she was still alive: the special biographical sketch he wrote for her was significantly longer than that he wrote for his wife, and he endorsed the decision by his nephews and nieces to mourn her as their aunt rather than a concubine. Posthumous honor in the form of a longer and more eulogic biography and being mourned with an upgraded ritual code by members of the younger generation, this bereaved polygamous husband hoped could somehow compensate his beloved concubine for her denied opportunity, as a result of her humble family origin, to enjoy the full status of a formal wife while alive. Mourning rituals, intended to be all about the order of social hierarchies, could also be employed to undermine those very hierarchies by appealing to the age-long argument that the ancient sages established rituals on the basis of feelings, a rationale many were more likely to appeal to when they found it advantageous for them to ignore the rigid codes of Confucian rituals.

I hope the several cases explored in this chapter give a sense of the wide range of ways deceased concubines could be remembered and mourned by their husbands, due to the spectrum of roles a concubine could assume in a polygamous family—from slave/maid, to entertainer, to minor wife, and even full-fledged wife in charge of managing an entire household. Precisely because of the ambiguities associated with a concubine, she is more likely than a formal wife to become a figure appropriated and even manipulated by her grieving husband, in the process of reconstructing her image from his memories, for a variety of agendas, many of which might be more related to his own self-image as a man. Li Yu's biography of his two concubines is an illuminating case despite its author's typical witty and sometimes exaggerated rhetoric, while Mao Xiang's memoir of Dong Xiaowan is a much more subtle and sophisticated project of self-vindication. It is a project of vindication as much as biography, and more about Mao Xiang himself in that it related a literati connoisseur's refined taste and his new aesthetics of concubinage.

Writing and exchanging of various elegiac works had become such an integral part of the social life of the literati that for many it served the important function of social networking. Because of the unique status of a concubine, her death and the ensuing mourning activities were more likely to become an important networking occasion for her husband and his literati peers, as we shall see in the next chapter.

CHAPTER 7

CIRCULATING GRIEF

By the seventeenth century, for many educated males, mourning had become a cherished, sometimes eagerly awaited, occasion for showcasing one's elegiac talent and enhancing one's social status. The monumental *Wumeng tang ji* compiled and published by Ye Shaoyuan is a case in point. This enormous book is comprised of individual collections of writings by Ye himself, his wife, and several of their children, with most of these collections, which already contain a large number of elegiac writings, followed by lengthy appendixes consisting mostly of similar writings by other family members, relatives, and friends in mourning of many of these same authors.[1] The entire book could be appreciated as a long mourning procession in which Ye's late wife and many of their deceased children appear as both the mourned and the mourners. Here, the distinctions between the two become rather blurred as, ironically, a mourner would later be mourned by yet another mourner, in part for his or her elegiac talent. If readers were struck by the early deaths of so many of Ye's family members, they might likely be more impressed by these authors' eagerness to write elegies whenever a family member passed away, as if the death of a family member were a long-anticipated occasion, or even an excuse to showcase elegiac talents.

It is interesting to note that among all the contributors who wrote elegies in mourning of Ye's younger daughter, Ye Xiaoluan 葉小鸞, only the ages of her three younger brothers, Shicheng 葉世偁, Ye Shirong 葉世傛, and Ye Shitong 葉世侗, are specifically noted by their father, Ye Shaoyuan, the editor: they are respectively fifteen, fourteen, and thirteen, presumably to show how young they were when they wrote these dazzling elegies. Anticipating possible doubt that they were really capable of writing these sacrificial litanies at such tender ages, Ye Shaoyuan goes out of his way to assure readers in a special note that these writings were printed verbatim exactly as written by these young children and received no later revision or embellishment.[2] For Ye Shaoyuan, the book was meant to showcase the literary and especially the elegiac talents of his entire family. Of course, the ultimate *daowang* master was Ye Shaoyuan himself, both as an author and the compiler of this grand book of family mourning. With the help of family members, he was able to turn his family tragedies into triumphant occasions for literary extravaganza. In many ways, *Wumeng tang ji* is all about the celebration of elegiac talents, pointing to the *daowang* fervor and the literati's obsession with their self-images as elegiac masters in the seventeenth-century Chinese literary world.

However, the seventeenth century was also the time when many discovered how difficult it was to stand out as an impressive *daowang* writer, given the accumulated burden of the long *daowang* literary tradition and the fact that so many were competing to impress others as gifted. To make a deeper impression, some even resorted to the practice of *jiju* 集句 (composing one's own poems by using exclusively poetic lines taken from the work of other poets, often on similar themes by celebrated masters in the past).[3] *Jiju* is considered a poetic exercise technically quite demanding, as one must compose a coherent poem with proper poetic patterns and rhyming from lines taken verbatim from poems written by other poets, often under different circumstances. While *jiju* as a poetic practice has a long history in premodern China, using this *jiju* method to compose *daowang* poems was a literary phenomenon relatively unique to the late imperial period, as the expression of deeply personal *daowang* grief now became the display of a poetic virtuoso. One's articulation of private grief over the loss of a spouse now had to rely on ready-made poetic lines from past *daowang* masters. Further, such *jiju* poems were often composed in large sets to underscore the author's mastery of the *daowang* poetic tradition, as if, to showcase one's elegiac talent, grief must be somehow quantified, even if in clever rearrangement of poetic lines by previous *daowang* authors.[4] This elegiac tendency toward quantification, however, was by no means confined to the *jiju* practice.

THE NEED TO QUANTIFY GRIEF

Upon the death of his concubine, Dong Xiaowan, Mao Xiang composed a long elegiac verse "Wangji Dong Xiaowan aici" 亡姬董小宛哀辭 (A Eulogy in Honor of My Deceased Concubine Dong Xiaowan) to mourn her. At the end of this eulogy, Mao Xiang profusely congratulated himself for having completed such a brilliant, long verse essay in such a short period of time:

> It was completed within the short span of two days and two nights. It is two-thousand-four-hundred-characters long, and two hundred forty different

rhymes have been employed. There have been no other *daowang* eulogies by anyone else that are as detailed as this one of mine.... Alas, Fengqian is heartbroken and Wentong's literary talent has been exhausted.[5]

Comparing himself to Xun Fengqian, who died of grief over the death of his wife, and Wentong (Jiang Yan 江淹 [444–505]), arguably one of the most famed writers of elegies in Chinese literary history, Mao Xiang declared he had composed a eulogy such as had never been attempted by others. Further, he called people's attention to the fact that he completed such a difficult long elegiac verse within the short period of only "two days and two nights," an eloquent testament to his poetic talent. And yet he still felt unsatisfied. To further outdo all other famous *daowang* writers in the past, Mao Xiang literally invented a brand new *daowang* form by producing the *Plum Shadow*, a much lengthier memoir in prose, which eventually secured his fame as one of the greatest *daowang* writers in premodern China.

Here, quantity of output is considered to be a key indicator of brilliance as an elegiac genius, as well as the depth of his feelings for his deceased spouse. Quantities mattered in terms of not only the length of a poem (how many words and how many different rhymes a verse contains) but also the total number of poems and prose essays one wrote in honor of the deceased. Indeed, many literati husbands were becoming increasingly voluminous in their outpouring of elegiac sentiments. It became quite common for them to write long sets of *daowang* poems and ever-longer memorial texts in prose. Mao Xiang's younger contemporary, Wang Shizhen, the poet and scholar-official, wrote a set of thirty-five poems to mourn his first wife and another two long sets to mourn his second wife and his concubine, respectively,[6] in addition to the long biographical sketches he wrote for all three of them.[7] Compared with Wang Shizhen, both Ye Shaoyuan and You Tong were even more voluminous in producing memorial writings on their deceased wives. Ye Shaoyuan wrote approximately one hundred and thirty *daowang* poems plus several memorial essays in honor of his late wife, while You Tong composed close to one hundred poems in addition to a long biographical sketch and other litanies in honor of his late wife.

A SELF-CLAIMED ELEGIAC MASTER

Mao Xiang's self-congratulatory rhetoric was not uncommon among elegiac authors of the time. Mao's younger contemporary, the poet and scholar Qu

Dajun 屈大均 (1630–1696), was even more deliberate and persistent in his endeavor to build up his image as a great *daowang* writer. In a postscript to a set of one hundred poems he wrote in mourning of his second wife, Wang Huajiang, Qu Dajun declared with great pride that he was doing something utterly unprecedented in literary history—in addition to the forty or so poems he had already dedicated to her when she was still alive, he was writing another one hundred poems eulogizing her now that she had passed away. Even the well-known ancient masters of *daiwang* poetry, such as Pan Yue, Jiang Yan, and Yuan Zhen, Qu insisted, had never attempted anything that came even close. He was absolutely confident that these poems would be read by many under Heaven.[8]

The outpouring of emotions after the death of Qu Dajun's second wife, Wang Huajiang, and his deep attachment to her were related in part to the unhappy experience of his first, very brief marriage. Although not much was said about his first marriage, we do know his first wife was a woman née Liu, not even mentioned in Qu's family genealogy.[9] A vague reference to his first wife was made in a poem about his taking refuge with his mother in the residence of a distant relative during the war, where he expressed his determination to remain single after his wife failed to return after a visit to her natal home,[10] probably part of the phenomenon of *bu luo jia* 不落家—a bride's refusal to return to the home of her husband after leaving for a visit to her natal family, a method of escape from an unhappy marriage popular in the Guangdong area at the time. Some of these women enjoyed deep bonding with other women and detested traditional marriage.[11] Liu's refusal to return must have hurt Qu Dajun so much that he swore he would never marry again.[12]

However, at the age of thirty-seven, Qu Dajun changed his mind when he was introduced to his future second wife, Wang Huajiang, the beautiful and talented daughter of a Ming general who had chosen to commit suicide rather than surrendering to the enemy after suffering defeat in a battle in defending the Ming monarchy. Deeply impressed by Qu's poetic talent, his friend, Li Yindu 李因篤 (1631–1692), a poet, introduced him to his future wife's uncle and aunt (they became her guardians after her parents had died). Li helped to bring about the marriage in part because he believed the girl, good at martial arts, might become helpful when Qu and others wanted to join the resistance movement against the Manchus.[13] Born and having grown up in the Qin area (what is now modern Shanxi province), Wang married Qu Dajun, a southerner from the Guangdong area, when the latter was visiting the northwest. Humiliated in his first marriage and embarrassed by his first wife's desertion, Qu must have had a special appreciation of Wang Huajiang to risk marrying again. Though apparently a very loving couple, their marriage lasted only twenty-eight months, as Wang died of miscarriage complications at the age of twenty-four.

Qu Dajun compiled a collection of *daowang* writings by different people in honor of Wang Huajiang, many of which were the results of his persistent solicitation. The volume was titled *Daoli ji* 悼儷集 (*In Mourning of My Wife*). Paying homage to his deceased wife and showing her what a great honor it was for her to have a book of *daowang* writings dedicated to her, Qu Dajun burned a copy of the book in front of her grave, declaring in a litany:

> *Daoli ji* was an unprecedented work and I was the first to assemble such a unique book of mourning. It is a book made of various elegiac writings by all the talented and virtuous men around the country to mourn your death. In the genre of poetry, there are songs of music bureau, ancient style poems [unregulated verse] and modern style poems [regulated verse]; in the genre of prose, there are prefaces, biographies, elegies, epitaphs and epitaphic essays; works of every genre are presented. . . . Alas, you were a woman and yet you have been celebrated in so many writings to eulogize you in the nether world! You should have no regrets dying so young. . . . There has never been a book such as *Daoli ji*. These virtuous and talented gentlemen from all over the country, thanks to my kind words for you, were eager to send me these writings praising you. I envy you. In the past Xun Fengqian died [of his deep sorrows over the death of his beloved wife] and more than forty famous gentlemen wrote elegies in memory of him. They covered up his mistakes as they were saddened over his overindulgence in his love for his wife. Should misfortune one day strike me and I have to leave this world, there would be many elegies and epitaphs being written to mourn me and these writings could be traced all the way back to the classic of *Lisao* [Encountering Sorrows]. And yet, whom could I expect to assemble them into a book [on my behalf]? Don't you think you have been very lucky![14]

One cannot help being struck by Qu Dajun's acute self-consciousness as a *daowang* writer and his self-congratulatory smugness. He is arguing that by virtue of his ritual act of *daowang*, which was occasioned by death, his dead wife had attained immortality.

Here the gendered implications of the act of mourning are hard to miss: Qu Dajun believed that Wang Huajiang was a woman who would have had little chance of being immortalized in a literary text, so she should rest content in death now that she had become the subject in the elegiac writings by so many famous male authors (not the least himself). It was the male author who possessed this immortalizing power. A deceased woman was saved from oblivion by her mourning husband and achieved immortality in his *daowang* writings.[15] On the other hand, if another book of mourning to commemorate Qu Dajun himself was ever produced after his death, the author of that volume would most likely be another man. Mourning, when considered an act capable of immortalizing the dead, was presented solely as a male prerogative. A woman should be deemed extremely lucky if her husband was a gifted *daowang* writer, or even better, one who could command enough prestige to secure *daowang* writings from so many well-known writers, and then be able to assemble them into a special book to honor her, exactly as Qu Dajun had done. By giving his wife immortality, Qu Dajun, as a brilliant poet and mourner, also secured his own position in literary history, even becoming immortalized himself. Often in his *daowang* writings, Qu Dajun appears to have been more concerned with his own image as a brilliant writer/mourner than that of the mourned. Sometimes it was the male mourner himself rather than the mourned female that became the main concern of *daowang* discourse. Such men as Qu Dajun probably never believed they would need a book of mourning written by others to immortalize them, having already achieved immortality by being a great mourner of several wives and concubines (besides those dedicated to the memories of his second wife, Qu Dajun also wrote many *daowang* poems and epitaphs for his other wives and concubines).[16] The question at the end of his litany—who will assemble a book of mourning for him after his death?—was largely a rhetorical one, raised to console his dead female subject, a hallmark of the effective mourning rhetoric on the part of a privileged male *daowang* writer.

After Wang's death, Qu Dajun married his third wife, Lishi; their marriage lasted only five years before she died, too, of illness. Qu Dajun actually spent only twenty-three months with her, as he was often away, participating in the resistance movement against the Manchus. In his biographical sketch of Lishi, Qu Dajun mentioned that before they were married Lishi had already begun to admire him after reading his *daowang* writings on her predecessor, Qu's second wife, which must have been circulated in his hometown.[17] The reader is meant to infer that Lishi was happy to marry him as his third wife partly out of her admiration for his literary talent as an elegiac writer. Not too long after the marriage, she died too, and thus became yet another subject of her husband's *daowang*. Lishi's marriage with Qu was something like a self-fulfilling prophecy. Like his previous wife, Lishi wished her name to be immortalized in her husband's elegies—though probably not so soon! And, clearly, Qu Dajun believed that all three of his immortalized wives were richly compensated (and perhaps should even be happy to have died since this gave him the chance to immortalize them).

A man of literary reputation, this mourning husband enjoyed the prerogative to grant eternal fame to all his wives and concubines through his *daowang* writings, although the ways these women could benefit from the grace of his writings had to fit their hierarchical rankings in the polygamous structure of his family, as carefully delineated in the collective epitaph he wrote for the four of his wives and concubines.[18]

There was a sense of friendly competition among many mourning literati husbands when it came to authoring various memorial writings on their own deceased spouses and those of their peers. After Wang Huajiang died, Qu Dajun's friend, the poet Chen Gongyin 陳恭尹 (1631–1700), composed a long poem of more than eight hundred characters to mourn her, in addition to writing an epitaph for her at Qu's request.[19] Later, after Chen's own wife passed away, Qu Dajun in return composed a long poem to mourn his friend's deceased wife. Qu, however, expressed uneasiness because this poem was only five-hundred characters long.[20] Once again, quantity mattered. What is so remarkable about Qu Daoqun is not so much his expressed grief over his deceased spouses but his insistence on the importance articulating such grief in various elegiac genres and the need to produce a large quantity of such elegies, as if there were a direct causal link between the depth of one's grief and the large number of elegies in various genres one wrote. In short, there was at the time a clear sense of competition among grieving literati husbands to see who could produce elegiac writings in ever larger quantities and ever greater variety.

THE SOCIAL CIRCULATION OF GRIEF

Such acute awareness of friendly competition was mixed with an even deeper sense of social obligation. When a friend suffered the misfortune of the death of a spouse, one was expected to compose and send poems of condolences to him at short notice. *Daowang* poems composed to mourn the death of the spouse of a friend, or composing such poems on behalf of someone else, (*wei moumou daowang* 為某某悼亡 or *dai moumou daowang* 代某某悼亡) became almost a poetic subgenre on its own.[21] On the other hand, a mourning husband would also actively solicit such poems and other elegiac writings from as many friends as possible because quantity was important. Then these writings were often assembled into a book, which was distributed, in turn, among friends for them to come up with even more colophons or endorsing poems to further expand this mourning project, seemingly perpetuating a literary exchange process that could last almost forever. After the death of his second wife, Wang Huajiang, Qu Dajun soon began to solicit poems and other elegiac writings from his friends. Then he carefully assembled them into a book and distributed the copies among his friends to seek more endorsement writings from them.[22] This is reminiscent of what Mao Xiang did after he completed his memoir in honor of his concubine Dong Xiaowan; he had the memoir printed as a book and distributed it among his friends, seeking their responses in writing. Most of their responses were reprinted in his *Tongren ji* 同人集 (A Collection of the Writings of Kindred Spirits), a massive collection of literary exchanges among Mao Xiang and his literati friends.[23] Now the memory of his deceased concubine became part of her surviving husband's large homosocial project of literati networking.

Daowang thus became a communal act—a public process through which literary participation of friends and peers of a grieving husband was desired, as well as expected. The mourning of the death of one's spouse was no longer a private act on the part of the bereaved. It became an occasion for validating or enhancing the grieving husband's cultural and social standing among his literati peers, and sometimes even an opportunity for self-reinvention.

Other factors contributed to the communal nature of the literati *daowang* endeavor. A late imperial educated man often had to travel far away to take civil examinations or serve in governmental office, and it was not uncommon that his spouse died while he was away. What added to the sorrow of the loss for those who had to be away was the guilt and helplessness they felt over their failures to be at the bedside when their wives died and the inability to bid in person farewell to the deceased, as in You Tong's case. Such shared social experience of loss and helplessness seems to have strengthened the homosocial bond among these grieving sojourners through the communal *daowang* process. In fact, quite a few of You Tong's friends had suffered similar pains of losing their spouses while far from home. Wang Shizhen, for example, had lost his first wife a few years earlier while serving as an official at the capital. Sending his condolences to You Tong, Wang must have had a deeper appreciation of the sorrows of You's bereavement. The two exchanged elegiac poems and wrote matching poems for each other's *daowang* poems.[24] A few years later, Chen Weisong, one of You Tong's friends and a *tongnian* of the special examination, also lost his wife while at the capital. Chen and You took turns writing elegiac essays in honor of each other's wives, and their friendship appears to have solidified in their shared loss of their spouses.[25] After news of

You Tong's wife's death reached the capital, many of his friends, also waiting to sit for the examination, expressed their condolences to You Tong. Their sympathy for the bereaved deepened even more because the grieving husband could not return to attend the funeral of his wife a thousand miles away. According to You Tong, more than one hundred people paid condolence calls to him at the capital, including many high officials, his *tongnian* friends, and fellow townsmen and relatives, and many of them contributed elegiac poems and essays, later collected in the special anthology *Aiyuan ji* 哀弦集 (the Sad String Collection) You Tong assembled.[26] Consequently, the mourning of You Tong's deceased wife became a big public event among his friends and the examination candidates, and many of them, like himself, were selected and invited by the imperial government to participate in the special examination by virtue of their prestige and reputation. The fact that so many famous and important men paid homage to his late wife must have been an experience You Tong cherished with great pride. In his biography of You Tong, the scholar and poet Pan Lei 潘耒 (1646–1708), one of his special examination *tongnian*, mentioned in particular You Tong's public mourning of his deceased wife and the special anthology of elegiac writings by his peers that he later compiled. This was now considered an important event in You Tong's life that was worth being recorded in his biography as a testimony to his prestige and fame.[27]

You Tong wrote voluminously to mourn not only his own deceased wife but also the deceased spouses of many of his peers, as his writings were actively sought by many grieving husbands. When presented with a volume of *daowang* poems that his friend Ye Feng 葉封 (1624–1687) wrote to mourn his late wife, You Tong felt obligated to come up with a preface for the volume, as he remembered how moved he was by Ye's condolence poems when his own wife, Caoshi, had died three years earlier. Now Ye was suffering the same misfortune of being stranded at the capital and unable to attend the funeral of his wife back home.[28] Apparently, You Tong considered responding to Ye's *daowang* poems with a preface as part of his obligation of returning social debt. A special examination *tongnian*, Fang Xiangying, whose condolence poem in honor of You Tong's deceased wife was also anthologized by the grieving husband in the special volume devoted to her, later sent You Tong a copy of the biographical sketch he wrote for his own recently deceased wife, and asked him to write a biography based on his sketch. You Tong duly fulfilled his obligation and produced an interesting biography of Fang's wife, in which he showed how Fang's wife reminded him of his own wife by carefully comparing the two. Here, mourning the death of a friend's wife became an occasion to commemorate his own late wife.

Indeed, mourning the death of one's own spouse as well as participating in the mourning of the deaths of the spouses of one's friends became an important part of a literatus's social life, whereas the ability to compose various types of memorial writings on demand and at short notice was crucial to his image as a cultured man, as reflected in the collected works of many literati. *Daowang* was an important shared social experience among the literati in that it enhanced their sense of the membership of a special homosocial community, where they not only shared the losses of loved ones but also had to demonstrate their special ability to articulate such mutual feeling of loss in a way that reaffirmed and solidified their standings as men of cultural sophistication. In the case of You Tong, many of those who exchanged *daowang* writings with him also happened to be those *tongnian* who participated in and passed the special "Erudite Scholarship Examination" sponsored by the imperial government in 1679. Since many of the candidates of this special examination, unlike the regular examination candidates, were specially recommended based on their already established reputations, most of them tended to be relatively advanced in age and, consequently, more likely to have suffered the losses of spouses. Whereas the fact that most of these specially selected examination candidates were nationally renowned scholars and officials only added to the exclusiveness of this community, the shared *daowang* experience must have further deepened such a sense of being a member of such an exclusive social club.

THE SPECTACLE OF GRIEF

Mao Qiling 毛奇齡 (1623–1716), another well-known scholar and participant in the 1679 special examination, launched an even more ambitious project of mourning and commemoration soon after the death of his concubine, Zhang Manshu. His commemorative project of his concubine was turned into a public spectacle, sometimes literally performed on stage.

Mao Qiling took Manshu as his concubine, under the arrangement of the Grand Secretary Feng Pu 馮溥 (1609–1692), while he was at the capital to participate in the special "Erudite Scholarship Examinations" sponsored by the imperial government. Manshu was the eighteen-year-old daughter of a local flower vendor when she became his concubine. She died at the age of twenty-four. Besides several poems in honor of her, Mao Qiling wrote a series of essays to mourn her: they include a formal epitaph, "Manshu zangming" 曼殊葬銘,[29] an alternative epitaph, "Manshu biezhi shuzhuan" 曼殊別誌書磚,[30] and an account of her miraculous resurrection, "Manshu huisheng ji"

曼殊回生記;[31] he even wrote a quite long letter addressed to his then-already-dead concubine, "Ji Manshu jinfang dixia shu" 寄曼殊禁方地下書.[32] All these memorial writings were part of Mao Qiling's deliberate and carefully choreographed attempt to build up Manshu's "legend" as a beautiful, talented, and, most important, faithful concubine of humble origin, who died a tragic death out of her faithfulness to her husband.

Except for in the letter, which was addressed to Manshu directly, Mao Qiling remained quite emotionally detached in his memorial writings, as if he were merely a storyteller telling a moving story about the life of an interesting but unrelated woman, a deliberate attempt to distance himself and present the life of Manshu as a tale. This was a tale for public consumption, so his own private emotions as a surviving husband were not a major concern. Zhang Manshu is presented in these private elegiac writings not so much from Mao Qiling's personal perspective (as her grieving husband) as from the perspective of a detached storyteller indulging in telling this tale of pathos.

According to Mao Qiling's epitaph for her, when the Grand Secretary Feng Pu tried to arrange to have him take Manshu as his concubine, the latter consented despite his much advanced age (he was about fifty-six at the time) because she was so impressed with his literary talent. This must sound familiar by now (as discussed in chapter 6, Li Yu offered a similar explanation as to why his young and beautiful concubine insisted on sticking with her old husband). Even when her mother, worrying that he was old and poor, began to regret the engagement after they heard Mao's wife was a jealous woman, Manshu herself never wavered. Although a daughter raised in the humble family of a flower vendor, Manshu was very gifted. She could imitate the singing of all kinds of bird and was very quick at learning needlework. After becoming Mao's concubine, she proved to be a quick learner of reading and writing as well. She could even compose poetry. She also became a quite good painter and could sing and play the songs composed by Mao Qiling after listening to them only a few times.[33] Here we are again reminded of Li Yu's combined biography of his two concubines.

The happy days, however, quickly came to an end when came the news that Mao Qiling's jealous wife was soon to arrive from the south. Without having given birth to a child during the past three years, Manshu found herself having no alternative but to move out of Mao Qiling's residence. Others suggested that she should be sent away. In the epitaph, Mao Qiling offers a very dramatic account of how Manshu responded to the prospect of being forced to leave:

> Before leaving for his hometown after retirement, the Grand Secretary Feng said to Manshu: "Originally I arranged to have Mr. Mao take you as

concubine because he had no son. In the past three years, you did not get pregnant and now his wife suddenly was about to arrive from the south. How do you think you would find accommodation for yourself? It is going to be quite impossible. Besides, Mr. Mao is advanced in age and is a man of limited means. Xiaoshan [Mao's hometown] is far away and he is too poor to take care of you. . . . If you don't ask to leave yourself, you are doing something quite unwise." His Excellency really cared about her and myself. He said this only out of his concern for us and nothing more. Manshu was in deep shock after hearing this. She thanked His Excellency but declined in tears, saying: "I believed Your Excellency had always instructed us to behave according to ritual propriety. How could you fail to hear the saying that a woman must not marry two husbands?"

At that time, a woman sitting next to her burst into laughter: "Really! Then who married you as a wife that you congratulated yourself so much?" Facing Manshu straight, she said: "Mr. Mao is not your husband!" Outraged, Manshu cried: "Heaven! If people do not consider me his wife, that is okay. However, I would rather die if I am said to have no husband!" Then she threw herself onto the ground. . . . An old female relative of mine in the capital tried to send her away under the false claim that she was acting upon my instruction. Manshu initially refused to believe but, after being repeatedly told so, she began to believe that instruction might have indeed come from me. She cried until she almost stopped breathing.[34]

Although there was no mention that Manshu was specifically persecuted by Mao's jealous wife, the fact that her arrival played a role in the former's tragic death was plausible. Her beauty, her talent, her loyalty, her humble origin, her so-called resurrection and, finally, her tragic death all helped create a tale of special pathos that must have reminded people of the popular legend of Feng Xiaoqing 馮小青, a talented and beautiful concubine persecuted by the principal wife of her husband, which saw wide circulation among the literati during the seventeenth century.[35]

Throughout this epitaph, there is virtually no description of Mao Qiling's own reactions or his emotions as her husband. There is even no reference to any direct interaction between Manshu and Mao himself, as if he were describing for us someone totally unrelated to himself despite, or precisely because of, the dramatic nature of his narrative (i.e., he was telling a tale). Was Mao himself present when all these events were taking place? The author did not give us much direct evidence to confirm this. The tale is told from the perspective of an omniscient narrator, who chose to omit such information. Overall,

CIRCULATING GRIEF | 147

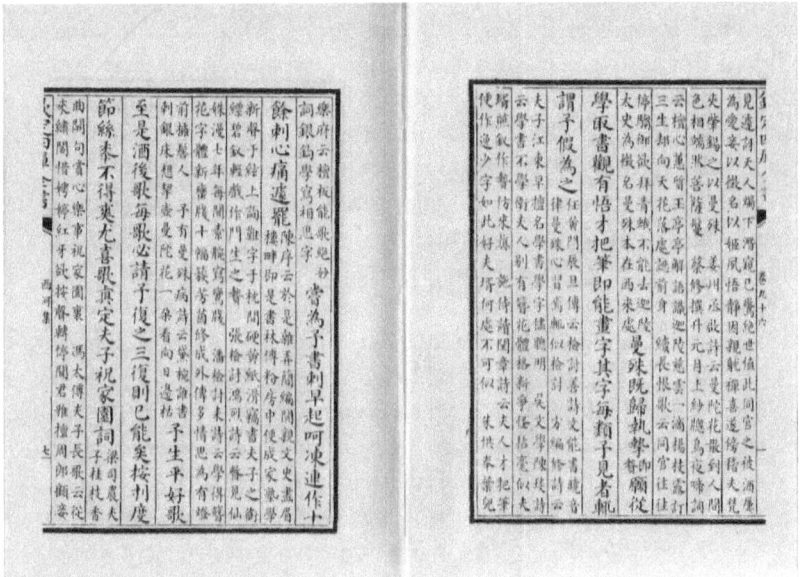

Figure 7.1 A scanned copy of two pages (96.6b and 96.7a) from "Manshu biezhi shuzhuan," collected in the *Siku quanshu* edition of *Xihe ji*.

the impression was that this was a kind of anecdotal or *chuanqi* 傳奇 tale that one might expect to find in a collection of random jottings (*biji* 筆記). That is probably one of the reasons why this epitaph and Mao's other pieces on Manshu were later selected to be anthologized in the popular *xiaoshuo* 小說 (fiction) collections *Yuchu xinzhi* 虞初新志 (The New Tales of Yuchu) and *Yuchu xuzhi* 虞初續志 (a continuation of the New Tales of Yuchu) compiled by Zhang Chao 張潮 (b. 1650) and others.[36] In fact, Mao Qiling himself mentioned that a theatrical play and drum-songs based on her life story had already appeared not long after her death.[37] The tragic death of his concubine was now being turned into a public spectacle on stage, due largely to Mao's effort.

If this *xiaoshuo*-like epitaph by Mao Qiling on Manshu is quite unusual in being so dramatic, then the "alternative epitaph" Mao Qiling wrote later is even more remarkable. It is partly rehash of what has been said in the epitaph, although its emphasis is now shifted onto her music and literary talents, while not so exclusively focusing on her moral virtue. What makes this alternative epitaph so intriguing is the large amount of annotations Mao inserted into the text. All these annotations were presented in the form of double-column interlineal comments (*shuanghang jiapi* 雙行夾批), such as in annotated editions of Confucian classics or commentary editions of literary works.³⁸ These comments are written or printed in characters smaller than those of the text proper, giving this epitaph a more formal typographic feel, as if it were a canonical text worthy of careful exegetic annotations (see fig. 7.1).

Often in this epitaph the lengths of these annotations are several times longer than the paragraphs or sentences they are supposed to annotate. The following is a passage from the epitaph (with annotations italicized):

> After she became my concubine, Manshu wanted to study and become my student. Not long after she started to learn how to read, she could already have adequate understanding of what she was reading. It did not take her long to learn to paint and write once she took up brush. Her handwriting was so much like that of mine that people thought I wrote for her.
>
> *Ren Chendan, the Supervising Censor, observes in her biography:* "The Examining Editor [Mao Qiling] is a master of poetry and prose, an excellent calligrapher, and an expert in music. Manshu was so devoted to learn from him that her style was just like that of the Examining Editor." *Fang Xiangying, the Compiler, remarks in his poem:* "Throughout the East of the River her husband's literary reputation became known a long time ago; a gifted student of reading and calligraphy Manshu herself turned out to be." *Wu Chenyan, the scholar, testifies in his poem:* "Refusing to learn Madam Wei's famous calligraphic style, she invented the new feminine style of her own. How close her writing style was to that of her husband one cannot help wondering; her handwriting could indeed be mistaken as that of her husband." *Shi Renzhang, the Reader-in-Waiting, writes in his poem:* "As soon as the Madam took up her brush, she wrote in the style of a handsome youth. With such a learned husband, how could she fail to imitate him?" *Zhu Yizun, the Academician for Court Service, declares in his poem in the style of* "Ye'er music bureau poetry": "With great gift for music she could sing beautiful songs, and in elegant style she wrote down words of deep love."³⁹

Most of these annotations are quotations of poems about Manshu composed by important contemporary literary figures or high officials, all of whom were Mao Qiling's friends or acquaintances. Their names (often with their official titles attached) constitute a who's who list of the cultural elite at the capital, allowing readers a glimpse into the large amount of literary writings devoted to Manshu that had been produced by various important poets, writers, and officials of the time. This epitaph of a deceased concubine was now turned into a detailed record of her surviving husband's homosocial exchanges with his male friends, serving as a testament to his high standing among the cultural elite in the imperial capital.

Each of this grieving husband's words about his deceased concubine needed to be elaborated on, augmented, and authenticated by the poetic testimonies of many others, as if Mao's firsthand memories of his own concubine were somehow actually based on these people's secondhand corroborations in a reversed order. Personal memory is here authenticated but simultaneously displaced by secondhand collective memories. Many of those who wrote about Manshu might have never met her in person and were only responding to Mao's own writings about her.

There was a peculiar power of persuasion associated with poetry when it came to the construction of the legend of a beautiful but humble concubine who had died a tragic death. With so many poems by so many different poets, and the sheer power of poetic repetition as a result, this legend somehow managed to acquire a unique romantic authenticity. And yet in this alternative epitaph, specially designed for public consumption and celebration, Mao had to repeatedly appeal to the authorities of these secondhand memories to reconstruct this alternative life-history of his own concubine. In the process, Mao Qiling's own personal memory became largely devoid of personal meaning, as her image was meaningful only when appreciated in the context of all the poetic responses from the peers of the bereaved husband. By authoring this special epitaph of his concubine, which constantly quotes as "comments" and "annotations" the endorsing poems by his literati peers and friends, Mao Qiling highlights the social and public nature of such a supposedly personal *daowang* undertaking; it had become a communal project celebrating literati culture and validating the elite status of each male participant, while the deceased herself was merely a character in a romantic tale of pathos.

As if this were not enough, Mao Qiling had to build up further the legend of his concubine by producing a special book to honor her. Mao mentioned in a note to this alternative epitaph that the death of Manshu prompted many at the capital to write numerous poems in addition to the long drum-song and play based on her tragic life. He promised that all these writings would be assembled into a book.[40] However, what remains today is a somewhat different volume, actually an album, that does not contain the long drum-song and play. Instead, it is an album made of a portrait of Manshu and many poetic colophons written by the famous and important (a biographical note of each contributor is duly provided to accompany the contributor's colophon lest the reader fail to appreciate the contributor's important status), as well as Mao's own elegiac writings in his own handwriting. Before she died, Manshu had a portrait of herself painted to be enjoyed forever by posterity. After her death, Mao began to solicit colophons for the portrait from many well-known poets and officials. He later assembled these colophons and his own writings on Manshu into an album.[41] The album is not composed only of his own writings but also contains a collection of calligraphic works that various people dedicated to the portrait of the deceased. The album is now a visual display and a spectacle of shared grief, intended to be read and gazed upon by its readers and viewers. Mao Qiling's memories of his deceased concubine and his grief were circulated in many different forms: literati poetic exchanges, *xiaoshuo*-like memorial writings, popular drum-songs, drama, painting, and calligraphic works. It was indeed a unique multimedia project of public mourning in seventeenth-century China.

Soliciting colophons for a painting or portrait from famous literati and scholar-officials was a networking practice quite popular among the educated elites of the time.[42] Another celebrated case is that of poet Chen Weisong a few years earlier. Chen had an affair with a female impersonator Xu Ziyun and had a portrait painted for him. Then he began to solicit colophons for the portrait. It was said that about eighty people contributed poems to Chen's project and, not surprisingly, Mao Qiling himself was one of them.[43] It then should not come as a surprise at all that Chen Weisong also contributed poems in honor of Mao Qiling's concubine, as Mao several times quoted in the "alternative epitaph." What is particularly intriguing, however, is that Mao Qiling's concubine originally did not have a formal name, and it was actually Chen Weisong who gave her the name "Manshu," while this name also happened to be the sobriquet of Xu Ziyun, Chen's then-already-deceased male lover. It was very likely that Chen Weisong named Mao's concubine with his own deceased male lover in mind, perhaps as a subtle way to mourn him as well, wittingly or unwittingly, highlighting the role as an "object" of the literati's literary exchanges assumed by both Xu Ziyun, a male servant/lover, and Zhang Manshu, a concubine.[44] This is probably why so many grieving husbands felt that writing individual pieces of *daowang* works such as a poem or a memorial essay was no longer enough. Now they needed to have a large project such as a book or an album dedicated to the deceased in order to stand out as a great *daowang* author and a mourning husband of great cultural sophistication. At the same time, to be part of such project by contributing colophons or poems was also a badge of honor for other participants.

THE DISPLACEMENT OF THE MOURNED

More than one hundred years later, a literatus of less stature, Chen Peizhi, came up with a book titled *Xiangyan xiaolu* 湘煙小錄 (*A Small Collection of Writings on the Deceased Lady Xiang*), which was composed of various elegiac writings by himself and others dedicated to the memory of his deceased concubine, Wang Zixiang 王紫湘. As many as fifty people later wrote endorsing poems for this book.

The central piece in the book is Chen's lengthy memoir *Fragrant Garden*, which is an unabashed imitation of Mao Xiang's *Plum Shadow*, as its title explicitly acknowledges (it also contains the word *yiyu*: remembrances). The influence of Mao Xiang is omnipresent in this work and happily acknowledged by the author. Chen wrote *Fragrant Garden* to mourn his concubine Wang Zixiang, who, like Dong Xiaowan, was once a courtesan.

In fact, even before Wang became Chen Peizhi's concubine, the latter had already reminded his friends of the famous Mao Xiang the moment the couple met each other. One of his friends compared their love at first sight to the first meeting between Mao Xiang and Dong Xiaowan almost a century earlier.[45] Elsewhere in the memoir, we are told that when other courtesans learned of Wang Zixiang's impending union with Chen Peizhi, they were so happy for her that they were all in tears, just like what happened in the story of Dong Xiaowan [為之喜極淚下, 如董青蓮故事].[46] An avid reader of Mao Xiang's *Plum Shadow* herself, Wang Zixiang shared Dong Xiaowan's love of moonlight.[47] Obviously, Wang was also consciously trying to emulate Dong Xiaowan as much as she could.

One of Dong Xiaowan's virtuous deeds mentioned by Mao Xiang in his memoir was her devotion to caring for him when he was struck by serious illness three times over a span of five years. In Chen Peizhi's memoir, Wang Zixiang was said to have assumed an even heavier load of caring for the sick, including her husband's grandfather, mother, and principal wife, Wang Duan. She probably worked herself into poor health and eventually died young by undertaking so much care for the sick. Compared with the marriage between Mao Xiang and Dong Xiaowan, theirs was even shorter, lasting only four years when Wang died at the age of twenty-two; like Dong Xiaowan, Wang Zixiang was also good at writing poems, which Chen repeatedly quoted in his memoir. In short, Chen Peizhi's marriage to Wang was largely meaningful to themselves, and many others, only when understood as a re-enactment of the marriage between the talented and beautiful pair celebrated in *Plum Shadow*. In this case, life indeed imitated art.

The early death of Wang Zixiang provided her husband with a long-awaited opportunity to produce an elegiac memoir to rival that by Mao Xiang, as one of Chen Peizhi's friends suggested to him that he should follow the example of Mao Xiang by producing another unforgettable elegiac memoir.[48] Apparently, the perceived similarities between himself and Mao Xiang were simply too tempting for Chen Peizhi not to produce another work in the style of *yiyu ti*, since his relationship with Wang Zixiang was largely inspired by the sad romance immortalized in *Plum Shadow*, as well as the late Ming courtesan culture associated with it.

A major difference, however, is that the courtesan past of Dong Xiaowan was presented in *Plum Shadow* as what the now exemplary concubine tried to forget and distance herself from, whereas in *Fragrant Garden* the courtesan past of Wang Zixiang was in fact celebrated as an integral part of becoming an exemplary concubine. With great pride, Chen told us how he and his concubine continued to maintain close relationships with other courtesans and how his concubine even encouraged him to continue to spread his love among her former "sisters" in the pleasure quarters. Chen actually took it upon himself to be the protector of all the talented courtesans.[49]

Unlike Mao Xiang, Chen Peizhi never had to worry about his concubine being rejected by his parents. It was actually his parents and his first wife who urged him to take a concubine, despite reluctance on his part. Chen Peizhi's father was none other than Chen Wenshu, the great promoter of female talent, famous for his active role in promoting women poetry as well as in serving as a teacher/mentor for many female students. Chen Wenshu's own wife (Chen Peizhi's birth mother), several of his concubines, and his daughters were all *cainü* 才女 (women of literary talents), with the most famous being his daughter-in-law, Chen Peizhi's wife, Wang Duan. It was said that Wang Duan encouraged Chen Peizhi to take a concubine because her literary and scholarly devotions, which were fully supported by her father-in-law and her husband, had prevented her from fulfilling various wifely duties. Being no exception, Wang Zixiang was also a *cainü*. As Chen Peizi recalled, she fell in love with him, her future husband, being willing to become his concubine, paradoxically, after reading his moving poems about why he had refused to take a concubine. This reminds us of the case of Qu Dajun's third wife, who began to admire her future husband after reading his elegies on his second wife. Both fell in love with their respective husbands after being impressed with their poetic talents, a common theme in popular literature at the time. As I have mentioned in discussion of Ye Shaoyuan in chapter 2, talent (*cai*) became an important component of womanhood celebrated in late Ming culture. Now in *Fragrant Garden*, nostalgic for the late Ming celebration of female talents and the golden days of courtesan culture, Chen Peizhi deliberately chose to present himself as a great connoisseur of female poetic talents associated with pleasure quarters.

A connoisseur of female literary talents, Chen Peizhi was even more thrilled at every opportunity to showcase his own poetic talent, especially his knack for elegiac writings afforded by the early but untimely (or timely) death of Wang Zixiang. Mourning his deceased concubine also became an occasion to recall and celebrate how his poems were admired by everyone, including the deceased. A significant part of the memoir consists of poems he wrote in the past on various romantic occasions. The celebration of literary talent is also a celebration of the power of writing, which endowed him with the ability to immortalize, while Wang Zixiang, as a woman and a concubine, should feel extremely lucky to be the subject of such writings and thus have her place secured in history. Indeed, besides Chen Peizhi's lengthy memoir in her honor, his parents, his principal wife, and other family members were all eager to produce writings to honor her. In their rush to mourn her and showcase their elegiac skills, Chen Peizhi's family members also did something quite unprecedented: his father wrote a eulogy, and his mother wrote a fairly long biography for their son's concubine, as carefully noted by one of Chen's friends.[50] It was also the mother who urged her son to reward his deceased concubine by immortalizing her in his *daowang* writing (*baoyi bimo* 報以筆墨) so that she could be remembered as other famous concubines in history, such as Zhaoyun, who was immortalized in the writings of her husband, the famous Song poet Su Shi 蘇軾 (1037–1101).[51] As I have pointed out, compared with other elegiac essays, such as an epitaph, a biography for a woman usually needed more justification, although women's biographies were becoming much more common by the early nineteenth century. However, it is nevertheless quite remarkable for a mother to write one for her son's concubine, who also happened to be a former courtesan. By the same token, it was equally rare for a father to compose a eulogy for his son's concubine, as Chen Wenshu did.

Like Qu Dajun and Mao Qiling, Chen Peizhi assembled these elegiac writings into a special book, *Xiangyan xiaolu*.[52] In several of its reprint editions, many colophons and other endorsing writings on its original edition are included. In these writings, much of the focus has been shifted from the mourned, the concubine, to the mourner, the husband Chen Peizhi. The celebration now concentrates on the literary talents of the mourner and compiler of the volume.

For Chen Peizhi and many others, the mourning ritual in the form of elegiac writings itself became more important than the subject of these writings—the mourned. Often the mourner usurped the place of the "protagonist" in the process and became the focus of his own mourning discourse. By allowing the mourning ritual itself to assume more importance than the mourned, remembrance became an act without an "object"—the act of remembering became more important than the one being remembered. That is, who remembers is more important than who is being remembered. Thus, mourning/remembering becomes intransitive, as mourners in the mourning ritual replace the mourned as the focus of the ritual. A mourner is now being celebrated at the expense of the mourned. Insisting that Chen Peizhi's own poems were much better than any of the endorsing poems he himself could come up with after reading his elegiac memoir in honor of his deceased concubine, one of his friends, Ge Zai, sent the grieving husband a set of sixteen *jiju* poems, all of which were composed exclusively of the poetic lines taken from many of Chen's own previous poems.[53] This friend did something quite unprecedented in the history of *jiju* composition of *daowang* poetry: unlike many practitioners of *jiju* mourning poetry before, such as the early Qing poet, Wang Xuling 王頊齡 (1642–1721), who, to mourn his deceased wife, complied fifty poems made exclusively of the lines taken from those famous *daowang* poems by the poets from the Tang dynasty,[54] Ge Zai added a twist to this particular subgenre of *daowang* poetry: he deliberately selected poetic lines from the grieving husband's own previous poems, many of which were not concerned with the *daowang* topic at all, and ingeniously reorganized them into "new" *daowang* poems to console their original author for the loss of his own concubine, as if Chen somehow had already unwittingly started to mourn his concubine long before she actually died. That is, the act of mourning had begun to unfold even before Wang Zixiang became the mourned. Here, what mattered most was the mourner and his act of mourning rather than the mourned! This friend's poetic ingenuity lies in his ability to "compile" these sixteen condolence poems on behalf of his friend by refusing to use the poetic lines other than those written by the very bereaved husband he was trying to console. Mourning the death of a concubine became an occasion for a delicate game of virtuosity between these two literati friends. The sixteen *jiju* poems were meant to be the ultimate tribute to the poetic talents of both the mourning husband Chen Peizhi and this friend himself, whereas the mourned, the supposed subject of their mourning discourse, Wang Zixiang, became no longer significant, almost irrelevant. The mourned was literally displaced through the process of mourning on behalf of someone else.

Reading through the book *Xiangyan xiaolu* and the poetic outpouring in reaction to it, one gets the impression that the development of Chinese *daowang* literature had reached a new milestone by the early nineteenth century. Death, especially the death of a spouse (or often a concubine), became almost something to be celebrated because a literati husband cherished so much this rare opportunity to showcase his elegiac talents, as well as those of his peers, and thus enhance his standing in homosocial solidarity.[55] Thus, the male mourner was now much better remembered than the mourned female.

Deceased concubines assumed a special function in this virtuoso exercise of self-promotion on the part of these male elegiac writers. A concubine, thanks to her lower and ambiguous status, proved to be a more convenient subject for this kind of communal literati *daowang* discourse, as her image could be more freely manipulated without much concern for Confucian decorum, unlike in the case of a deceased formal wife. Here the aforementioned act of naming of Mao Qiling's concubine on the part of Chen Weisong alerts us to an interesting fact—this kind of communal mourning project with the participation of many in the form of poetic colophons dedicated to a portrait of the deceased became more popular among the literati partly because the mourned was a concubine, whose status, in many ways, resembled that of Chen's male lover, a servant boy, thus someone more easily objectified. While Qu Dajun, You Tong, and many others also solicited *daowang* poems from their friends for their deceased wives, publically requesting colophons for the portrait of one's own deceased wife might be considered by some to be an act not so discreet. The case of a concubine was different: a concubine could perform the usual role of a wife under certain circumstances and yet, at the same time, she could also be a maid or even an entertainer, who was otherwise accessible in the public sphere outside the family compound, as in the case of Dong Xiaowan and Wang Zixiang, two former courtesans.

This also helps explain why in premodern China a man's own deceased parents seldom became the subjects of his *daowang* writings, except in more functional or practical writings, such as epitaphs and biographical sketches (epitaphs for burial and biographical sketch for epitaph writers), and why instead his spouses became the main subject in his *daowang* poems. However, compared with a deceased wife, a late concubine tended to occupy a more prominent place in the social circulation of grief among the literati. In the hierarchy of a family, a concubine occupied a position much lower than that of the principal wife. On the other hand, a concubine could still be considered a man's spouse to qualify as the subject in traditional *daowang* discourse normally reserved for a wife. At the same time, precisely because of her lower status, a concubine could more easily become an object in this circulating process of grief, which tended to pay attention to her sexual appeal and other not-so-wifely qualities (such as Dong Xiaowan's aesthetic tastes) without much scandal among the more conservative. Strangely enough, it seems that, like the case of a female chastity martyr (as in Qian Chengzhi's hagiographic project on his late wife), a concubine, especially when she was also a former courtesan, was more likely to become a figure celebrated in more public elegiac discourses, here not so much in the form of a Confucian hagiography as in a romantic tale (*chuanqi* 傳奇). In both cases, intimate memory became devoid of much of its personal meaning, as what was now at stake was the public implications of the life of the deceased and, especially in the case of a deceased concubine, the narcissistic elegiac gesticulations of the male mourner.

In the gradual shift of focus from the mourned to the mourner in the development of *daowang* writings in late imperial China, the concubine and her death appear to have performed a unique function. As a female figure to be mourned, she proved to be a favorite metaphor in her mourning husband's project of self-celebration—her "life" as constructed and construed by her male mourner was presented largely as an illustration of his own virtues as a husband, and, more importantly, as a man of literary brilliance, as unabashedly boasted by Li Yu, Mao Qiling, and many others. Her death was an excuse for the male mourner's self-promotion and self-invention.

CHAPTER 8

REMEMBERING SISTERS

Thus far we have focused on mourning men writing about their deceased spouses. A look now at how such men mourned their married sisters allows us a basis for comparison. How did male mourners' epitaphs, biographies, and other writings change when the subject was not a deceased wife but a deceased sister? Did brothers tend to mourn their sisters differently from how they mourned their wives? If so, what change in perspective caused this difference?

When writing about the life of his sister, a man found himself in a position in which he would be more likely to look at things from the perspective of a woman, as he became more inclined to identify himself with his sister in examining her relationships with her husband and affinal kin.[1] In mourning and remembering a married sister, the issue of what qualities constituted a good wife could invite a different kind of scrutiny. By the same token, the likelihood that a mourning brother would scrutinize more closely the duties of his brother-in-law as a husband was also significantly increased, in part because of his close relationship with the latter's wife.

CONFLICTING IDENTITIES AND OBLIGATIONS

A sister was a close family member, but she later became, by virtue of marriage, a member of another family, and yet her relationship with her natal family was often not completely discontinued. It was this ambiguity associated with a married sister—she had been but at the same time she was no longer a member of his family—that made her relationship with her brother particularly intriguing, allowing us to examine the complexities of a late imperial man's conceptualization of womanhood in a slightly different context.

Wang Shizhen, one of the best-known literary figures of the second half of the sixteenth century, wrote an epitaph and a sacrificial litany in honor of his deceased sister, drawing our attention to a married woman's possible dilemma of her divided loyalty to her natal family and that of her husband. According to Wang Shizhen's epitaph, his sister was a precocious child deeply loved by her parents. Raised in a nurturing family environment of high cultural sophistication, she could already read quite well when she was very young. She was also very good at doing needlework. Not long after she married, she moved north to live with her parents, where her father was serving as an official, because her mother missed her so much and because her husband happened to be studying at the imperial university. During the many crises in her father's tumultuous public career, she became literally indispensable to her mother. Their father said that she was almost a son to him while his two sons were often far away. However, his sister felt torn between her obligations toward her parents-in-law and those to her own parents: "I had married into the Zhang family but now I returned to be a daughter again. Who should take care of my parents-in-law now?"[2]

Her health began to decline rapidly after Wang's father was thrown into prison due to his loss of the battle at Luanhe to the enemy as the commander of the imperial army in 1559. She eventually died of a broken heart at the age of thirty-one, not long after their father was executed under the order of the emperor for failing in his official duties. Before she died, her husband swore to her that he would never remarry after her death. Wang Shizhen quoted his sister as having replied: "You care so much about me. Don't you care about the need to continue the Zhang family line?"[3] This was presented as a strong testament to her wifely virtue and her unselfish understanding of the importance of a male heir to the family of her husband.

While in his epitaph for his sister Wang Shizhen tried to present a more balanced image of his sister as a dutiful daughter-in-law as well as a virtuous wife from the perspective of her husband's family and as a filial daughter to her own parents from the perspective of a brother, he showed no such concern for balance in his sacrificial litany in honor of his sister, as he explicitly acknowledged there. In his epitaph, he had much less to say about his sister's filial devotion toward her original family, the Wang family.[4] This was because, when writing the epitaph, he was constrained by the fact that the epitaph would become part of her tomb at the gravesite of the Zhang family, since, strictly speaking, as the wife of Zhang Yuling, she was a member of the Zhang family and was supposed to be buried as such. Consequently, in the epitaph, she had to be presented first of all as an exemplary daughter-in-law of the Zhang family, even though Wang still managed to say quite a lot about how filial she was as a daughter of the Wang family. Now, the litany was a personal "communication" between his then-already-deceased sister and himself. Here the author felt he was no longer bound by the constraints associated with an epitaph on a married sister. The litany was solely about his sister's role as a member of the Wang family and what she continued to mean to her parents even after she had married into another family. The litany detailed how she devoted herself to the care of her parents while living with them for a long period of time after she got married. She insisted on tying her fate with that of her natal family as a daughter. In the eyes of Wang Shizhen, his sister died for their father, and she was celebrated first of all as an exemplary daughter:

> How Sad! You died but your brothers survived. You died to follow our father into the underground. Do ghosts know that? We two brothers are two men of great guilt under heaven, clinging to our lives. You died and you are now dead, whereas I am dead too even though I am [physically] still alive. How can I be compared with you![5]

Overall, the focus of Wang Shizhen's memory was his sister's female exemplariness despite the conflicting obligations she had to assume as a daughter and a daughter-in-law.

THE REMARKABLE EPITAPH OF AN UNREMARKABLE SISTER

In fact, a bereaved brother might feel less pressured to use the perceived exemplariness of his deceased sister to justify his fond remembrance of her due in part to the fact there was less a presence of discursive Confucian convention to constrain him. Unlike the all-important brother–brother relationship,[6] not so much had been said in Confucian prescriptive writings about the brother–sister relationship. After all, a sister was someone who would eventually become a member of another family, as far as the brother was concerned. Probably more importantly, a grieving brother was far less vulnerable to the possible criticism of being "overindulgent" or "selfish" (*si*) in mourning his sister as a grieving husband would be in mourning his wife due to the strong Confucian suspicion of the role of a wife in a patriline family, as discussed earlier. Thus, the image of a sister reconstructed through her brother's memory was even more likely to be that of a woman not necessarily known for her exemplariness.

Qian Chengzhi's epitaph of his deceased elder sister is particularly compelling precisely because of the utter unremarkableness of its female subject.

The epitaph was relatively long, underscoring how much Qian as a brother felt he had to say about his rather unremarkable sister, who did not seem to have many worthy Confucian virtues to boast of. Qian mourned her simply because she was an elder sister he had been very close to.

This epitaph is quite unusual in that it reads more like the author's personal memoir of his sister, where his unique perspectives and feelings are constantly underscored. Qian Chengzhi's father had six children, among whom his elder sister was the only daughter, a possible reason why the mother doted on her so much. When she married, their mother almost exhausted their family fortunes to prepare for her dowry. With her new home only twenty *li* away, whenever she needed something, the mother would have the servants deliver it immediately. This became almost a routine. Unfortunately, her husband, though enjoying a reputation as an intelligent child when he was very young, failed to pass the provincial examinations after as many as ten attempts. He died a frustrated examinee at the age of forty-seven. The family's fortunes went downhill rapidly, as bandits began to ravage the area when the country was thrown into chaos during the violent dynastic changeover, and their residence was eventually burned down. They had to live away from their hometown. The situation became even more difficult for his sister with the death of their mother; getting help from her natal family was not that easy anymore.

According to Qian, when their mother was still alive, if his sister disliked any of her own maids, their mother would simply choose a good one among those of her own and have that maid sent over to serve her. As a result, the number of maids serving his sister was several times larger than that of those serving all the brothers. After their mother died, within a few years, all the maids of his sister were gone: they either died or ran away, as Qian informed us that his sister was a mistress "lacking generosity" (*shao'en* 少恩), implying she might have treated them harshly.[7] Due to her relatively easy life when her doting mother was still alive, she appeared for quite some time to be ill equipped to deal with hardships later in her life after her natal family could no longer help her as before:

> When my sister became old, she suffered a lot of hardships and had to do all the chores herself. She once said to me in tears: "Good Heaven! How did I become like this!" And she sighed: "I did not know this before: from clothing to food and even very tiny things, you need money to buy everything."[8]

Here we are presented with a picture that is hardly flattering: his sister was a woman originally from a relatively rich family, who, even after she got married, for a long period had been somewhat spoiled by her mother. She had hardly any sense of money until late in her life when she was confronted with economic hardships and was forced to do all the family chores herself, especially with all her maids gone (perhaps partly due to her mistreatment of them).

This image of his sister becomes even more interesting when Qian Chengzhi goes out of his way to emphasize, elsewhere, in his biographical sketch of their mother, how strict their mother was in raising her children and how efficiently she managed the household.[9] Although Qian Chengzhi's main intention of mentioning his mother's doting on his sister here in this epitaph was to show how precious her sister was to the former, the reference to doting complicated the mother's image considerably, as in fact such doting contributed to the sister's later misery when it took her so long to learn how to manage a household. One thing she never learned was how to supervise her servants and maids, which her mother was apparently very good at. Writing about his mother, Qian Chengzhi told us in detail how effectively she supervised all the servants and the maids, even though she was actually quite kind to them,[10] a sharp contrast to the clumsiness on the part of his sister, who might have mistreated her maids. Obviously, Qian Chengzhi was far more candid in presenting his sister, whereas, in writing about his mother, in contrast, presumably out of his filial reverence, he was celebrating her as an exemplary mother. Reading these two biographical essays side by side should help draw our attention to the different strategies a literati author often adopted when he remembered and wrote about his different female relatives, compelling us to appreciate even more Qian's candor in writing about his sister.

His sister's misery was compounded by the fact that her own daughters-in-law were not nice to her, or, in the words of Qian Chengzhi: "Her daughters-in-law did not serve my sister as well as the latter served her mother-in-law."[11] Qian's elder brother, You'an, heard about this and tried to intervene. However, his sister stopped him before he could reach their house, telling him that recently her daughters-in-laws had changed their behaviors for the better. As a result, You'an returned without uttering a word to her daughters-in-law. Qian Chengzhi attributed part of the reason for the bad behavior of her daughters-in-law to his own sister's practices of appeasement.

Qian was by no means trying to speak ill of his sister. He was just describing her as an ordinary woman who was far from perfect. In fact, for the most part, Qian presented her in very loving terms, betraying his deep attachment to his sister:

> My sister was twelve years my senior. When I was little, I was sick all the time. She often carried me in her arms while I was crying and she seldom put me

down. I do not remember that well the time when she got married [since I was too young]. I could only recall the day when she returned to visit us for the first time after the wedding: All dressed up and with the tingling sound of her bracelets, she got off from the cart and entered through the door. Looking at her, my mother was so happy that she was in tears.[12]

In Qian's vague memory, his much older sister was almost like a mother figure to him, although she moved away after her marriage before he was old enough to remember her that well (he was only four when she got married at the age of sixteen).

After the death of her husband and the quick decline of the family fortunes, his sister also aged quickly: "Although she was barely over fifty and her hair had not turned grey completely, she looked so old and worn-out that she was simply a copy of our mother in her old age, only much more haggard."[13] Qian attributed his sister's eventual death to her shock and sadness over the untimely death of his own son. That is, she died while still closely associated with her natal family:

> The year before she died, I told my sister: "Our mother and our brothers all died before they reached seventy. On your seventieth birthday next year, I would like to invite you over and celebrate your birthday with a party with all the members of the younger generations." My sister agreed. However, who would expect that my son would be killed by the bandits the winter of that year? The sad news shocked her and worsened her illness and she died. She did not live to the age of seventy after all.[14]

There are not too many explicit expressions of love on the part of the author, and yet in his carefully restrained narrative the reader could feel a deep sense of attachment on the part of this younger brother.

Even when Qian Chengzhi was trying to compliment his sister, he seldom sang direct praise of her virtues; instead he would allow "facts" to speak for themselves. Qian told us that his sister had a daughter who was a hunchback. Almost everyone in the family wished that she would die as soon as possible. However, his sister loved her deeply. Later her daughter died. For several years, she cried over her death, asking "Why has Heaven been so cruel in depriving me of my daughter?"[15] This is certainly a portrait of a very loving mother.

Although his sister herself was not well educated, she cherished the value of education and always encouraged others to study hard:

The time when my sister was growing up was a peaceful period undisturbed by chaos. For generations, men in our family had been scholars. At home she would consider a man almost an alien if he was not dressed in scholar gown. Ever since the upheavals [the fall of the Ming dynasty], many of us had to change our careers. My sister would still judge things by the old standards: she was always upset that her sons could not fulfill their father's wishes. Once pointing to me, she told her sons: "In the past, I saw your uncle studying. When it was becoming dark, my mother would give them lamp oil after measuring it. When the lamp oil was burned out at mid-night, children knocked at the door of the room of our mother for reward. She would give reward to the ones who had studied hard. In addition, she would treat them to porridge. However, those who had been sitting there playing got nothing for reward. Now I am old but yet I still weave during the night. It has been quite a while since I heard people reading aloud in the family."

Then she recalled how I could not count money when I was young. I had a problem counting money as late as when I was ten. What I did was always reading and people considered me stupid. [She would wonder] why people nowadays were so obsessed with calculating and counting [money].[16]

Here Qian Chengzhi was remembering how his sister recalled his childhood, an indirect way of showing the reader how very early on he himself was destined to become a Confucian scholar. On the other hand, such admiration for Confucian learning on the part of his sister certainly testified to her good understanding of the importance of learning, an indication that this was in the genes of Qian's family and a reconfirmation of his sister as a member of the same Qian family, even though she married into the family of another man a long time earlier.

This is indeed a very personal memoir rather than a typical scripted epitaph, where the deceased woman was supposed to be eulogized in abstract terms of her Confucian exemplariness. Qian Chengzhi never showed any concern that he needed to apologize for writing such a lengthy epitaph for such an unremarkable woman. He wrote it simply because she was a sister whom he loved; as he said in the concluding verse, he authored this epitaph so that "A woman sharing the same birth mother/the future generations would know her."[17] Although Qian Chengzhi never explicitly blamed his brother-in-law or his family for the miseries of his sister, the reader could still feel that her husband's career failures contributed to her suffering. Compared with his biographical sketch of his own late wife, Qian's epitaph of his late sister, interestingly enough, reads much more personal, even more intimate, a possible result of the deliberate distance Qian tried to keep from his late wife as a biographical subject as he was trying to convince his readers that he was writing as an objective historian about the life of a remarkable chastity martyr rather than his own wife, while here he was writing a personal memoir about his late sister, an ordinary woman characterized by her seemingly unremarkable life.[18] His memoir of his sister was so compelling precisely because of her ordinariness and the unique freedom with which he wrote about her simply as his sister. He wrote this epitaph of his sister as a private memoirist rather than a public historian of female chastity, a stance he deliberately took when he wrote about his own wife, as we saw in chapter 3.

UNHAPPY MARRIAGES

In the remainder of this chapter I look at several cases in which mourning brothers explicitly argue that the miseries their deceased sisters experienced in their lives were directly caused by the families they were married into and by the incompetent, or sometimes irresponsible, behaviors of their husbands. It is interesting to see how their unique perspectives as brothers shaped their sad memories of their sisters as members of another man's family.

In his epitaph of his elder sister, "Wangzi Sun ruren muzhiming" 亡姊孫孺人墓誌銘 (The Epitaph of My Deceased Sister, Lady Sun), the Ming scholar-official Sun Cheng'en, whose elegiac writings on his spouses we have examined in chapter 6, was quite blunt in blaming his brother-in-law for all the miseries his sister suffered in their family. Unlike the wording of the titles of the epitaphs of their sisters authored by Wang Shizhen and Qian Chengzhi, to show that he was identifying his sister as a member of the Sun family rather than her husband's family, in the title of the epitaph, Sun simply omitted the name of her husband and referred to his sister as "Sun ruren." This was quite unusual given the fact that epitaphic convention dictated that in the title of the epitaph of a married woman she should be identified as the wife of a particular man. Obviously, this brother was deliberately trying to demonstrate his contempt for her husband, who, as he would show in the epitaph, had caused his sister so much misery.

According to Sun Cheng'en, her sister's husband, as the youngest son in the family, had been spoiled by his father ever since he was a young child. He grew up a good-for-nothing. He became much worse when no one could restrain him after the death of his father. Sun's sister had to weave and do needlework to help pay for the household expenditure in order to survive, while her husband continued to party and squander away money, completely neglecting his responsibilities as a man. According to Sun, his sister and her family eventually even had to worry about daily survival. The family almost had nothing left when his sister became a widow at the age of thirty-nine. However, through hard work, his sister was able to raise her son, give him an education, and arrange his marriage. Gradually, the mother and the young couple were able to build a more stable life when the son took on the job of a tutor after becoming a *xiucai* degree holder. Just when things were improving, her son suddenly died of illness, and ten years later the sister herself passed away.

Before she died, Sun Cheng'en asked her sister where she would prefer to be buried. She told him she wanted to be buried with her son. Earlier, when her husband died, they were so poor they could not afford a piece of land as his burial place. They had to make do by burying him in the gravesite of their distant ancestors. Later, when the son died, they could afford a piece of land for his burial near their home. Considering that the husband's gravesite was quite distant and in poor condition, Sun decided to follow his sister's wishes to bury her near her son's grave and moved her husband's grave to the same place so that the husband and the wife could be buried together. This, however, seems to have reversed the hierarchical order of husband and wife, symbolically suggesting that now the husband had to follow his wife after their deaths.

If this move of the grave of his brother-in-law was only a ritually symbolic censure of the husband for his failure to fulfill his duty as a man while alive, Sun was much more literal and explicit in his indictment of his unworthiness as a husband at the conclusion of his epitaph:

> Someone might say that extolling the virtues of one's own sister while exposing the misdeeds of her husband (*suotian* 所天) [in this epitaph] may not be in full accordance with ritual propriety. However, Mr. Tang failed miserably in his role as a husband (*butian shenyi* 不天甚矣) by behaving so irresponsibly and caused my sister so much misery. Out of sympathy for my sister, I have to record the facts without any concern for niceties. The principle behind Confucius's *Spring and Autumn Annals* dictates there are situations where concealment is appropriate and there are situations where concealment is not proper. I have nothing to conceal for Mr. Tang. If this is the case, then why should I conceal?

Furthermore, the conventional verse that usually concludes an epitaph here is employed to further defend the author's unusually frank indictment of his deceased brother-in-law:

The intent to follow the son,
And the principle of having to be buried together with the husband:
With the moving of Mr. Tang's grave,
Fulfilled was the intent and followed was the principle.
To ruin Mr. Tang's reputation is not my intent,
Even though I cannot say that I do not blame him.
On the left there is the ravine,
On the right, there is the stream.
A thousand years later people should know
This is the grave of Yizhai's sister,
And it they should not damage.[19]

While continuing to defend his unusual decision to move Mr. Tang's grave so that he could be buried together with his sister, Sun insisted that the deceased should be remembered as Yizhai's sister (i.e., *his* sister) rather than as the wife of Mr. Tang, even though in a joint grave, it was usually the husband who was supposed to be the main occupier while his wife occupied the subordinate position. This may explain why at the beginning of the epitaph little information is offered about her husband's family except that her husband was a fellow villager. Obviously, Sun felt his brother-in-law was not worthy of his sister and that in posterity she should be associated with her natal family rather than her husband's family. Sun's sense of injustice done to his sister was apparently exasperated by the fact that even as a powerful high governmental official he felt powerless to help his sister because, strictly speaking, as a married woman his sister was now a member of another family. The death of his sister and the chance to write an epitaph for her became almost an awaited opportunity for Sun to vent his frustrations as a helpless brother over the injustice done to his sister. Mourning and writing about his sister became an act of vindication—to vindicate his sister as a member of her natal family.

It was relatively rare for the author of a commissioned epitaph on a woman to so openly and vehemently denounce her husband. Here the fact that the author of the epitaph was her own brother was certainly an important factor; he was trying to seek justice for his sister, whom he defended as if she were still a member of his own family, while the target of his criticism, her husband, was a man from another family. Sun was even willing to risk being criticized for "airing the family's dirty laundry" (*jiachou waiyang* 家醜外揚) because, for him at least, the dirty laundry was that of another family.

More than a century later, the famous early Qing poet Qian Qianyi wrote an epitaph for his sister, which, though much more restrained, also criticized her husband for causing her misery. Qian's grandfather and father had close relationships with the Yan family, which is why his father arranged the marriage between his sister and her future husband, Yan Zhiruo. However, by the time they were married, the Yan family was already in decline. Yan Zhiruo failed repeatedly in his examination attempts but was obsessed with book collecting. While he spent a lot of money buying and collecting books, he was extremely stingy when it came to daily household expenditures. When the kids cried because there was so little to eat, he just covered his ears. His sister toiled day and night trying to run the household. She once bitterly complained: "I have worked enough as a hard laborer for the Yan family. When will be the year when I can finish returning all my debt [i.e., when she no longer must labor for the Yan family as if she owed them a lot]?"[20]

In his rush to show how miserable his sister had been, Qian Qianyi even directly quoted his sister's bitter complaint about her unfortunate fate of marrying an utterly incompetent husband, which might compromise her image as a virtuous wife in the eyes of the more conservative, as they would expect her to endure hardship with grace.

Qian Qianyi titled his epitaph, "The Epitaph for the Joint Tomb of My Deceased Younger Sister Lady Yan." Traditionally, for a husband–wife joint tomb, in the title of the epitaph the husband was always mentioned first, followed by his wife. In the eyes of the conservative, even this practice was considered a violation of the ancient ritual codes, since, according to them, the wife should not be mentioned in the title at all, even in the case of a joint tomb.[21] To make it worse, here in the title of this epitaph for a joint tomb, Qian Qinayi not only prominently mentioned his own sister but completely dropped the name of her husband—just the opposite of what the conservative would insist on. Of course, the content of this joint tomb epitaph focuses on his sister, the wife, while her husband is mentioned only as someone causing her misery. Once again, mourning and epitaph writing became an attempt on the part of a brother to seek vindication on behalf of his deceased sister, who had the misfortune of being trapped in an unhappy marriage. Here the wife was presented as someone who had at least the right to complain loudly if her husband failed to fulfill his duty.

THE BONDING OF NATAL FAMILY

If the cases of Sun Cheng'en and Qian Qinayi show how frustrated and helpless a brother could feel over his sister's unhappy marriage, a man's memorial writings on his sister could sometimes also shed light on how deeply involved a natal family could be in trying to help a daughter or a sister trapped in such an unhappy situation, testifying to the close relationship between a married woman and her natal family at that time, as we have seen in the case of Qian Chengzhi's epitaph on his sister.[22]

Fang Bao had five sisters (two of them were step-sisters by the first wife of his father). It appears they all married into families that were suffering economic hardships,[23] and none of these marriages could be considered happy, to say the least. Fang Bao, as a brother, had to help them whenever he could and, apparently, he was quite close to many of them. His elder step-sister, Qie, married the son of the Bao family, but her husband's birth mother was his father's concubine and this caused a lot of misery for this daughter-in-law. She had to behave with extra caution in front of the mother-in-law (the principal wife of her father-in-law) in order to avoid causing problems for his husband's birth mother. Her sister-in-law, whose husband was the son of the principal wife of the father-in-law, was able to take advantage of his sister's vulnerable position in the family, and often mistreated her. And yet Fang Bao's sister never said anything about her difficult situation to the members of her natal family. Fang Bao felt particularly guilty over being unable to help his sister more because she was almost a mother figure to him when he was young. About twelve years his senior, she was the person who babysat him and took care of him.[24] We are reminded here of Qian Chengzhi's special relationship with his late elder sister.

Fang Bao's biography of his youngest sister is more revealing about the hardship a woman had to endure in an unhappy marriage. This became even more significant when we recall Fang Bao's professed reluctance to write epitaphs for women when asked by their male relatives, as discussed in chapter 1. He must have felt he had something so important to say about this sister that he did not want to wait for the opportunity afforded by the need to mourn her. This biography, though not an elegiac essay or an act of mourning, is nevertheless worth a look here, as it is an interesting case in which a married woman chose to live with her natal family largely because of the poverty of her husband's family, despite the fact that her husband was still alive. According to our biographer, when his younger sister married her husband, the financial situation of the Xie family, though already in decline, was still stable. However, her husband had many bad habits typical of a spoiled son from a rich family. To make it worse, he took a dislike of Fang Bao's sister because her personality was quiet and reserved, whereas such personality was usually associated with a virtuous woman. He even abused her physically. However, the sister tried her best to prevent her parents from hearing about her difficult situation. Even when Fang Bao directly asked her about it, she, with tears in her eyes, refused to reveal anything. In a few years, her husband's family was quickly reduced to sheer poverty, and they had to rely heavily on the financial help from Fang Bao's family. Once when her husband was seriously ill, Fang Bao went over to visit his younger sister and found her in total despair. Fearing that she had no one to rely on there, the sister moved back to live with her natal family. Then Fang Bao began to describe how, staying in her natal family, the sister began to take on the job of caring for their mother until the latter died. She used the money she had saved from selling what was left to her by their mother to buy a concubine for her husband, and the latter soon gave birth to a son, whom the sister treated as her own. At that time, Fang Bao often had to make sure that they would offer help to the Xie family on a regular basis while the sister continued to stay in her natal family. However, according to Fang Bao, feeling guilty over not sharing times of hardship with the family of her husband, his sister was still worried about the well-being of the Xie family and would visit them several times a year, bringing them money and clothing.[25]

Obviously, Fang Bao was trying to present his younger sister as an exemplary wife as well as an exemplary daughter despite the predicament she found herself in, as he concluded the biography by explaining that he decided to write this biography over the possible objection of his younger sister herself because he wanted people to have some common standards when they try to understand what constituted a virtuous woman. His younger sister's most admirable virtue as a wife, he seems to suggest, was her lack of jealousy and her ready embrace of her husband's polygamous privilege: since she had no son of her own, she took the initiative to use her own money to buy a concubine for her husband despite his abusiveness in the past and then later cared for the concubine's son as if he were her own; even though she now lived with her natal family, she was concerned enough about the well-being of her husband's family to visit them quite frequently. After moving back to her natal family, she performed her filial duty impeccably, becoming indispensable to her mother when the latter became old and sick.

However, an important question that remains is how a woman could be extolled as a virtuous wife after she decided to move back to live with her natal family (she was separated from her husband) merely for the reasons mentioned in the biography (i.e., her husband was abusive and the family was poor). Our biographer did not explain in detail the immediate reason why she moved back to live with her natal family except saying that when her husband was dying (and he later apparently recovered), "fearing having no one to rely on, she moved back to her natal family, and was no longer able to take care of the mother-in-law." This could hardly be the most compelling justification for abandoning her dying husband and her mother-in-law (here the biographer was not particularly forthcoming about exactly when she left—was it after or before her husband had recovered?), given the traditional Confucian emphasis on the unconditional sacrifice on the part of a wife for the sake of husband or on the part of a daughter-in-law for the sake of her parents-in-law. Our biographer is in fact arguing that by coming back to live with her natal family, which was in a much better financial situation, her sister was in a better position to help the Xie family financially. As her brother, Fang Bao must have felt that his younger sister was perfectly justified in moving back to her natal family due to the dire poverty of the Xie family and the abusiveness of her husband, suggesting a more liberal, as well as more pragmatic, notion of the obligations of a wife: a woman should have the right to move back to live with her natal family if her husband was abusive and if his family was poor. When read in parallel with the hagiographies of the female chastity martyr widely promoted at that time, where a woman would commit suicide to vindicate her loyalty to her husband or even her fiancé upon the latter's death, Fang Bao's biography of his sister was certainly written with a far different set of expectations in mind; whether his sister should prepare to commit suicide to vindicate her chastity when her husband was dying is never an issue in this biography. Of course, her husband was totally incompetent, and worse, abusive. However, in a typical hagiography of a chastity martyr, whether the husband was a loving spouse was often not the primary concern of a chastity martyr when she decided to commit suicide to vindicate her faithfulness. Apparently, Fang Bao must have felt that he was writing a biography of his own sister rather than a hagiography of a chastity martyr, although he had expressed admiration for such chastity martyr figures himself, as many Confucian literati routinely did.[26] An argument could be made that writing about his own sisters from a brother's perspective, Fang Bao became a biographer much more sensitive to the sufferings of his female subjects, a unique situation in which hagiographical concerns were not foremost on his mind.

READING HAGIOGRAPHY TOO LITERALLY

This leads us to arguably the most famous sacrificial litany dedicated to the memory of a sister from the late imperial period, "Ji mei wen" 祭妹文 (A Sacrificial Litany to My Younger Sister) by the prominent eighteenth-century poet Yuan Mei, in which he tells us that his sister also moved back to live with her natal family because of the abuses of her husband. Ironically, Yuan Mei attributed the tragedy of his sister in large part to her having read too many hagiographies of chaste women, because, he was convinced, her tragic marriage was something that could have been prevented if she had not insisted so much on practicing literally what she had read in these Confucian books of female exemplariness.

To better understand this litany, we should read it side by side with Yuan Mei's biography of this same sister. While the litany, in which, as dictated by convention, the author addresses his already deceased sister directly, focuses on his close personal relationship with her, the biography provides more detailed information on her tragic life and the factors directly contributing to it. Yuan Mei devoted approximately one-third of the biography to an account of how the marriage between his sister, Suwen, and her future husband was arranged between the two families. Yuan Mei's father once worked on the personal staff of Mr. Gao Qing, a county magistrate. However, after Gao Qing suddenly died, his family members were jailed because the county's treasury was found short of a large sum of money (Gao Qing apparently used the money to curry favor with his superiors, a practice not uncommon among officials of the time). After learning of this, Yuan Mei's father traveled all the way there to help. Gao Qing's family was eventually released, thanks to Yuan Mei's father's intervening. To show his deep appreciation for the help of Yuan Mei's father, Gao Qing's brother suggested that if his pregnant wife gave birth to a son, that son would marry Yuan Mei's younger sister, who was a one-year-old at the time. A gold locket was given to Yuan Mei's father as an engagement present.

For many years following, the two families had not been in touch with each other, and then suddenly Yuan Mei's father received a letter from the would-be father-in-law, saying that his son was sick and unable to marry Suwen. He asked Yuan Mei's father to consider the engagement annulled:

> My father hesitated. My sister stood by him. With the gold locket in hands and with tears in her eyes, she refused food. Not eating, my father also began to cry. After my father informed the Gao family of my sister's intention, they were surprised and happy, believing that they were going to get a model daughter-in-law. Then her future father-in-law died and later his nephew wrote to us: "Your future son-in-law actually was not sick. He has been behaving like an animal. Once my uncle almost beat him to death. Afraid that your kindness would be requited with ingratitude, my uncle had to use

an excuse to annul the engagement. Hope your daughter won't bring misery upon herself." My sister went ahead and married [her fiancé] as if she had never heard about all this.²⁷

Her husband turned out to be worse than one could imagine. He was ugly in looks but much worse in character and personality. He often behaved as if he were not a human being. Whenever he saw books, he got upset. Thus, Suwen could not write poems anymore; she could not do needlework because that would upset him too. He often forced Suwen to sell things from her dowry to provide money for his various activities of indulgence. If his sister failed to comply, he would pinch, kick, and burn her. He even broke off one of his own mother's teeth when she tried to save his wife from his abuse. Deep in gambling debt, he tried to sell Suwen. Yuan Mei's father went to the courts and secured a divorce for Suwen after he leaned what was happening to her. Finally, Suwen was able to return to her natal family.

After returning home, Suwen became the constant companion of their mother, but she remained despondent. She became a vegetarian; she never dressed in colors, never had her hair done, and never listened to music. When sick, she refused treatment and often cried when alone. Whenever people visited from the hometown of her husband's family, she would ask about her mother-in-law and send food or clothing there. She became sick after her husband's death and died at the age of forty. Though generally refraining from commenting on this issue directly, Yuan Mei poignantly concludes the biography with a reminder that among the manuscripts his sister left upon her death was a copy of the book *Lienü zhuan* 列女傳 (*The Biographies of Women*) that she herself had copied and edited (*shoubian* 手編).²⁸ It is this ultimate symbol of the rigid Confucian womanhood that defines her tragedy as the result of her willful determination to imitate Confucian female exemplars by allowing her own life to be destroyed. The pain and suffering were, in a way, self-inflicted.

To fully appreciate the causes of his sister's tragedy, one must turn to Yuan Mei's litany in memory of his sister:

> Because of your insistence on the idea of chastity, you married an evil person and suffered the fate of being abandoned. This caused you all the miseries and loneliness. Although this was predetermined by your fate, Heaven certainly played a role in your misfortune. However, I was not completely blameless in your having suffered so much.
>
> When I was studying the Confucian classics as a child with my tutor, you often sat next to me and you liked to listen to those stories about loyalty

and chastity. When you grew up, you literally put into practice what you had learned. Alas, if you had been illiterate, you might not have insisted so steadfastly on being chaste and faithful.²⁹

In the biography, Yuan Mei did not explain in detail why his sister insisted on marrying her fiancé, even though she had been warned repeatedly by the members of the fiancé's family that the proposed marriage would bring tremendous misery upon herself (*ziku* 自苦). Here in the litany he was directly attributing his sister's almost masochist decision on her marriage to her reading too many Confucian stories of chaste women, implicitly suggesting that one should not literally practice what one read in those exemplar biographies. Yuan Mei even blamed himself because his sister was able to read these books while she was studying with him.³⁰

If Yuan Mei was quite constrained as a biographer of Suwen, he became very emotional as a mourning brother in the litany in honor of this same person, addressing directly his deceased sister and recalling the good time the two shared together when they were young:

> While I was trying to catch the cricket, you were gesticulating wildly; after the cricket was frozen to death in the cold weather, we two bade it farewell together in front of its grave. The scene many years ago reappeared vividly before my eyes now I am trying to bury you. When I was nine-year-old, I was taking a break in my study and there came you in silk blouse with your hair braided. We began to read together the chapter of "Ziyi" 緇衣 (The Black Robes) from *The Book of Odes*. Just at that time, the teacher came in. He smiled and praised us when he heard two children reading the book so beautifully. That happened on the fifteenth of July. In the underworld you must still remember it clearly.
>
> At the age of twenty, I was about to leave home for my trip to Guangxi. Clinging to me, you were so sad. Three years later, I came back a *jinshi* degree holder. With plates still in hands, you rushed out [to greet me] from the room on the east wing. All the family members were laughing and staring [at you]. I don't remember exactly what you said first. You probably were talking about the letter announcing my success in the capital arriving too slowly or too quickly.³¹

Here Yuan Mei was recalling happy childhood moments he shared with his sister—how they played and studied together. However, his happiest memory of his younger sister was associated with his glorious return home as a *jinshi* degree holder after he had passed the civil examinations at the national level, marking the beginning of his public career as a government official, the ultimate goal every educated male at that time aspired to but very few could actually reach. A milestone in Yuan Mei's life as a Confucian male, his glorious home return ironically punctuated the moment when his younger sister was about to enter her disastrous marriage, a tragic turning point in her life. These parallel turning points in the respective lives of a brother and sister point to the often different fates waiting for a boy and a girl, even though both were from the same family—a man could help shape his own destiny, while a woman's fate was usually sealed when her marriage was arranged. In the case of his sister, her fate was sealed when she was only a year old. A much deeper irony was that her fate was not completely sealed at that time, as she had an opportunity to escape the pre-arranged marriage; but she chose to stick to the arrangement her father had made, even after learning that her future husband was not a good man. She did this because she was an unquestioning student in the teachings of the Confucian classics. Yuan Mei did not hesitate to bring this irony home to his readers, suggesting that his sister's tragedy lay in her insistence to read too literally the Confucian biographies of female exemplars.

Later in the litany, Yuan Mei attempted to present his sister as a member of his own family and mourn her as such, a strategy adopted by many other mourning brothers, including Sun Cheng'en and Wang Shizhen, as we have seen earlier:

> Since I read your poem mourning the death of your nephew [Yuan Mei's son] in the year of *wuyin* 戊寅 (1758), I have not been able to have another son born to me. . . . Ah Pin [Yuan Mei's cousin] was serving as an official stationed in the distant Henan and he does not have any children of his own. The Yuan family male lineage might not be able to continue. Now you are dead and I am burying you. Who is going to bury me when I die?[32]

When Suwen died, neither Yuan Mei nor his cousin, Yuan Shu, had a son. He was deeply worried about the possible discontinuation of the Yuan family patriline. Although as a woman, his sister was, strictly speaking, a member of the Gao family after her marriage, despite the later separation, Yuan Mei nevertheless tried to mourn her as a concerned member of the Yuan family by mentioning in the litany the Yuan family's problem of a male heir because he assumed that this must have been something she also cared deeply about.

As many of the previously examined cases show, due to his special relationship with his sister, a brother was more likely to dwell on the "unhappy" aspects of her marriage if he felt she was unfairly treated by her husband or his family was unworthy. That is, family tension or marriage tension, a topic infrequently broached when a man wrote about his own wife, could be an issue receiving much more discussion and exposure when a brother wrote about his married sister, and the notion of wifely virtues could also be renegotiated accordingly.

A brother and his sister were siblings and members of the same family until the latter was married and became a member of another family. Unlike a man's relationship with his wife, which was relatively complete in itself—he usually began to know her only after they were married, and their relationship continued until one of them passed away—his relationship with his sister underwent a drastic change, or a sort of rupture, when she married into another man's family and moved away. Thus, for a man, his sister could be someone quite close to him, but she would leave him for another family once she grew up. An important part of his memory of her often involved their shared childhood, as vividly described in Yuan Mei's litany to his sister. This memory of the intimate time he shared with his sister during their childhood often formed a sharp and sometimes unhappy contrast to that of his adult sister when she became the wife of someone else in another family, giving rise to a deep sense of loss. At her death, he might feel he had lost her a second time, this close family member he had already lost once before. The tension between the inclination to mourn one's sister as a member of his own family and the realization that she had married into another's man's family and her Confucian obligation was above all to her husband's family could be a difficult issue, one confronted by Wang Shizhen and Yuan Mei.

It seems that in mourning one's late sister, a male literatus often enjoyed a unique freedom regarding what and how he could write about the life of a woman: while he could still claim the advantage of knowing his female subject as a close relative, he felt far less pressure to present her as a female exemplar in part because, as a grieving brother, he was much less vulnerable to the accusation of being selfish or indulgent, as might happen when writing about his wife in his capacity as a grieving husband. Unlike a sister, a wife was a family member scrutinized with much more suspicion in Confucian patriarchic discourses, in part because of her perceived ability to lead astray her husband from his sacred roles as a son and a brother in relation to his parents and male siblings. Without such suspicions hovering over him, a male mourner could describe a deceased close female relative, such as a sister, from a far-different perspective, allowing his readers to see aspects of the life of a woman they otherwise could not see.

EPILOGUE

A WIFE'S REMEMBRANCES

This study has been concerned primarily with late imperial Chinese men's elegiac memories of their female kin, especially their spouses. A related topic is how a late imperial Chinese woman mourned and wrote about her close male kin, such as her husband. Granted, this should be the topic for a different research project and await a separate occasion; that said, it might be helpful, at the conclusion of this study, to take a quick look at an early nineteenth-century woman's biography of her recently deceased husband. It should shed light on some of the possible issues involved in such a future project and the directions it might take.

In chapter 7, we have already had an opportunity to acquaint ourselves with Wang Duan's husband, Chen Peizhi, in our discussion of his memoir of his deceased concubine, Wang Zhixiang. Chen himself died in 1826. The following year, Wang Duan edited and published a collection of his poems, to which she appended a lengthy biographical sketch of him titled "Mengyu sheng shilüe" 夢玉生事略 (A Biographical Sketch of Mr. Mengyu) that she herself authored.[1] Around seven thousand Chinese characters in total, this is probably the longest biography authored by a woman in premodern China (very few women wrote biographies of their deceased husbands).[2]

Wang Duan was quite deliberate in her decision to present the life story of her husband from the perspective of someone other than that of his wife, a result of careful manipulation of some of the rhetorical conventions associated with traditional biography. Besides its sheer length and comprehensiveness (it covers his childhood precocity, his filial acts, his literary talents, his impressive literary output, his wide social circles, and his pubic careers), what impress the reader most about this elegiac biography are some of its rhetorical features that direct his or her attention to the biographer's emphasized stance as an intellectual peer of the biographical subject. At the same time, the fact that the biographer is also the subject's grieving wife is presented almost as an afterthought in the biography.

Usually a surviving wife tends to refer to her deceased husband in the title of her elegiac writings either by his official title (if he had one) or simply as "my husband."³ Using instead his sobriquet "Mengyu" 夢玉 to refer to her deceased husband in the title, Wang Duan appears to have gone out of her way to underscore her stance as a friend or an intellectual peer of her biographical subject, while obscuring her identity as his wife. Furthermore, as we learn in another biography of Chen Peizhi, "Chen Xiaoyun sima zhuan" authored by his friend, Xu Shangzhi 徐尚之, Chen adopted this sobriquet, Mengyu, because, as a *ci* (lyrical song) poet, he always followed the poetic style of two famous poets from the Southern Song Dynasty (1127–1279): Wu Wenying 吳文英 (ca. 1200–1260) and Zhang Cai 張采 (1248–1320). Mengchuang 夢窗 is the sobriquet of the former, while Yutian 玉田 is that of the latter. Chen's sobriquet, Mengyu, is composed of two characters, *meng* 夢 and *yu* 玉, taken respectively from the sobriquets of these two poets.⁴ However, Xu Shangzhi fails to inform us specifically who coined this sobriquet of Chen's, giving the misimpression, perhaps inadvertently, that Chen Peizhi himself thought it up. As if to rectify this possible misimpression by setting the record straight, Wang Duan, in her biographical sketch, reminds everyone that it was she herself who coined this sobriquet for her husband.⁵ The fact that both Xu Shangzhi's biography and Wang Duan's biographical sketch are appended to this collection of Chen Peizhi's poems makes her "correction" even more significant precisely because of Xu's apparent omission: Wang Duan is insisting on the significance of her own "naming" act. We may recall the naming act performed by Li Yu in his biography of his two concubines discussed in chapter 6—his insisting on his prerogative as a polygamous husband to define the meanings of the lives of his concubines. Here, however, the roles are reversed: by virtue of this naming act, Wang Duan, as a female biographer, is insisting on her prerogative as an intellectual peer of her husband to interpret the meaning of his life in her capacity as a biographer. What complicates the implications of these two different naming acts is, however, the gender difference implied: while these concubines remained "nameless" until their polygamous husband/biographer, Li Yu, performed his naming act, Wang Duan's naming act is much more limited in its ability to define the meaning of her husband's life because Mengyu was only one of several names that Chen Peizhi adopted—a husband would never be "nameless," as a concubine could. In other words, symbolically, as a woman and as his wife, Wang Duan could not claim to be the sole meaning-giver in defining the meaning of the life-history of her late husband, as Li Yu apparently had done with regard to his deceased concubines. At the same time, it is precisely the gender hierarchy implied in such difference that is being challenged by Wang Duan's biographical/naming act. After all, Chen Peizhi's decision to adopt "Mengyu" coined by Wang Duan as one of his sobriquets spoke volumes of the intellectual equality assumed between herself and her husband. The title suggests that the life story of Chen Peizhi as told in this particular biographical sketch is being presented from the unique perspective of someone who is insisting on addressing him by his sobriquet Mengyu rather than as "my husband." First and foremost, she was his intellectual equal.

Throughout the biography, Wang Duan refers to Chen Peizhi as *jun* 君 rather than my husband,[6] and refers to herself by her own style name, Yunzhuang, which tends to function here more as a third-person pronoun, as if Yunzhuang were someone other than the biographer herself. While such use of *jun* by a biographer to refer to his or her biographical subject and reference to oneself by one's own name or style name (rather than first-person pronoun) were not uncommon in classical Chinese writings, they do help obscure the nature of the relationship between the writer and the person he or she is writing about.[7] Consequently, that the biographer is also the wife of her biographical subject remains a fact rather de-emphasized or obscured, a fact Wang Duan somewhat obligatorily acknowledges only at the end of the biography, when she tries to legitimate her biographical act by observing that Yunzhuang, as his wife, should be the person who knows best the biographical subject and is therefore the most qualified to author this biography.

Here are some of the examples of Wang Duan's deliberate rhetoric of detachment: Having heard about her future husband's literary fame and having read his literary writings, "Mr. Wang Qiantian decided to have his second daughter engaged to him. Her name was Duan and her style name was Yunzhuang. At that time, he was only fourteen."[8] Note she refers to her own father as Mr. Wang Qiantian and mentions Yunzhuang's engagement to Chen as if this Yunzhuang were someone other than she herself. Everything is presented from a third-person perspective. Another example is the way in which she records the death of her husband:

> He died in the early morning of the seventeenth day of that month in the Chu area. His clan cousin Zeyuan and sworn brother Xu Yudao were the only two people who were there to attend to the funeral matters, while his parents, wife and child (*qi'nu* 妻孥) were unable to bid farewell to him in person.[9]

By referring to herself and their child by the conventional term *qi'nu*, Wang Duan deliberately avoids the need to describe her own immediate reactions as a wife to her husband's death at that time, reinforcing the reader's impression that she is merely recording the death of her biographical subject as a detached biographer, refusing to allow her status as the surviving wife of the deceased (*weiwang ren* 未亡人) to come into significant play.[10] Such deliberate rhetoric of detachment becomes all the more striking if one compares Wang Duan's account of Chen's death to the account of his death in Xu Shangzhi's biography, and especially to the much more emotional account in the biographical sketch "Peizhi shilüe" 裴之事略, authored by her father-in-law, Chen Wenshu.[11]

More significantly, this calculated rhetoric of detachment seems to have also provided cover for the biographer when she praises her biographical subject and herself together as a perfect couple of matching literary talents by mentioning that someone once compared them to the well-known literary couple from the Song dynasty, Wang Yuan and his wife Huangshi.[12] Then, more interestingly, she adds: "However, many said that the couple's literary talents were far greater than those of Wang and Huang."[13] Although such self-promotion is being presented under the excuse of praising her biographical subject, Wang Duan shows no hesitation when Yunzhuang (i.e., she herself) is also included as one of the recipients of such praise. Furthermore, at the same time, the reader is also indirectly reminded that, unlike Huangshi, who played only a subservient role in her relationship to her husband (as it is said that she was ready to prepare the ink for her husband whenever he had literary inspirations), the Yunzhuang as presented here was very much an intellectual equal of her husband. This rhetoric of presenting herself as another person helped to shield her from the possible complaint that she was being arrogant in singing praises of herself.

Such a display of self-confidence and self-celebration reaches a new level of audacity when our biographer goes out of her way to reflect on Yunzhuang's literary scholarship as she recounts the frequent scholarly exchanges between her biographical subject and herself:

> At that time Yunzhuang was deeply engaged in her project "Selected Poems of the Thirty Masters from the Ming Dynasty." From a very young age on, following her family tradition, Yunzhuang has read widely in history. One could find no traces of the languid and flowery style typical of boudoir poetry (guige xiannong zhi xi 閨閣纖濃之習) in her collection of poems *Poetry from the Studio of the Naturally-Inclined to Learn*. After marriage, under the instructions of Mr. Yidao she made more progress in learning while often exchanged her views with him [her husband]. She is especially familiar with the different literary trends and poetic schools since the Tang and Song dynasties. In her discussion with him about the development of Ming poetry, she

once argued that Ming poetry reached its apex during the reign period of Hongwu (1368–1398). However, starting from the reign periods of Zhengde (1506–1521) and Jiajing (1522–1566), Li Mengyang began to promote the false poetic style. He usurped the leadership in the literary circle and began to suppress true talents. He was followed by Wang Shizhen and Li Panlong. They tried reshuffling and caused chaos in the literary world. All this led to the decline of the quality of poetry produced during the Ming. However, the Ming loyalist poets began to exhibit a profound poetic style that was much loftier than that of their Song loyalist counterparts during the period of Song-Yuan transition. Among those compilers of the selections of Ming poetry, Qian Qianyi was quite biased while Zhu Yizun was comprehensive but not selective enough. None of these poetry anthologies are satisfactory. Shen Deqian, in his *Mingshi biecai* (An Alternative Selection of Ming Poetry), was especially wrong to promote He Jingming and Li Mengyang while being over critical of Kao Qi. This is a serious wrong that has to be rectified. This is why she purchased so many Ming poets' collected works and did careful selecting, starting from the works of Liu Ji and ending with those of Xia Wanchun (1631–1647). The selection is divided into part 1 and part 2. They contain the poems selected from the works of thirty poets and the poems of another seventy poets are included in the appendix. Brief biographies with comments are provided for each poet.[14]

This is an unusually long autobiographical digression into a celebration of her own scholarly achievement on the part of the biographer in a biography of her husband. Note she refers to her father-in-law as "Mr. Yidao," just as she has referred to her own father as "Mr. Wang Tianqian" in the previously discussed passage. Such rhetoric can be justified only because she is writing from the perspective of a detached biographer rather than that of a wife, daughter, or daughter-in-law. Recalling the scholarly exchanges between her husband and herself has afforded her an excuse to digress with great pride into a detailed description of her own achievements. Here Wang Duan, stepping out of her role as a biographer of her husband, becomes a bragging autobiographer. Writing about her deceased husband became an autobiographical occasion for her to present in detail her bold views on Ming literary history as a literary historian and call the reader's attention to her own extraordinary achievement in literary scholarship. She is exhibiting the kind of exuberant self-confidence not commonly seen in a woman's writing at that time.[15] This is even more remarkable during a period of mourning, when a grieving wife was expected to present herself as a humble widow, explaining why she had not decided to die with her husband to vindicate her chastity, or swearing loyalty and faithfulness to him by promising not to marry again, as other female elegiac authors had done.[16] Apparently, Wang Duan is suggesting that her best expression of her wifely virtue as a mourning widow is her assuming the editorship of her husband's works and getting them published. Here the usual hierarchical gender roles in a conjugal mourning process are reversed: instead of a literati husband publishing his deceased wife's literary works as an ultimate mourning gesture, as Ye Shaoyuan and Jiang Tan did with the works of their respective late wives, now it was Wang Duan, the wife, who assumed this conventional role of a literati husband in attempting to bring literary immortality to her deceased husband. She not only edited and published his works but also authored his life history. Keenly aware of the gender implications of her literary endeavors, she makes a special point in the biography about the style of her own poetry being distinctly different from the typical style of women's poetry at the time (*guige xiannong zhixi*). She considered herself a scholar and poet whose work could not be fully appreciated in terms of the traditional notion of female literary talent. She was, by implication, a woman who could not be defined merely in terms of her traditional role as a wife.

That she was by no means a typical traditional wife who excelled at managing household matters is a fact she happily acknowledges in the biography: she tells us that she was so absorbed in her work on the Ming poetry project that she began to suffer serious insomnia and that she could hardly attend to any family chores; she also slept in a separate room, away from her husband.[17] This was the reason she urged her husband to take a concubine. As we may recall, this is also basically what Chen Peizhi himself has told us in his memoir of his concubine, Wang Zixiang (discussed in chapter 7). However, the implication of Wang Duan's version of the story is different: in Chen's memoir, this information (that she urged her husband to take a concubine) was presented by Chen Peizhi as evidence of Wang Duan's wifely virtue—the virtue of lacking jealousy—and also intended to show that he himself was a reluctant polygamist. However, interpreted in the context of Wang Duan's autobiographical agenda in this biography, while presenting herself as an independent woman of great literary achievement, the same information (that she urged her husband to take a concubine) can be seen as her attempt at finding a substitute for herself in her role as Chen Peizhi's wife so that she could devote herself whole-heartedly to the pursuit of her intellectual interests without having to bear the burden of being a wife. Finding her husband a concubine, an act of Confucian wifely virtue, paradoxically became a married woman's attempt to gain self-independence in a polygamous society.

What further complicates Wang Duan's gender self-perception is the fact that she sometimes liked to identify herself more as a man. According to her father-in-law, Chen Wenshu, before her death, Wang Duan declared that in her previous incarnation she had been a man and, therefore, she gave the specific instruction that people should not have her wear earrings as she was dying because she would be reborn as a man again in her next life.[18] By implication, then, her existence as a woman in this life was only temporary. This is not inconsistent with her insistence on her own poetic style being distinctly different from the typical style of boudoir poetry, as pointed out before, and the masculine rhetoric she deliberately adopted for her biographical sketch for her deceased husband.

In many ways, Wang Duan's decision to write a biography—a choice that had been largely relegated as a male prerogative—and her deliberate masculine rhetoric of detachment are unique among the very limited number of late imperial female elegiac authors who attempted to construct the life-histories of their deceased husbands in the form of a prose essay. Zuo Xijia 左錫嘉 (1831–1894) wrote an epitaph for her deceased husband fifteen years after the latter's death when he received a formal reburial in his hometown. The epitaph focuses on the public career of her husband and emphasizes his stellar moral character, with the last section being an account of how she had been dutifully carrying out her responsibilities as a widow, bringing back his coffin to his hometown through a long and treacherous journey, taking good care of his parents and raising their children, almost a widow's report to her deceased husband in the underworld as to what she had accomplished as a virtuous widow since his death.[19] A woman, in this case, almost always had to define, or felt the constant pressure to justify, her continual existence after the death of her husband in terms of the need to take care of the latter's parents or raise his children. This is exactly the kind of apology, Wang Duan, remarkably, did not feel she needed to make. She was writing about her deceased husband not so much as a widow but as an intellectual peer. Her status as a renowned woman scholar and her having her own successful literary career must have made her feel different about herself, helping to explain the extraordinary self-confidence exhibited in her biography of her deceased husband.[20] Wang Duan, however, is a rare case, albeit a significant one. It demonstrates how far a late imperial Chinese woman had come in successfully launching her own scholarly career and being able to claim to be an intellectual equal to her husband. Wang Duan's biography of her husband gives us a unique glimpse into the self-expressive potentials of late imperial women's elegiac writings, especially works in those more formal and more public prose genres, such as elegiac biography, which most women apparently shunned.[21]

In contrast to the case of grieving husbands writing about their deceased wives, it was quite rare for grieving wives to dwell on the intimacy of private life when they wrote about their deceased husbands. This is understandable given the much more intense pressure of decorum on women authors and the fact that men were much more likely to have a public career, thus the greater need for the bereaved women to talk about the public lives of their deceased husbands. A unique work by a female elegiac author, Wang Duan's "Mengyu sheng shilüe" should help us better appreciate the gendered meanings of a grieving wife's elegiac act as it is being turned into an autobiographical act of self-expression and even self-promotion. In her case, when she was promoting herself in the biography of her husband, she had to do it discreetly, presenting herself, at least rhetorically, as someone other than herself. Even though she was not trying to hide the fact that she was the wife of her biographical subject, the rhetoric of presenting herself as another person does help her to assume the appearance of a discreet woman author, while such need for discretion was apparently much less a concern for grieving husbands in writing about their deceased spouses, as we have seen in cases such as that of Li Yu. Here rhetoric mattered even more for a female elegiac author.

In late imperial China, women were far more likely to choose poetry as a medium for expressing their elegiac sentiments, a phenomenon consistent with the situation of women's writings in general—they wrote predominantly in the form of poetry. In his study of the late Ming poetess Bo Shaojun's 薄少君 (d. 1626) "One Hundred Mourning Poems" in memory of her husband, Wilt Idema notes the grieving poetess's deliberate choice of a masculine poetic style, a choice that helped her poems assume a more "public" tone, rendering her less vulnerable to possible complaint that she wrote the poems for selfish reasons. Wang Duan appears to have made a similar choice, adopting the more masculine style of a detached biographer and presenting herself as a friend of her husband's, de-emphasizing the significance of her role as his wife. Unlike Bo Shaojun, who expresses respect for her husband almost as if he was her teacher, Wang Duan never hesitates to present herself as an intellectual equal to her husband. Her deliberately chosen style of detachment has added gendered personal meanings.

In this regard, also pertinent is Grace Fong's reading of the *daowang* poems by the nineteenth-century poetess Qian Shoupu 錢守璞, Wang Duan's younger contemporary:

> In comparison with men, who take the inner chamber as the locus of their grief, women's *daowang* series, as exemplified by Qian Shoupu's sequence of

eight poems, situate their husbands and themselves in a broader context of family and society; they adopt a more "public" face as they celebrate or lament their husbands' lives and their roles in them.[22]

This "public" dimension of women's *daowang* poetry noted by Fong may have been related in part to the more public life of their male subjects as well as to the more intense pressure for discretion on women writers. This must have been the same pressure Wang Duan, as a biographer of her husband, felt when she deliberately adopted the detached biographical rhetoric, or "a more public face." She was writing about her husband as his "literati peer" rather than his wife. Despite the different literary genres (whether poetry or prose) in which they chose to inscribe their elegiac memories and the different contexts within which they produced their respective works, we could see the same pressures these authors were under as women elegiac authors and their shared auto/biographical strategies. For late imperial Chinese women, when writing about someone as close as their own husbands, the choice of style and rhetoric often had gender implications, partly because they, as writing women, were scrutinized much more closely. Our knowledge of late imperial Chinese women's elegiac writings is still quite preliminary. There are too few *daowang* works, especially works of prose narrative, by women that are known to be still extant to offer the necessary foundation for any meaningful generalizations or large understandings. Much more work of excavation, re/discovery, and research remains to be done before we will be in a position to adequately address the important questions on how the gender differences between men and women of the period helped to shape their respective elegiac memories and how differently they inscribed such memories.

NOTES

Introduction

1. "Xianshi Cao ruren xingshu" 先室曹孺人行述, *Xitang zhazu sanji* 西堂雜組三集, 7.13a (rpt. in *Xitang wenji*).
2. "Xianshi Cao ruren xingshu," 7.18b.
3. To mention only a few of these important studies: Patricia Ebrey, *The Inner Quarters: Marriage and the Lives of Chinese Women in the Sung China*; Dorothy Ko, *The Teachers of the Inner Chambers: Women and Culture in Seventeenth-Century Period*; Susan Mann, *Precious Records: Women in China's Long Eighteenth Century* and *The Talented Women of the Zhang Family*; more recently: Beverly Bossler, *Courtesans, Concubines, and the Cult of Female Fidelity: Gender and Social Change in China, 1000–1400*.
4. See some of the essays collected in Ellen Widmer, Kang-I Sun, ed. *Writing Women in Late Imperial China* and the more recent volume, Grace Fong and Ellen Wimder, eds. *The Inner Quarters and Beyond: Women Writers from Ming through Qing*; see also Grace Fong, *Herself an Author: Gender, Agency, and Writing in Late Imperial China*; Wilt Idema and Beata Grant, *The Red Brush: Writing Women of Imperial China* is the most extensive English anthology of premodern Chinese women's writings to date.
5. *Daowang*, broadly defined, means "mourning the deceased." However, narrowly defined, it refers specifically to "mourning the death of a spouse." Cf. Hu Xu, *Daowang shi*, 1.
6. "Feng yiren wangqi Zuoshi muzhiming" 封宜人亡妻左氏墓誌銘, Li Mengyang, *Kongtong ji*, 45.10a. For further discussion of this epitaph by Li Mengyang, see chapter 1.
7. Many other terms have been used to refer to biographical sketches, including *xingshu* 行述, *xingshi* 行實, and *shilüe* 事略.
8. In her recent article "Personal Writings on Female Relatives in the Qing Collected Works," Weijing Lu has called attention to the kinds of rich information about women in Qing China one may find in Qing literati writings focused on female relatives. Rania Huntington's article "Memory, Mourning and Genre in the Works of Yu Yue" is a careful look at how personal memory is enacted and preserved in the massive collected writings by the late Qing scholar Yu Yue 俞樾 (1827–1907), mainly focusing on his poems and *biji* (random notes), drawing our attention to his unique deployment of the genre of *biji* in relation to his remembrances and mourning of his close female kin.
9. "Quli shang" 曲禮上, Wang Meng'ou, anno. & ed., *Liji jinzhu jinyi*, 19; James Legge, trans., *Li Chi: Book of Rites*, 77.
10. For a general account of biographical writings on women in premodern China, see Yi Ruolan, *Shixue yu xingbie: Mingshi lizhuan yu Mingdai nüxing shi zhi jiangou*, 151–253.

11. Harvey Cox, *The Secular City: Secularization and Urbanization in Theological Perspective*, 15.

12. The Chinese scholar Song Xiren 宋希仁, in his article "Guanyu shisuhua de duanxiang," argues that *shisuhua* also has the meaning of *fei daodehua* 非道德化 (people become less inclined to view things in exclusively strict moral terms) and *fei zhengzhihua* 非政治化 (depoliticization; people, tired of everything being politicized during the Mao era, exhibit the tendency to interpret certain things from an apolitical perspective). Post-Mao China was thought to have undergone a process of *shisuhua* due to the belief that during the Mao era the dominant Maoist ideology functioned in almost the same way in its persistent suppression of the individuality of a person as religion was supposed to have done during the Dark Ages of the medieval period in the West.

13. For a discussion of the secularization of Confucianism during the late imperial period, see Chen Lai陳來, "Mengxue yu shisu rujia lunli." For a more historical look at the tendencies toward "worldly concerns" (*rushi* 入世) exhibited by various religions and Confucianism during the same period and their relationships with the rise of the merchant class, see Yu Yingshi 余英時, "Zhongguo jinshi zongjiao lunli he shangren jingshen." More directly relevant to my contention here is the argument about the *shisu hua* process Chinese biographical writings underwent during the mid- and late Ming outlined by Chen Lancun 陳藍村 in the section titled "Mingdai zhonghouji shimin zhuanji de shisuhua qingxiang" 明代中後期市民傳記的世俗化傾向 in Chen Lanchun et al., *Zhongguo zhuanji wenxue fazhanshi*, 301–315. My argument here, however, centers on the "secularizing" function of "intimate memory"—how intimate memory helped secularize various forms of biographical writings in late imperial China.

14. For a study of the biographies of female exemplars in *Mingshi* 明史, the official history of the Ming dynasty compiled by the Qing government, see Yi Ruolan, *Shixue yu xingbie*. In her discussion of what she has called the "conquest generation memoirs" during the mid-seventeenth century in her article "Chimerical Early Modernity: the Case of 'Conquest Generation' Memoirs," Lynn Struve notes that these authors of memoirs "distinguish clearly between the work of the historian (as broad in view, objective in stance, and documentary in mode) and what they are doing: writing down what they know from personal experience" (340–341) and that this reflects "the gradual, centuries-long liberation—to flourish in the late Ming—of subjective, personal narrative voice from the definitive objectivity and impersonality of history-writing" (340). The memoirs Struve has examined may point to a different aspect of this same "secularization of memory" process in late imperial China that I am trying to outline here and in more detail in chapter 1. She explores the increasing awareness of the important implications of an individual's personal experiences in understanding large historical events.

15. For a discussion of the revalorization of *qing* or emotions/feelings in late imperial China, see Martin Huang, *Desire and Fictional Narrative in Late imperial China*, 23–56; Dorothy Ko explores this phenomenon in term of its impact on the gender relationship in seventeenth-century China in *Teachers of the Inner Chambers*, 78–96 and 110–112. Cf. Ko's characterization of companionate marriage as "a union between an intellectually compatible couple who treat each other with mutual respect and affection" that often involved "an elevation of a woman's cultural level to a plane equal to or even surpassing that of her husband" (*Teachers of the Inner Chambers*, 179). In his recent article "Marriage and Mourning in Early Qing Tributes to Wives," Alan Barr observes (178): "a rather

different picture of marriage in seventeenth-century China emerges if we consider partnerships between men and women of less exalted social standing. In these cases, while the notion of a union between a couple who 'treat each other with mutual respect and affection' often holds true, it appears that the idea of intellectual compatibility, to the extent that men set store by it at all, may have hinged more upon consultation and shared decision-making than a close literary fellowship." As Barr shows in his article, and as this study further demonstrates, such consultation and shared decision making were sometimes concerned with practical matters in daily life rather than literary activities.

16. Much has been written on the female chastity cult in late imperial China. For a survey of the scholarship on this topic, see Paul Ropp's introduction to the special theme issue of *Nan Nu: Passionate Women: Female Suicide in Late Imperial China*; see also Ju-K'ang T'ien, *Male Anxiety and Female Chastity in Late Imperial China* and Weijing Lu, *True to Her Word: The Faithful Maiden Cult in Late Imperial China*.

17. Such Confucian female exemplar discourse was characterized by a significant narrowing of the concept of virtue in women's biographies collected in official histories produced in late imperial China when compared with the much earlier *Lienü zhuan* 列女傳 (Biographies of Women) attributed to Liu Xiang's (c. 79–8 BC), where a greater variety of female virtues were in fact celebrated. Some late imperial writers had perceptively pointed out that there appeared to be a graduate shift from valuing *lie* 列 (variety) to a narrowing focus on *lie* 烈 (martyrdom) in women's biographies in official histories of later ages; see the Qing scholar, Zhang Xuecheng 章學誠 (1738–1801), "Da Zhen xiucai lun xiuzhi dier shu," *Wenshi tongyi xinbian*, 719. His view was anticipated by some earlier scholars, such as Xie Zhaozhe (1567–1624; discussed in chapter 1). For a detailed study of the greater variety of female virtues celebrated in Liu Xiang's *Lienü zhuan* and the gradual diminishing of such variety in writings about women that followed, see Lisa Raphals, *Sharing the Light: Representations of Women and Virtues in Early China*.

18. Cf. Susan Mann's brief discussion of the tension between mother-in-law and daughter-in-law in eighteenth-century China, *Precious Records: Women in China's Long Eighteenth Century*, 11–12.

19. The late Ming neo-Confucian thinker, Liu Zongzhou 劉宗周 (1578–1645) wrote an epitaph for his deceased wife titled "Liuzi ji pei gaofeng shuren Xiaozhuang Zhangshi hezang yuzhi" 劉子暨配 誥封淑人孝莊章氏合葬預志 (An Epitaph Written in Advance for the Joint Grave for both Mr. Liu and His Wife, Zhangshi, with the Imperial Title of Lady of Virtue), claiming that those who wanted to know about his own life could get much relevant information from this epitaph, which was mostly about his deceased wife despite what was explicitly suggested by its title (namely, it was an epitaph for a joint grave). See *Liu Zongzhou quanji*, vol. 4, 188.

20. Besides Weijing Lu's "Personal Writings on Female Relatives in the Qing Collected Works" mentioned earlier, Katherine Carlitz's article "Mourning, Personality and Display: Ming Literati Commemorate Their Mothers, Sisters and Daughters" is also an interesting attempt in this regard.

Chapter 1

1. Wang Wan, "Yuren lun muzhiming zhuangai shu" 與人論墓誌銘篆蓋書, *Dunweng xugao* 鈍翁續稿, *juan* 12, in *Wang Wan quanji jianjiao*, 1404.

2. Huang Zongxi, "Tinggao" 庭誥, in *Huang Zongxi quanji*, vol. 10, 521–522.
3. Fang Bao, "Liu Zhonghan ruren Zhoushi mumiao" 劉中翰孺人周氏墓表, *Fang Bao ji*, 384.
4. For another example of such reluctant compliance, see Fang Bao, "Linmu Zheng ruren mubiao" 林母鄭孺人墓表, in *Fang Bao ji*, *juan* 13, 392.
5. Huang Zongxi, "Yishiguan xianbi Yao taifuren shilüe" 移史館先妣姚太夫人事略, *Huang Zongxi quanji*, vol. 10, 543–546.
6. For a discussion of the general Confucian biographical imperative on exemplariness, see D.C. Twitchett, "Chinese Biographical Writings," especially, 101–103.
7. Tang Shunzhi, "Da Wang Zunyan" 答王尊嚴, *Jingchuan xiansheng wenji*, *juan* 6, 119. Li Le 李樂 (1532–1618) also complained about the "overpopularity" of epitaphs, *Jianwen zaji*, *juan* 3, 285.
8. It is worth our special notice here that Tang Shunzhi himself was quite involved in publishing. The publication of collected writings of individual literati authors was closely related to the development of *jiake* 家刻 or private printing (more literally, printing funded or sponsored by a private family); see Kai-wing Chow, *Publishing, Culture, and Power in Early Modern China*, 62–63 (here Chow is arguing about the blurring boundaries between private printing and commercial printing (*fangke* 坊刻); Chow (19–56) attributes part of the reason behind the rapid expansion of private and commercial printing during the late Ming to the declining cost of printing (especially the low cost of paper). The booming of private and commercial publishing certainly contributed to the secularization of the Ming society in general.
9. According to Chen Chao 陳超, in the massive collectanea *Siku quanshu* 四庫全書 compiled by the Qing government in the eighteenth century, there are approximately 1100 epitaphs and other kinds of funeral writings on women (most of them are devoted to a single woman, with some being joint epitaphs for husbands and wives buried together in the same grave (*hezang* 合葬). See Chen Chao, "Mingdai nüxing beizhuanwen yu pin'guan mingfu yanjiu," 26.
10. Gui Youguang 歸有光 (1507–1571), "Taixuesheng Chenjun qi Guoshi ruren muzhiming" 太學生陳君妻郭氏孺人墓誌銘, *Zhenchuan xiansheng ji*, 499. For a similar request by another dying woman, see Huangfu Fang 皇甫汸 (1497–1582), "Xu Wenmin gong jishi shuren Yushi muzhiming" 徐文敏公繼室淑人郁氏墓誌銘, *Huangfu sixun ji*, 55.1a–b.
11. Wang Shizhen, "Ku wangmei Wangshi wen" 哭亡妹王氏文, *Yanzhou sibu gao*, 105.19a.
12. Zhu Yizun, "Zhang Yiren zhuan" 張宜人傳, *Pushu ting quanji*, 899; Wang Maoling, "Wang yiren zhuan" 王宜人傳, *Baichi Wutong ge wenji*, 5.18a–5.19b. Both are about the same woman, despite one referring to her by the last name of her natal family and the other the last name of her husband's family.
13. You Tong, "Wu ruren zhuan" 吳孺人傳, *Xitang zazu sanji*, 16.23a–16.25b, rpt. in *Xitang wenji*.
14. For Chen Que's biography, see *Chen Que ji*, 280–281; Alan Barr discusses this biography in his article "Marriage and Mourning," 164–176.
15. See Chen Zi's own note at the end of this biography, "Neizi Yajun zhuan" 內子雅君傳, *Shanhou wenji*, 10.19a.
16. Most biographies of women produced at the time tended to be about women known for having performed acts of extraordinary Confucian virtues; their biographies were often

categorized as *jiefu zhuan* 節婦傳 (biographies of chaste widows) or *lienü zhuan* 烈女傳 (biographies of female chastity martyrs). Words such as "chastity" (*jie*) and "martyrdom" (*lie*) were often prominently exhibited in the titles of these biographies in order to boost these women's worthiness as subjects of these kinds of honorific writings.

17. Sun Cheng'en, "Dingxi hou furen Zhangshi muzhiming" 定西侯夫人張氏墓誌銘, *Wenjian ji*, 58.4a–b; see also "Dongmu Zhang ruren muzhiming" 董母張孺人墓誌銘 and "Wang ruen Tanshi muzhiming" 王孺人談氏墓誌銘, *Wenjian ji*, 56.3a and 56.6b.
18. Li Panlong, "Ming Meng yiren muzhiming" 明孟宜人墓誌銘, *Changming xiansheng ji*, 23.535.
19. Xie Zhaozhe, "Renbu si" 人部四, *Wuzazu*, 153.
20. Cf. Dorothy Ko's extensive discussions of the emergence of new womanhood in the late Ming, *Teachers of Inner Chambers*, 115–250.
21. Huang Zongxi, "Zhang jiemu Ye ruren muzhiming" 張節母葉孺人墓誌銘, *Huang Zongxi quanji*, vol. 10, 380. The famous poet Qian Qianyi 錢謙益 (1582–1664) seems to have shared this view of gendered features associated with many biographical writings concerning women. He argued that in their writings about women, male writers in the past often concentrated on trivial things in their lives in order to present big pictures (*juexi yi zheng da* 舉細以徵大); see his "Xiucai Sun Han qi Wangshi muzhiming" 秀才孫銲妻王氏墓誌銘, *Chuxue ji*, juan 58, *Qian Muzhai quanji*, 1433.
22. Cf. Bei Jing 貝京, *Gui Youguang yanjiu*, 109–153 (esp. 134–136). However, Gui Youguang's writings on women are not confined to traditional biographical genres such as epitaphs and biographical sketches. He is also known for embedding his memories of his female relatives in essays ostensibly devoted to his recollections of his family residences, and they are not explicitly biographical, such as his famous essays "Xiangji xuan zhi" 項脊軒誌 (the Xiangji Studio) or "Shimei tang houji" 世美堂後記 (The Later Record of the Hall of Shimei), *Zhenchuan xiansheng ji*, 429–431 and 423–425.
23. Xie Zhaozhe, "Wangshi Zheng anren muzhiming" 亡室鄭安人墓誌銘, *Xiaocao zhai ji*, juan 18, 400.
24. Li Chengzhong, "Wangqi Wang anren muzhiming" 亡妻王安人墓誌銘, *Baiyunchun wenji*, 3.30a.
25. Mao Jike, "Tong tairuren xinglüe" 童太孺人行略, *Huihou xiansheng wenchao*, 12.4b.
26. See Sun Cheng'en, "Zhaomu Liu ruren muzhiming" 趙母劉孺人墓誌銘, "Gaoshi Zhangshi ruren muzhiming" 高室張氏孺人墓誌銘 and "Dingxi hou furen Zhangshi muzhiming," *Wenjian ji*, 57.6a–b, 57.11a, and 58.4a–b.
27. Sun Cheng'en, "Chifeng ruren wangqi Wushi muzhiming" 敕封孺人亡妻吳氏墓誌銘 and "Wangqie Xieshi kuangzhi" 亡妾謝氏壙誌, *Wenjian ji*, 56.15a–17b and 58.10a–12a. I compare these two epitaphs in more detail in chapter 6.
28. Fang Bao, "Wangqi Caishi aici" 亡妻蔡氏哀辭, in *Fang Bao ji*, 17, 504.
29. "Xianshi Gong yiren zhuan" 先室龔宜人傳, *Yidao tang wenchao*, juan 13, "Fu" 附.
30. For a discussion of this aspect of the epitaphic tradition in premodern China, see Yu Zhanghua 俞樟華 and Xu Jinpin 許菁頻, *Gudai zazhuan yanjiu*, 86–94.
31. Fang Xiangying, "Wangshi Wu ruren xingshu" 亡室吳孺人行述, *Jiansong zhai ji*, 14.22b–23b.
32. You Tong, "Wu ruren zhuan" 吳孺人傳, *Xitang zaju sanji*, 16.23a–25b (rpt. in *Xitang wenji*).

33. For a discussion of the general suspicion toward "wife" in a patriarchal family as articulated in many popular collections of household instructions or *jiaxun* from the late imperial period, see Martin Huang, *Negotiating Masculinities in Late Imperial China*, 186–89.
34. These lines are from the Confucian classic *Shijing* 詩經 (*The Book of Odes*): "Chexia" 車舝, "Xiaoya" 小雅, *Shijing*. For the Chinese text and English translation, see James Legge, trans. *The She King, The Chinese Classics*, vol. 4, 392–393.
35. Fang Bao, "Wang ruren shouxu" 汪孺人壽序, *Fang Bao ji*, 210.
36. *Guifan* 閨範, *juan* 1, *Lü Kun quanji*, 1457–1458. This passage is usually attributed to Liu Xiang's *Lienü zhuan*, as quoted in the Song dynasty book *Taiping yulan* 太平御覽; see "Hunyin xia" 婚姻下, "Liyi bu ershi" 禮儀部 20, reprinted in *Taiping guangji*, *juan* 541, 2453.
37. See Gu Dashao 顧大韶 (b.1576), "Fangyan si" 放言四, *Bingzhu zhai gao*, p.533.
38. Guan Tong, "Daowang tu ji" 悼亡圖記, *Yinji xuan wen chuji*, 7.9a.
39. "Zhaoqi Wenshi muzhiming" 趙妻溫氏墓誌銘, *Kongtong ji*, 44.13b.
40. Cf. Chen Jianhua 陳建華, "WanMing wenxue de xianqu: Li Mengyang."
41. For a survey of the development of *daowang* poetry in premodern China, see Hu Xu, *Daowang shi shi*, although it is not terribly analytical.
42. Li Kaixiang's preface to the anthology was dated 1566. The extant copy of this anthology is in the form of a hand-copied manuscript. However, the editor of the modern edition of Li Kaixiang's collected works, Li Jianzhong, believes that Li Kaixiang must have it published. See Li Jianzhong, "Tiyao," and Li Kaixian, "*Daonei tongqing* xu," *Daonei tongqing ji*, *Li Kaixian quanji*, 1811 and 1813.
43. In his biography of Li Mengyang, "Li Kongtong zhuan" 李崆峒傳, Li Kaixian mentioned that he only managed to have a letter sent to Li Mengyang through a mutual friend when the latter was bedridden in his death bed. *Li Kaixian quanji*, 770.
44. For example, it was quoted by Li Kaixian's contemporary, Huangfu Fang 皇甫汸 (1497–1582). "Tan anren xinglüe" 談安人行略, *Huangfu sixun ji* 皇甫司勳集, 57.24b; it was also referred to or quoted in several of the epitaphs on the deceased ladies written by the famous scholar-official and writer Wang Shizhen 王世貞 (1526–1590) at the request of their grieving husbands; see, for example, "Yushi Wujun yuanpei Wang ruren muzhiming" 御史吳君元配王孺人墓誌銘, "Lin dafu yuanpei Bao yiren muzhiming" 凌大夫元配包宜人墓誌銘, "Huang ruren muzhiming" 黃孺人墓誌銘, "Wushan Lujun jipei Gao ruren hemu zhiming" 吳山陸君暨配高孺人合墓誌銘, and *Yanzhou xugao* 弇州續稿, 98.24a, 106.10b, 106.11a and 120.21b.
45. "Feng yiren wangqi Zuoshi muzhiming" 封宜人亡妻左氏墓誌銘, Li Mengyang, *Kongtong ji*, 45.10a; see also *Daonei tongqing ji*, *Li Kaixian quanji*, 1815. The status of Li Mengyang's epitaph as a classic was later secured when it was anthologized as a model essay in He Xiazheng's 賀夏征 (b. 1600), *Wangzhang bianti huixuan* 文章辨體彙選 (Selected Essays of Different Genres), 716.17b–716.20b.
46. See Hu Xu, *Daowang shi*, 302–313 and Geng Chuanyou 耿傳友, "Yige bei wenxueshi yiwang de zuojia: Wang Cihui jiqi shige yanjiu," 117–123.
47. Geng Chuanyou, "Yige bei wenxue shi yiwang de zuojia," 118.
48. For a discussion of the formation of the *daowang* poetic conventions in China, see Jiang Yin 蔣寅, "Daowang shige xiezuo fanshi de yanjin."

49. One phenomenon illustrative of how the writing of *daowang* poems had become so conventionalized as well as the resultant difficulty faced by a late imperial *daowang* poet trying to be innovative under the burden of the long tradition of *daowang* poetry was the emergence of the practice of *jiju* 集句 (compiled lines) poems on the *daowang* theme: a poet, often himself a mourning husband himself, would compose a long set of elegiac poems, which were exclusively made of poetic lines taken from the works by different famous *daowang* poets of the previous dynasties (Cf. Hu Xu, *Daowang shi*, 235). More on *daowang* poems composed by using the *jiju* method in chapter 7.
50. See Qian Chengzhi's letter, "Jiaoyou chidu" 交遊尺牘, "*Nanlei shiwen ji* fulu" 南雷詩文集附錄, in *Huang Zongxi quanji*, vol. 12, 291.
51. For Ming scholars' observations on the generic features of various memorial writings, see the relevant entries in Wu Na 吳訥 (1372–1457) and Xu Shizeng 徐師曾 (1517–1580), *Wenzhang bianti xushuo Wenti mingbian xushuo* 文章辨體序說, 文體明辨序說, 49–54 and 144–155.
52. See Sun Xiaoli 孫小力 and Cai Weiyou 蔡維友, "Hanfu yu yiyou: Wan Ming Jiangnan funü de jiating juese xinbian." They argue (144) that although comparing one's wife to a friend could also be found in the Song literati's writings, such comparison was largely invoked to underscore a wife's moral exemplariness.
53. Mao Xiang had the memoir printed as a book and distributed it among his friends, as Chen Hongxu 陳弘緒 (1597–1665) told us: "This spring, Mao Bijiang [Mao Xiang] from the Zhigao area, mailed me several newly printed books and one of them is this book (*zhi* 帙) titled *Yingmei an yiyu*, "*Yingmei an yiyu* tici" 影梅庵憶語題詞, Mao Xiang, comp. *Tongren ji*, 3,54b.
54. See Zhao Shaokuang 趙苕狂 (1892–1953), "*Yingmei an yiyu* kao" Mao Xiang et al., *Yingmei an yiyu, Fusheng liuji, Xiangwai lou yiyu, Qiudeng suoyi*, 40–41.
55. The four extant chapters of *Fusheng liuji* are already more than thirty thousand characters long, almost three times as long as *Yingmei an yiyu*, although it is not exclusively on his late wife (the last chapter is mostly about his own travels around the country).
56. "Sanqian beihuai" 三遣悲懷, *Yuan Zhen ji*, 98. Different from the Tang poet Yuan Zhen, who recalled the earlier life of poverty he shared with his late wife later, after he became an official and was enjoying a much better life, Shen Fu remained poor throughout his life. *Six Records* was a memoir by a poor man about his lifelong poverty. He did not have the luxury of expressing wishes that his late wife could enjoy the present glory, as Yuan Zhen and many other grieving husbands did when mourning their wives who had experienced great hardships in their earlier married life (as captured in the Chinese phrase *zaokang zhi qi* 糟糠之妻 or "wife of chaff and husks," as their husbands were yet to achieve success in their careers) and these wives did not live to enjoy the belated successes of their husbands.

Chapter 2

1. See the appendix to *Zhu Bangxian ji*, 9b–13a and 18a–21b.
2. "Wangqi Tangshi xingshu" 亡妻唐氏行述 and "Jishi Shenshi xingzhuang" 繼室沈氏行狀, *Zhu Bangxian ji*, 9.16a–9.19b and 10.1a–10.3b.
3. "Sanqian Beihuai," *Yuan Zhen ji*, 98.

4. "Ji wangshi Shen xijun wen" 祭亡室沈細君文, *Zhu Bangxian ji*, 11.4b–11.5a.
5. "Jishi Shenshi xingzhuang," *Zhu Bangxian ji* 10.2b.
6. "Xiaofu Lushi zhiming" 小婦陸氏誌銘, *Zhu Bangxian ji*, 8.19b. In this brief epitaph he wrote for his concubine Lushi, Zhu Bangxian tells us he decided to take this concubine to ensure he would have more sons partly because his wife, Tangshi, who was still alive at the time, was not a jealous woman.
7. "Gu taixuesheng Xianggang Zhu jun muzhiming" 故太學生象崗朱君墓誌銘, appended to *Zhu Bangxian ji*, 5b.
8. Zhu Bangxian referred to his mother's anxiety over his not having many sons in the epitaph he wrote for his concubine Lushi, "Xiaofu Lushi zhiming," *Zhu Bangxian ji*, 8.19b.
9. It is not uncommon for a late imperial Chinese man to assert his loyalty to his wife by insisting on sleeping with a particular prostitute presumably because the latter resembled the former, regardless whether his wife was still alive (as in the case of Shen Fu at the turn of the eighteenth century, discussed in chapter 4) or already dead (as in the case of the late Ming writer Song Maocheng 宋懋澄 [d. 1620], who became attached to a courtesan whom he believed to be the reincarnation of his deceased wife, as discussed by Lynn Struve, "Song Maocheng's Matrixes of Mourning and Regret," 91). A husband could insist on his very act of betrayal as a demonstration of his faithfulness to his wife because it was his memory of his wife that made him choose this particular prostitute over another!
10. There are quite a few *daowang* poems in his collected works, but most of them were devoted to his second wife, Shenshi, while only one was written in memory of his first wife, Tangshi. I am grateful to Sarah Schneewind and Katherine Carlitz for first drawing my attention to Zhu Bangxian's elegiac poems, which led me to his elegiac works in prose.
11. "Ji Wangqi Weishi wen" 祭亡妻韋氏文, *Yuan Zhen ji*, 630.
12. Cf. Dorothy Ko's discussions of Ye Shaoyuan and Shen Yixiu in terms of "companionate marriage," *Teachers of the Inner Chambers*, 187–190.
13. Ye Shaoyuan, *Wumeng tang ji*, 1.
14. "Bairi ji wangshi Shen anren wen," "Fulu" 附錄, *Lichui* 鸝吹, *Wumeng tang ji*, 211.
15. In his preface to Ye Wanwan's (his eldest daughter) collected works, *Chouyan* 愁言, Ye Shaoyuan faulted the "Neize" 內則 (Prescriptions for the Inner Chamber) section in the Confucian classic *Liji* (The Book of the Rites) for its failure to include essay and poetry as what a woman should also practice, "Xu" 序 *Chouyan* 愁言, *Wumeng tang ji*, 237. Interestingly, this is the very text on which many later Confucian thinkers, such as Zhu Xi 朱熹 (1130–1200), based their stricter prescriptions for women (stricter in comparison with what is presented as exemplary in Liu Xiang's *Biographies of Women*). Cf. Raphals, *Sharing the Light*, 255.
16. "Wangshi Shen anren zhuan" 亡室沈安人傳, "Fulu," *Lichui*, *Wumengtang ji*, 229.
17. "Wangshi Shen anren zhuan," ibid., 228.
18. For another example of good female mannerism of "refraining from laughter" (*bugou yanxiao*), see Wang Wan, "Song lienü zhuan" 宋烈女傳, *Wang Wan quanji jianjiao*, 733. In this hagiography, Wang apparently tries to present such good female mannerism as a telling sign of his biographical subject's impeccable Confucian moral character, whose ultimate expression is the act of chastity martyrdom (*lie* 烈). It should be noted that in

Ban Zhao's *Nüjie* it is specifically mentioned that a woman should not indulge in banter and laughter (*buhao xixiao* 不好戲笑). "Nüjie," "Cao Shishu qi" 曹世叔妻, "Lienü zhuan" 列女傳, *Hou Hanshu*, 2789. For an English translation of *Nüjie*, see Wilt Idema and Beata Grant, *The Red Brush*, 36–42.

19. "Bairi ji wangshi Shen anren wen," 210; "Wangshi Shen anren zhuan," 226.
20. "Wangshi Shen anren zhuan," 226.
21. "Bairi ji wangshi Shen anren wen," 210.
22. "Wangshi Shen anren zhuan," 225–226. Ye Shaoyuan's account of the role of his mother in his wife's misery was corroborated by his brother-in-law (Shen Yixiu's younger brother), Shen Zizheng 沈自徵, who was much blunter in describing his sister's hard life due to her harsh mother-in-law: "[My sister] had to be very cautious and was in constant fear of displeasing her mother-in-law. They had a large number of children and whenever some of them did something upsetting their grandmother, it was my sister who had to kneel down begging for forgiveness on their behalf, something she had always to do throughout her life." *Lichui ji* xu 鸝吹集序, *Lichui, Wumeng tang ji*, 17–18.
23. See, for example, Luo Hongxian's "Dian wangshi Zeng ruren wen" 奠亡室曾孺人文, *Luo Hongxian ji, juan* 24, 950, where he acknowledged that throughout their thirty-five years of married life he had lived together with his wife (i.e., sleeping in the same bed) for only a few years (*yuzi jushi zhe buguo shunian er* 與子居室者不過數年耳). Note that Luo Hongxian chose to describe such private feelings in a *jiwen* or *dianwen* 奠文 rather than the formal epitaph he wrote for his wife; cf. "Minggu wangshi Zengshi ruren muzhiming" 明故亡室曾氏孺人墓誌銘, *Luo Hongxian ji, juan* 22, 880–881.
24. Wang Ji, "Wangshi chunyi Zhangshi anren aici" 亡室純懿張氏安人哀辭, *Wang Ji, juan* 20, 649. See also the scholar-official Xiang Qiao's 項喬 (1493–1552) reference to the fact that he and his wife did not have much a sex life due to his poor health, "Ji gaofeng yiren wangqi Zhangshi wen" 祭誥封宜人亡妻張氏文, *Xiang Qiao ji*, 459.
25. She apparently had complained in some of the poems in her collected writings personally edited by Ye Shaoyuan himself. See, for example, her *ci* poem "Huanxisha: He Zhongshao jiyun" 浣溪沙——和仲韶寄韻, *Lichui, Wumeng tang ji*, 153–154. This was a poem his wife wrote while he was serving as an official near Beijing, but she could not join him because she had to take care of her mother-in-law, who did not like to live in the capital in the north, where the weather was cold and dry. She did so in poems probably because the mother-in-law usually did not read her poems. She did not have to worry too much about her mother-in-law being unhappy about her writing poems now that her husband had become an official by passing the *jinshi* examinations.
26. Disinterest in sex can also be understood as a hallmark of a man's masculinity, as popularized in the famous Ming novel *Shuihu zhuan* 水滸傳 (Water Margins); see Martin Huang, *Negotiating Masculinities in Late Imperial China*, 107–109.
27. "Wangqi Caishi aici" 亡妻蔡氏哀辭, *Fang Bao ji*, 17, 503.
28. "Xianshi Cao ruren xingshu" 先室曹孺人行述, *Xitang zhazu sanji* 西堂雜組三集, 7.13a., rpt. in *Xitang wenji*.
29. "Xianshi Cao ruren xingshu," 7.6b–7.17a. It appears that of the eight children, only two boys and three daughters survived into adulthood.
30. "Ji xianshi Cao ruren wen" 祭先室曹孺人文, *Xitang zazu sanji*, 8.120a; see also "Qizhong zai ji wangshi wen" 七終再祭亡室文, ibid., 8.20a–8.21b.

31. Poem no. 33, "Ku wangfu Cao ruren shi liushi shou" 哭亡婦曹孺人詩六十首" *Aixuan ji* 哀絃集, 4a, rpt. in *Xitang shiji*.
32. "Xianshi Cao ruren xingshu," 7.18b.
33. Poem no. 15 in "Ku wangfu Cao ruren shi liushi shou" *Aixuan ji*, 2b.
34. "Xianshi Cao ruren xingshu," 7.14a–b.
35. "Xianshi Cao ruren xingshu," 7.6a–b.
36. Cai Jingpin suggests that the birth mother of one of Ye Shaoyuan's daughters, Ye Xiaofan 葉小繁, about whom we know very little, was actually his concubine rather than his wife Shen Yixiu. See Cai Jingpin, *MingQing zhiji Fenhu Yeshi wenxue shijia yanjiu*, 54–55.
37. Ye Shaoyuan mentioned that he once promised his late wife that he would remarry, "Bairi ji wangshi Shen anren wen," 213.
38. Wang Shunmin, "Ji wangshi Jiang yiren wen" 祭亡室江宜人文 and "Gao Jiang yiren wen" 告江宜人文 *Jingxuan xiansheng wenji*, 15.7b–15.9a and 15.10b–15.11a.
39. Fang Bao, "Jihai siyue shi Daoxi xiongdi" 己亥四月示道希兄弟 *Fang Bao ji*, 479–480.
40. "Jihai siyue shi Daoxi xiongdi," 477.
41. "Jihai siyue shi Daoxi xiongdi," 480–481.
42. Cf. Katherine Carlitz's observation on some of the general features of the epitaphs on Women from the Ming: "Epitaphs for model wives and mothers (and every woman became a model in her epitaph) tell us about their genealogy and progeny, demonstrating that the husband's family had chosen well, and that its choice had been rewarded. The women eulogized are presented as having significant agency, but their actions all express devotion to their families of marriage. . . . The aim of the epitaph was to raise the family's standing by making a public display of domestic virtue." "Advertisements for Ourselves: The Reproduction of Elite Status in 16th-century Chinese Epitaphs," paper presented at the conference on "Lifewriting," Sheffield, England, March 2008. The issue of how the author of the epitaph of the woman being her bereaved husband conditioned its writing was, however, not the main concern of Carlitz's paper. My thanks to Carlitz for sharing this paper with me.
43. See, for example, the scholar-official and neo-Confucian thinker, Nie Bao 聶豹 (1487–1563), "Chifeng ruren jin yiren Songshi muzhiming" 敕封孺人進宜人宋氏墓誌銘, *Nie Bao ji*, juan 6, 152 and Wang Ji, "Wangshi chunyi Zhangshi anren aici," *Wang Ji* 648.

Chapter 3

1. See Ju-K'ang T'ien, *Male Anxiety and Female Chastity in Late Imperial China*, Fei Siyan, *You dianfan dao guifan: cong Mindai zhenjie lienu de bianshi yu liuchuan kan zhenjie guannian de yangehua* and Weijing Lu, *True to Her Word: The Faithful Maiden Cult in Late Imperial China*.
2. "Xie Jifang zhuan" 謝季方傳, *Fang Bao ji*, 501–502. More on this biography in chapter 8.
3. Huang Zongxi, "Zhang jiemu Ye ruren muzhiming," *Huang Zongxi quanji*, vol. 10, 380.
4. The compiler of the "Lienü" 列女 (exemplary women) section in *Mingshi* (The History of the Ming dynasty) notes a trend--the penchant for the eccentric and the sensational in chaste women writings. "Lienü yi" 列女一, *Mingshi*, 7689. See also Weijing Lu, *True to Her Words*, 51.
5. Fei Siyan has noted that during the Ming some wives would pledge to die together with their husbands, who were seriously ill, and that they actually committed suicide first

to demonstrate their determination to keep their words. However, she does not give any specific examples. See her *You dianfan dao guifan*, 8. There is a biography of such a chastity martyr who was survived by her husband in the Qianlong edition of the Sui'an county gazetteer: "Xu liefu Maoshi zhuan" 徐烈婦毛氏傳, *Sui'an xianzhi*, 10.28–10.29a. It is interesting to note this biography was authored by her own brother, Mao Huikai 毛彙愷. He rationalized that his sister's suicide should not be considered unfortunate or unnecessary just because her husband later recovered since it was her death in place of her husband that resulted in his miraculous recovery and, furthermore, her death also brought good luck to her husband later—the husband later remarried and was able to have many sons by his second wife. In short, according to her brother, her act of chastity martyrdom had not been in vain at all even if the rationale for such an extreme act no longer existed (her husband did not die). The dates of Mao Huikai were not known, but there were brief biographies of him and his grandfather, Mao Qiying 毛奇英, in this same gazetteer, "Xiaoxing" 孝行, "Renwu" 人物, *Shui'an xianzhi*, 7.10a. Mao Qiying was an early Qing scholar, thus Mao Huikai might have lived in the late Kangxi (1661–1722) and Yongzheng (1722–1735) reign periods.

6. "Wangqi Li ruren kuangzhi" 亡妻李孺人壙誌, *Qitian ji*, 8.23a–8.24b.
7. "Wangshi Li ruren xinglüe" 亡室李孺人行略, *Qitian ji*, 12.20b–12.29a.
8. "Wangshi Li ruren xinglüe," 12.23b–12.24a.
9. "Wangshi Li ruren xinglüe," 12.25b.
10. Huang Zongxi, "Anqiu Zhangmu Li ruren muzhiming" 安丘張母李孺人墓誌, *Huang Zongxi quanji*, vol. 10, 502–503.
11. "Caoshi Li ruren mubiao" 曹室李孺人墓表, *Qitian ji*, 9.24b. Here, *qingyu* reminds us of *ernü zhiyan*, the phrase You Tong used to characterize his own biography of his late wife, discussed earlier. I translate the Chinese term *mubiao* as "epitaph" as well, even though a *mubiao* was supposed to be carved on the stone erected above the grave rather than being carved on a stone tablet buried in the grave, as in the case of *muzhiming*. I have used the same English word, "epitaph," to translate *mubiao* and *muzhiming* because the difference in their meaning is not significant for my discussion.
12. "Qingci fumo" 請辭副墨, *Qitian ji*, 13.25b–13.26a.
13. Ibid., 13.25b–13.26a.
14. Huang Zongxi, "Anqiu Zhangmu Li ruren muzhiming," *Huang Zongxi quanji*, vol. 10, 503.
15. "Qingci fumo," *Qitian ji*, 13.26a.
16. See his comments on his friend, An Zhiyuan's (1629–1702) epitaph and birthday tribute in honor of the latter's wife, An Zhiyuan, "Shou qi Li ruren qishi xu" 壽妻李孺人七十序, *Jicheng wengao* 紀城文稿, 1.41b and "Qi Li ruren muzhi" (bingming) 妻李孺人墓誌（并銘）*Jieyin* 蠽音, 10b (both works reprinted in *Siku cunmu congshu* series). For a discussion and English translation of An Zhiyuan's epitaph on his wife, see Allan Barr, "Marriage and Mourning in Early Qing Tributes to Wives," 141–149.
17. "Wangshi Li ruren xinglüe," 12.25a–b.
18. "Anqiu Zhangu Li ruren muzhiming," *Huang Zongxi quanji*, vol. 10, 503.
19. "Qingci fumo," *Qitian ji*, 13.25b.
20. For a discussion of the complicated implications of *qing* (love) in the debate of "faithful maidens" (*zhennü*, women committing suicide to vindicate their faithfulness to their fiancés who had passed away), see Weijing Lu, *True to Her Word*, 145, 148, and 152–156.

21. At the end of his biography of a filial daughter-in-law, the Qing scholar-official Wang Youdun 汪由敦 (1692–1758) goes out of his way to remind the reader that he has omitted many details associated with his female subject as recalled by her father-in-law, such as her literary talent, because they are not illustrative of her virtue of filiality, the central concern of this hagiographical project. See "Lu xiaofu zhuan" 魯孝婦傳, *Songquan wenji*, 19.6a. This can be considered another case of the need to "forget," as prescribed by the hagiographical agenda.
22. In the biographical sketch, Qian Chengzhi often uses the words *zei* 賊 and *bing* 兵 interchangeably. Roaming bandits (*liukou* 流寇) is another term he uses. All this makes it difficult to tell whether it was the Manchu soldiers or the bandits who caused his wife to commit suicide. In his chronological biography of Qian Chengzhi, his son, Qian Weilu 錢搗祿, is still not clear when he uses both the words *di* 敵 and *zei*; see "Qiangong Yingkuang fujun nianpu" 錢公飲光府君年譜, *Suozhi lu*, 188. However, Huang Zongxi, in his account of this episode in his epitaph for Fangshi, which was based on Qian's biographical sketch, is quite unequivocal in saying that Qian's wife committed suicide when approached by the bandits. Huang specifically tells us that the bandits (*tukou* 土寇) began to roam in that area, taking advantage of the chaos created by the coming south of the Manchu troops (*dabing* 大兵); she drowned her daughter and herself when the bandits (*zei*) got onto their boat. "Tongcheng Fang liefu muzhiming," *Huang Zongxi quanji*, vol. 10, 474–475. At the same time, it is quite inconceivable that these authors would still use the term *zei* to refer to the Manchus in their writings when it was already well into the Kangxi reign (1654–1722). The issue of whether it was the Manchu soldiers or the bandits that caused Fangshi to commit suicide should not change the likelihood that Qian Chengzhi wrote this biography of his wife from the perspective of someone who still held Ming loyalist sentiment.
23. "Yu Pan Shuzao shu" 與潘蜀藻書, *Tianjian wenji*, 81–82.
24. Qian Chengzhi, "Xianqi Fangshi xinglüe" 先妻方氏行略, *Tianjian wenji*, 564.
25. "Xianqi Fangshi xinglüe," 565–566.
26. "Xianqi Fangshi xinglüe," 565.
27. See, for example, Mao Jike's biographical sketch of his own daughter, who repeatedly tried to commit suicide after the death of her husband, "Wangnü jielie shu" 亡女節烈述, *Anxu tang wenchao*, 24b.
28. "Xianqi Fangshi xinglüe," 565.
29. "Xianqi Fangshi xinglüe," 567.
30. "Xianqi Fangshi xinglüe," 568.
31. "Fu Lu Yiwang shu" 復陸翼王書, *Tianjian wenji*, 84.
32. "Xianqi Fangshi xinglüe," 569.
33. "Xianqi Fangshi xinglüe," 569.
34. For a discussion of suicide poems by women during violent periods in late imperial China, see Grace Fong, "Signifying Bodies: The Cultural Significance of Suicide Writings by Women in Ming–Qing China."
35. "*Mingmo zhonglie jishi* xu" 明末忠烈紀實序, *Tianjian wenji*, 212–213.
36. "*Mingmo zhonglie jishi* xu," 213.
37. "Shangxin shi" 傷心詩, *Cangshan ge ji*, 134.
38. "Bayue shiqi ri ku Zhongyu" 八月十七日哭仲馭, *Cangshan ge ji*, 132–133; see also "Xianqi Fangshi xinglüe," *Tianjian wenji*, 567.

39. "Guo Zhenze kou hao ji'ai" 過震澤口號紀哀, *Tianjian shiji*, 452.
40. "Tongcheng Fang Liefu muzhiming" 桐城方烈婦墓誌銘, *Huang Zongxi quanji*, vol. 10, 473–476.
41. *Mingshi*, "Lienü san" 列女三, 7761.

Chapter 4

1. Jin Zhaoyan, "Wangshi Jin ruren zhuan" 亡室晉孺人傳, *Zongting guwen chao*, 4.5b.
2. Chen Wenshu, "Xiaohui Wang yiren zhuan" 孝慧汪宜人傳, Wang Duan, *Ziran haoxue zhai shichao* 自然好學齋詩鈔, Hu Xiaoming, et al. *Jiangnan nuxing bieji erbian*, 306–319. For a discussion of Wang Duan's life and scholarship, see Ellen Widmer, *Beauty and Book: Women and Fiction in Nineteenth-Century China*, 106–107 and 117–127. Chen Wenshu's wife even wrote a biography in honor of the deceased concubine of their son Chen Peizhi (Chen Peizhi also wrote a long memoir of this concubine, which I examine in detail in chapter 6). It was quite rare for a woman to write a biography for her daughter-in-law, especially when that daughter-in-law was the concubine of her son and a former courtesan. This might suggest a less rigid view of familial hierarchy shared among certain sections of the society and a new trend in the development of the elegiac writing at the time.
3. Chen Wenshu, "Xianshi Gong yiren zhuan" 先室龔宜人傳 *Jidao tang wenchao*, appendix to *juan* 13, 2a and 6a–b.
4. "Xianshi Gong yiren zhuan," 6b.
5. "Xianshi Gong yiren zhuan," 5a.
6. "Xianshi Gong yiren zhuan," 10a–b.
7. "Xianshi Gong yiren zhuan," 5b.
8. "Xianshi Liu gongren muzhiming" 先室劉恭人墓誌銘, *Long Qirui shiwen ji jiaojian*, 450–451.
9. "Ji xianshi Liu gongren wen" 祭先室劉恭人文, *Long Qirui shiwen ji jiaojian*, 505.
10. For a study of autobiography in traditional China, see Pei-yi Wu, *The Confucian's Progress: Autobiographical Writings in Traditional China*. This study, however, does not cover works after the seventeenth century.
11. All quotations of the English translation of *Fusheng liuji* are from Shen Fu, *Six Records of Floating Life*, trans. Leonard Pratt and Su-hui Chiang, with Wide-Giles Romanization being changed to that of *pinyin* and with minor modifications whenever I feel necessary. References to the Chinese text of *Fu Sheng liuji* are to Shen Fu, *Fusheng liuji* (1991). Page references are provided in parentheses, with the first number being that of the Chinese text and the second the English translation.
12. The translation of the last sentence is mine.
13. Here I have modified the English translation.
14. See, for example, Zhu Bangxian's description of his second wife in his "Jishi Shenshi xingzhuang" (*Zhu Bangxian ji*, 10.1b–2a) discussed in chapter 2.
15. I have modified the English translation here based on my interpretations of the original Chinese text.
16. Elsewhere (93; 65), Shen Fu shows his apparent disdain for the civil examinations, as he tells us that when he and his friends got together one of the topics considered to be too vulgar was the eight-legged examination essays and yet, ironically, the rules of the drinking

game they played were all worded in the vocabularies of the civil examinations. Besides the inescapability of the examination culture being implied here, the reader wonders whether any mention of the civil examinations would become a painful reminder to Shen Fu of being denied a chance for even trying it due to his father's insistence on his being a *muyou*.

17. For a different reading of the "small spaces" in the *Six Records*, see Steven Owen, *Remembrances: Experience of the Past in Chinese Classical Literature*, 99–113.
18. See, for example, Lai Zhide 來知德, *Zhouyi jizhu*, 5.9a. For a brief discussion of the association of travel and manliness in Ming culture, see Martin Huang, "Male Friendship and *Jiangxue* (Philosophical Debates) in Sixteenth-Century China," 149–150.
19. Gong Weizhai, "Da Ganlin zhi" 答甘林侄, *Xuehong xuan chidu*, in Xu Jiacun and Gong Weizhai, *Qiushui xuan, Xuehong xuan chidu*, 303.
20. For a brief discussion of the gender anxiety some literati had over their *muyou* careers, see Martin Huang, *Negotiating Masculinities in Late Imperial China*, 58–59.
21. Gong Weizhai, "Da Yunfang liudi" 答韞芳六弟, *Xuehong xuan chidu*, 305.
22. For a chronological account of Shi Yunyu's life, see Sui Jun 眭駿, *Shi Yunyu nianpu*.
23. *Langyou* is also the word Shen Fu's more famous contemporary, the poet Huang Jingren 黃景仁 (1749–1783), employed to describe his experience of traveling around the country to visit various famous places, as well as his *muyou* activities. See Huang Jingren "Zixu" 自敘, *Liangdang xuan ji*, 1.
24. The same kind of deep attachment among the wives in a polygamous family is also the theme of the novel *Lin Lan Xiang* 林蘭香 (Three Women Named Lin, Lan, and Xiang) (tentatively dated as a work from the Kangxi period [1662–1722]). Despite various explicit descriptions of their love, which are often erotic, nothing physical is mentioned to have happened among these wives. For a discussion of the lesbian theme of this novel and its similarities with Li Yu's play, see Martin Huang, *Desire and Fictional Narrative in Late Imperial China*, 184–205. In her article "If Chen Yun Had Written about Her 'Lesbianism': Rereading the Memoirs of a Bereaved Philanderer," Helen Dunstan argues that nothing lesbian was going on between Yun and the courtesan, and that Yun arranged to have Shen Fu take her as a concubine as a way to keep him in check after his "philandering," rather than out of her attachment to another woman. While I appreciate the value of Dunstan's caution that Shen Fu as an autobiographer can often be unreliable, her readings between the lines are not always persuasive.
25. Gui Youguang, "Shimei tang houji" 世美堂後記, *Zhenchuan xiansheng ji*, 423–424.

Chapter 5

1. Shen Shanbao 沈善寶, "Xuji xia" 續集下, *Mingyuan shihua* 名媛詩話, in Wang Yingzhi, et al., eds., *Qingdai guixiu shihua congkang*, 602. For a discussion of the implication of this Chinese term in relation to the Western concept of "companionate marriage," see Dorothy Ko, *Teachers of the Inner Chamber*, 187.
2. See, for example, the several poems she wrote in honor of the well-known poetess Shen Shanbao 沈善寶 (1808–1862), Guan Ying, *Sanshi liu furong guan shicun*, 1461, 1463–1464, 1466, 1468, 1470, and the prefaces she wrote for the collections of poems by other poetesses, 1497–1501.
3. Cf. Susan Mann, "The Virtue of Travel for Women in the Late Empire." Grace Fong discusses seventh-century Chinese women's travel writings, *Herself an Author*, 85–120.

4. Zhu Jianmang, comp. *Meihua wenxue mingzhu congkan*.
5. Guan Ying's writings and Jiang Tan's elegiac works dedicated to her are reprinted in Hu Xiaoming, et al., eds., *Jiangnan nüxing bieji sibian* (2014), which are the main primary sources I rely on for discussions of this chapter.
6. Chen Jicong, "Jiang wenxue Tan" 蔣文學坦, Idem., *Zhongyi jiwen lu*, 26.9a.
7. Zhu Jianmang, "*Qiudeng suoyi* kao" 秋燈瑣憶考, in *Qiudeng suoyi*, in Zhu Jianmang, comp., *Meihua wenxue mingchu congkan*.
8. Li Huiqun, "*Qiudeng suoyi* xinkao." See also her book, *Guige yu huafang: Qingdai JiaqingDaoguang nianjian de Jiangnan wenren he nüxing yanjiu*, 232–234.
9. Li Huiqun, *Guige yu huafang*, 234.
10. *Qiudeng suoyi*, 1526.
11. Zhang Ruiqing, "*Qiudeng suoyi* yu *Fusheng liuji*," 222. Zhang argues that Jiang Tan apparently had in mind the legend associated with Su xiaomei, the younger sister of Su Shi (1037–1101), one of the best-known Song-dynasty literary figures. It was said that Su xiaomei was trying to quiz her groom, the poet Qin Guan 秦觀 (1049–1100), by asking him to compose poems during their wedding night. This beginning of *Fragments* is considered farfetched because Jiang Tan and Guan Ying had known each other pretty well before they were married, while Su xiaomei had reasons to find it necessary to test her groom, Qin Guan, because she did not know him until they were married. For the vernacular story based on the legend, see the eleventh story, "Su Xiaomei sannan xinlang" 蘇小妹三難新郎, Feng Menglong, *Xingshi hengyan*, 217–231. Apparently, Jiang Tan was presenting Guan Ying and himself as a "perfect literary couple" by comparing themselves to the legendary Song literary couple.
12. *Chouluan ji*, in Hu Xiaoming, et al., eds, *Jiangnan nüxing bieji sibian*, 1503.
13. "Daowang bashi shou," Jiang Tan, *Chouluan ji*, 1505.
14. "Chumen ershi shou" 出門二十首, Jiang Tan, *Chouluan ji*, 1515.
15. "You bashou," Jiang Tan, *Chouluan ji*, 1510–1511.
16. Xun Fengqian eventually died of a broken heart after the death of his wife. See "Huoni" 惑溺, Xu Zhen'e, ed. & comp. *Shishuo xinyu jiaojian*, 489–490. By the time of the late Ming and early Qing, Xun Fengqian had become the familiar figure of a loving and sometimes overindulgent husband. Ye Shaoyuan also repeatedly compared himself to Xun Fengqian in his elegiac writings; see, for example, "*Qinchai yuan* xiaoyin" 秦齋怨小引 and "Nianpu xuzuan" 年譜續纂, *Wumeng tang ji*, 595 and 856; see also Ko, *The Teachers of the Inner Chambers*, 160–161. As discussed in chapter 7, in their elegiac writings, Mao Xiang and another early Qing wirter, Qu Dajun, also appealed to the legend of Mr. Xun in constructing their own images of a grieving husband.
17. "Shu fu bing huai" 述婦病懷, Wang Cihui, *Yiyu ji*, 2.5.
18. *Qiudeng suoyi*, 1526–1527.
19. *Qiudeng suoyi*, 1519.
20. *Qiudeng suoyi*, 1519.
21. *Qiudeng suoyi*, 1529.
22. "Daowang bashi shou," *Chouluan ji*, 1505.
23. Grace Fong, "Writing and Illness: A Feminine Condition in Women's Poetry of the Ming and Qing," 44–47.
24. "Daowang bashishou," Jiang Tan, *Chouluan ji*, 1506.
25. *Sanshi liu furong guan shicun*, 1455.

26. "Shisan jian lou ye zhuo tong Lüqiong mei" 十三間樓夜坐同侶瓊妹, GuanYing, *Sanshi liu Furong guan shichun*, 1469.
27. Chen Jicong, "Jiang wenxue Tan," *Zhongyi jiwen lu*, 26.7a.
28. "Taochan shishou" 逃禪十首, Guan Ying, *Sanshi liu Furong guan shicun*, 1455.
29. "Wobing," *Sanshi liu Furong guan shicun*, 1463.
30. Chen Jicong, "Jiang wenxue Tan," *Zhongyi jiwen lu*, 26.9a.
31. Chen Wenshu, the father of Chen Peizhi and the father-in-law of Wang Duan, knew Jiang Tan quite well and wrote a preface to Jiang's collected poems. Chen was also a friend of Jiang's father and the tutor of his mother; see Li Huiqun, *Guige yu huafang*, 241–245.
32. "Mengying lou ci zixu" 夢影樓詞自序," Guan Ying, *Sanshi liu Furong guan shicun*, 1496.
33. "You bashou" 又八首, *Chouluan ji*, 1511 and *Qideng suoyi*, 1523. For a discussion of Tanyangzi, see Ann Waltner, "T'an-yang-tzu and Wang Shih-chen: Visionary and Bureaucrat in Late Ming China."
34. *Qiudeng suoyi*, 1521.
35. "Daowang bashi shou," *Chouluan ji*, 1506.
36. "Chumen ershi shou," *Chouluan ji*, 1516.
37. "Doawang shi baishi shou," *Chouluan ji*, 1505.
38. *Qiudeng suoyi*, 1522.
39. "Sanshi chudu yougan" 三十初度有感, *Sanshi liu furong guan shicun*, 1466.
40. "Chumeng ershi shou," *Chouluan ji*, 1514.
41. *Qiudeng suoyi*, 1529.
42. "You bashou," *Chouluan ji*, 1510.
43. Wang Cihui, "Beiqian shisan zhang" 悲遣十三章, idem., *Yiyu ji*, 2.10.
44. "Daowang bashi shou," *Chouluan ji*, 1505.

Chapter 6

1. For a discussion of the extant epitaphs composed by husbands for their wives and concubines from the Tang dynasty, see Chen Shangjun, "Tangdai de wangqi yu wangqie muzhi." According to Chen's estimate (p. 43), among the extant epitaphs from the Tang dynasty, there are eighty-seven for wives authored by their husbands but less than twenty for concubines.
2. Beverly Bossler, "'Concubines' in Song and Yuan Funerary Inscriptions," 4–5.
3. In his PhD dissertation, "The Domestication of Concubinage in Imperial China," Neil Ennis Katkov argues that the status of concubines improved in late imperial China as the institution of concubinage was gradually domesticated. Based on her examination of Chinese legal history from the Song to the Qing, Kathryn Bernhardt notes "an elevation in the legal status of concubines—from a little more than a sexual servant to a kind of minor wife," *Women and Property in China: 960–1949*; see especially her detailed discussions of the legal status of concubines in late imperial China, 168–178. A similar trend of "elevation of status" is also noted by Jin Huihan 金蕙涵 in her study of the practice of "joint burial" of husbands and concubines during the Ming. "Qing yu de: lun Mingdai Jiangnan diqu de ceshi hezang mu."
4. Relying on the *muzhiming* data available in the *Siku quanshu*, Bossler notes a steady increase of reference to *qie* (concubine) from the Han dynasty to the Ming dynasty. "Concubines in Song and Yuan Funeral Inscriptions," 3.

5. Cf. Kathryn Bernhardt's observation: "Legally, she exists somewhere between a maidservant of the household on the one hand and a full-fledged legal wife on the other. Where exactly she was located along the continuum was open to varying constructions, depending on the circumstances." *Women and Property in China*, 162.
6. "Wangqie Xieshi kuangzhi," *Wenjian ji*, 58.10a.
7. "Wangqie Xieshi kuangzhi," *Wenjian ji*, 58.11a.
8. "Wangqie Xieshi kuangzhi," *Wenjian ji*, 58.12a
9. "Chifeng ruren wangqi Wushi muzhiming" 敕封孺人亡妻吳氏墓誌銘, *Wenjian ji*, 56.15a–15.17b.
10. "Shefeng ruren jin yiren Songshi muzhiming" 敕封孺人進宜人宋氏墓誌銘, *Nie Baoji*, 152–154.
11. "Wangqie Wangshi Taojie kuangji" 亡妾王氏桃姐壙記, *Nie Bao ji*, 207.
12. "Qiao Fusheng Wang Zailai erji hezhuan" 喬復生王再來二姬合傳, *Liweng yijia yan wenji*, *Li Yu quaji*, vol. 1, 95–101.
13. During the late imperial period, *jiayue* 家乐 (also known as *jiaban* 家班) or family theater troupe was usually maintained by a rich person to perform and entertain for his private enjoyment. However, in Li Yu's case, his family theater troupe also performed in private for other rich people for the sake of deriving income in various forms. Consequently, their performances were semi-public. See Huang Guoquan, *Yasu zhi jian: Li Yu de wenhua renge yu wenxue sixiang yanji*, 52–60.
14. "Qiao Fusheng Wang Zailai erji hezhuan," 98.
15. "Qiao Fusheng Wang Zailai erji hezhuan," 100.
16. For an account of Li Yu's family members (his wife and numerous concubines), see Shen Xinlin, *Li Yu xinlun*, 69–81.
17. "Qiao Fusheng Wang Zailai erji hezhuan," 100–101.
18. For a study of Li Yu's writings in terms of his obsession with self-invention and his witty style, see Patrick Hanan, *The Invention of Li Yu*. Hanan observes that "His gift, in both talking and writing, was less narrative than discursive; he was the exponent of witty, cogent, unorthodox opinion rather than a raconteur" (p. 41).
19. "Hou Duanchang shi shishou" 後斷腸詩十首, *Liweng yijia yan shici ji*, *Li Yu quanji*, vol. 2, 216.
20. "Wangji Dong Xiaowan aici," Wu Dingzhong, *Dong Xiaowan huikao*, 47. Unlike remembering a late wife, a literati husband, in writing about his late concubine, was usually more likely to acknowledge her physical attractiveness, validating the impression that physical appeal was understood to play a much more conspicuous role in a polygamous husband's relationship with his concubine. Chen Shangjun notes that unlike the epitaphs on their wives, which tended to emphasize moral virtues, these Tang grieving authors were much more likely to refer to the physical appeal of their deceased concubines in their epitaphs, "Tangdai de wangqi yu wangqie muzhi," 54. This is probably one of the reasons Mao Xiang was so adamant that his love for his concubine was based on her virtue rather than her sex appeal.
21. Cf. Paul Rouzer's discussion of this work by Song Yu in his *Articulated Ladies: Gender and Male Community in Early Chinese Texts*, 53–58.
22. "Qiao Fusheng Wang Zailai erji hezhuan," 97.
23. See Chen Hongxu, "*Yingmei an yiyu* tici," Mao Xiang, *Tongren ji*, 3.54b.

24. Mao Xiang, *Yingmei an yiyu*, reprinted in Li Baomin, et al., ed., *Ming Qing yuqing xiaopin xiezhen*, 581.
25. *Yingmei an yiyu*, 581.
26. *Yingmei an yiyu*, 584.
27. *Yingmei an yiyu*, 589.
28. "Maoji Dong Xiaowan zhuan" 冒姬董小婉傳, Mao Xiang, *Tongren ji*, 3.44b.
29. *Yingmei an yiyu*, 591.
30. Mao Xiang continued to take other concubines after Dong's death. For a brief account of Mao Xiang's other concubines, see Wu Dingzhong, *Dong Xiaowan huikao*, 78.
31. "Ji laoqi Su ruren wen" 祭老妻蘇孺人文, *Chaomin wenji*, 7.25a–7.36b.
32. "Wangshi Zhou furen shilüe" 亡室周夫人事略 and "Wangji Xie shuren shilüe," 亡姬謝淑人事略, *Erzhi xuan wencun*, 30.24b–3026a and 30.26b–30.30a.
33. "Wangji Xie shuren shilüe," 30.30a; for the origin of the last phrase, see Wang Mengou, "Tangong shang" 檀弓上, *Liji jinzhu jinyi*, 92.
34. This reminds people of Chen Wenshu's relationship with his concubine Guan Yun 管筠. According to Chen's biography of his late wife, Guan Yun assumed the responsibility of running the household after his wife became sick and an alcoholic, as discussed in chapter 4. By skillfully managing various properties, Guan was instrumental in helping Chen return the large debts he incurred; see Chen Wenshu, "Xianshi Gong yiren zhuan," *Yidao tang wenchao*, appendix to *juan* 13, 4b–5a. For many years, Guan Yun was de facto mistress of the household. Chen's relationship with Guan was quite equal, as he demonstrated great respect for her intellectual ability since they shared a common strong interest in Buddhism and Daoism and especially since she sometimes appeared to have shown a better understanding of the issue of religious transcendence. In her preface to a work Chen compiled, Guan Yun even teasingly advised her husband against publishing too much of his own writing and suggested that most of his writing should be burned instead, mocking his worldly attachment. "Xu" 敘, *Xiling xianyong* 西泠仙詠, 3.4a. Chen Wenshu and his concubine Guan Yun sometimes did appear to be comrades in their common pursuit of religious transcendence. In fact, Chen revealed that he planned to conduct a formal ceremony to formally promote Guan Yun to be his formal wife, Chen Wenshu "Xiaohui Wang yiren zhuan," Wang Duan, *Zirang haoxue zhai shichao*, 314–315.

Chapter 7

1. The modern reprint of *Wumeng tang ji* published in 1998 is a book of more than eight hundred thousand Chinese characters. Of course, this reprint also includes other works not collected in the earlier editions of *Wu Mengtang ji* published by Ye Shaoyuan.
2. "Fuji," *Fansheng xiang* 返生香, in Ye Shaoyuan, *Wumeng tang ji*, 378–381.
3. For a historical study of the general practice of *jiju* in traditional China, see Zhang Minghua and Li Xiaoli, *Jiju shi shanbian yanjiu*.
4. See, for example, Wang Xuling 王頊齡 (1642–1721), "Daowang ji Tang wushi shou" 悼亡集唐五十首, *Shi'en tang shiji*, 10. 9b–10.21b.
5. "Wangji Dong Xiaowan aici," Wu Dingzhong, *Dong Xiaowan huikao*, 47.
6. "Daowang shi sanshi wu shou" (Ku Zhang yiren zuo) 悼亡詩三十五首（哭張宜人作）, "Daowang shi shi'er shou" (Ku Chen ruren ji nü Gong zuo) 悼亡詩十二首（哭陳孺人

及女宮作）, "Daowang shi ku Zhang ruren shi'er shou" 悼亡詩哭張孺人十二首, *Wang Shizhen quanji*, 866–870, 1109–1110, and 1302–1304.

7. "Gaofeng yiren xianshi Zhangshi xingshu" 誥封宜人先室張氏行述, "Wangshi Chen ruren xingshi" 亡室陳孺人行述, "Wangshi Zhang ruren xingshi" 亡室張孺人行述, *Wang Shizhen quanji*, 1690–1695, 1900–1902, and 2275–2277.
8. "Ai Huajiang shi baishou ba" 哀華姜詩百首跋, *Wengshan wenwai*, 翁山文外, *juan* 9, *Qu Dajun quanji*, vol. 3, 173.
9. "Qushi zupu" 屈氏族譜, "Fulu san" 附錄三, *Qu Dajun quanji*, vol. 8, 2115.
10. "Fengmu ru Longzhou binan yu congdi yinqin Linshi guan youfu" 奉母入瀧州避難寓從弟姻親林氏館有賦, *Wengshan shiwai*, 翁山詩外, *juan* 5, *Qu Dajun quanji*, vol. 1, 218. This poem was probably written in 1663, when the Manchu government forced many residents along the coast of southern China to move 50 *li* inland in order to separate them from the anti-Manchu forces stationed in Taiwan. See Chen Yongzhen, *Qu Dajun shici biannian jianzhu*, 162. See also Wu Qingye, *Qu Dajun nianpu*, 10–11.
11. See Zhang Jie, *Zhongguo gudai tongxin lian tukao*, 491–521; for relevant studies in English, see Marjorie Topley, "Marriage Resistance in Rural Kwangtung" and Janice Stockard, *Daughters of the Canton Delta*.
12. This was corroborated by Qu's friend Mao Qiling in a preface to his condolence poem to him on the death of Wang Huajiang, when Mao described Qu as "never wanting to get married" (jueyi hun 絕意婚), "Wei Qusheng daowang" 為屈生悼亡, "Touzeng ji" 投贈集 "Fulu er" 附錄二, *Qu Dajun quanji*, vol. 8, 2047.
13. Wang Fupeng, *Lingnan san da jia yanjiu*, 61–62.
14. "Fen *Daoli ji* guwen" 焚悼儷集古文, *Wengshan wenwai*, *juan* 13, *Qu Dajun quanji*, vol. 3, 220–221. This book is apparently no longer extant.
15. In fact, Qu Dajun's celebratory rhetoric of the immortalizing power of the elegiac writings of a grieving husband had become quite common by that time. It was also employed by one of Mao Xiang's friends to praise his memorial writing on his concubine. That friend wondered how lucky Dong Xiaowan must have been as a woman since she attained eternal fame by becoming the subject of her husband's long elegiac memoir. Chen Hongxu 陳弘緒 (1597–1665), "*Yingmei an yiyu* tici" 影梅庵憶語題詞, Mao Xiang, *Tongren ji*, 3.54b.
16. For the *daowang* poems he wrote for his other concubines, see, for example, the fifteen poems grouped under the titles "Ai Liangshi Wenji" 哀梁氏文姞 and "Dao Liangshi Wenji" 悼梁氏文姞, *Wengshan shiwai*, *juan* 8, *Qu Dajuan quanji*, vol. 1, 669–670 and 675–676. For various epitaphs on his wives and concubines he composed, see "Wangshi furen muzhiming" 王氏夫人墓誌銘 "Huajiang yiji zhongzhi ming" 華姜衣笄冢誌銘 Wangying Chenshi muzhiming" 亡媵陳氏墓誌銘 in *Wengshan wenwai*, *juan* 8, "Wangqie Liangshi kuangzhiming" 亡妾梁氏壙誌銘 in *Wengshan wenchao* 翁山文鈔, *juan* 5, and "Qumen si shuoren muzhiming" 屈門四碩人墓誌銘 in *Wengshan yiwen* 翁山佚文, *Qu Dajun quanji*, vol. 3, 149–152, 376–377, 474.
17. "Jishi Lishi ruren xinglüe" 繼室黎氏孺人行略, *Wengshan wenwai*, *juan* 3, *Qu Dajun quanji*, vol. 3, 116.
18. "Qumen si shuoren muzhiming," *Wengshan yiwen* 翁山佚文, *Qu Dajun quanji*, vol. 3, 474.
19. "Wang Huajiang aici" 王華姜哀辭 and "Huajiang muzhiming" 華姜墓誌銘, *Dulu tang ji*, 104–106 and 777–779. It is interesting that in the titles of these two works, Chen

identified her by her own name rather than as the wife of Qu Dajun. Chen's long poem is presented in the voice of Wang Huajiang, who is directly addressing Qu Dajun, an ingenious "mourning" poem.

20. "Ai Chen gongren shi xu" 哀陳恭人詩序, *Wengshan wenwai, juan 2, Qu Dajun quanji*, vol. 3, 74.
21. Hu Yu, *Daowang shi shi*, 235; see also the relevant poems collected in "Touzeng ji" 投贈集, Fulu er 附錄二, *Qu Dajun quanji*, vol. 8, 2022, 2030, 2041–2042, 2047, and 2075.
22. For example, one of his friends, Huang Sheng, in the foreword to his endorsement poems mentioned that he wrote the poems after receiving the book; see Zhu Zejie, "Sanzhong tiyong lei Qingshi zongji yizhu xuba jikao," 76–80 (esp. 77).
23. "Yingmei an daowang tiyong" 影梅庵悼亡題詠, *Tongren ji*, 6.12a–31b; see also various prefaces or postscripts by different people reprinted in the same book, 3.54a–3.55b and 3.57a–3.59b.
24. You Tong, "Ti Wang Yuanting shidu daowang shi hou sanshou," *Yujing ji* 于京集, 1.9a–b, *Xitang shiji*; Wang Shizhen, "Wei You Chan daowang sanshou," *Wang Shizhen quanji*, 897.
25. See "Youmu Cao ruren lei" 尤母曹孺人誄 in honor of You Tong's deceased wife written by Chen Weisong (*Chen Jialing liti wenxi* 陳迦陵儷體文集, 10.23a–10.26a, in *Chen Jialing wenji*]) and "Chen ruren lei" 陳孺人誄, the elegiac essay on Chen Weisong's deceased wife composed by You Tong one year later (*Xitang zazu sanji*, 8.7b–8.9b; in *Xitang wenji*).
26. "Qizhong zaiji wangshi wen" 七終再祭亡室文, *Xitang zazu sanji*, 8.21a
27. Pan Lei, "You shijiang Genzhai zhuan" 尤侍講艮齋傳, *Suichu tang wenji*, 18.6b.
28. "Ye Jingshu daowang shi xue" 葉井叔悼亡詩序 *Xitang zaju sanji*, 4.10b–4.11a.
29. "Manshu zangming," *Xihe ji*, 96.2a–96.3a.
30. "Manshu biezhi shuzhuan," *Xihe ji*, 96.3b–96.11a.
31. "Manshu huisheng ji," *Xihe ji*, 67.18a–67.20b.
32. "Ji Manshu jinfang dixia shu," *Xihe ji*, 17.15b–17.17a.
33. "Manshu biezhi shuzhuan," *Xihe ji*, 96.7a.
34. "Manshu zangming," *Xihe ji*, 96.1b–96.3a
35. See Ellen Widmer, "Xiaoqing's Literary Legacy and the Place of the Woman Writer in Late Imperial China."
36. "Manshu biezhi shuzhuan" is anthologized and reprinted in Zhang Chao, comp. *Yuchu xinzhi, juan* 13; "Manshu zangming" and "Manshu huisheng ji" are collected in Zheng Shuruo 鄭澍若, comp. *Yuchu xuzhi, juan* 1; see He Yuchun, comp. *Shuohai*, 535–540 and 734–737. Note Zhang Chao's comment on "Manshu biezhi shuzhuan" that once he also wrote a set of fifty poems to mourn the death of his wife, and many of his friends also contributed endorsing poems (540). Apparently such *daowang* networking practice was quite common among the literati at that time. Here "fiction," the word often used to translate the Chinese term *xiaoshuo* could be misleading because fictionality is not a hallmark of traditional Chinese *xiaoshuo*, which was instead often defined by its "unofficial" nature in comparison with the official histories produced by the imperial government. Consequently, many traditional *xiaoshuo* works were not necessarily produced as "fictional" but rather as works dealing with those topics or issues usually not considered very important by the Confucian historians and thus ignored in official histories. *Xiaoshuo* often was characterized by its "anecdotal" and "strange" nature. As the

term itself suggests, *xiaoshuo* (small talk) was a minor discourse, supplementary to official histories.
37. "Manshu biezhi shuzhuan," 96.10b.
38. For a brief discussion of this form of commentary and annotation as practiced by fiction commentators in premodern China, see David Rolston, ed., *How to Read the Chinese Novel*, 54–55.
39. "Manshu biezhi shuzhuan," *Xihe ji*, 96.6b–96.7a.
40. "Manshu biezhi shuzhuan," *Xihe ji*, 96.10b.
41. The original manuscript copy of this album containing the portrait and all the colophons as well as Mao Qiling's own handwritten elegiac writings dedicated to Manshu was found in Japan in the early twentieth century. Later, in 1930, a facsimile reprinted edition of the album was published in Shanghai. See Zhang Jusheng's 張菊生 postscript to this facsimile edition at the end of the book, Mao Qiling, *Manshu liuying (fu mingzhuan bing mingren tiba)*.
42. For a general study of this literati networking phenomenon during the late imperial period, see Mao Wenfang, *Tucheng xingle: Ming Qing wenren huaxiang tiyong xilun*.
43. Cf. Sophie Volpp, "Literary Consumption of Actors in Seventeenth-Century China."
44. Mao Qiling's contemporary, the well-known poet Fang Wen 方文 (1612–1669), was another one of those who tried to turn the death of his concubine into a public event of literati social networking. According to Fang Wen, after his principal wife, Zuoshi, suddenly died of a stroke, his in-laws began to take over their properties and even killed his concubine, Jinyuan, who was pregnant at that time, wrongly accusing her of having a hand in the death of Zuoshi. See Fang Wen's long narrative poem, "Shu'ai" 述哀, *Fang Tushan shiji*, juan 2, 69–72. Later Fang Wen had a portrait painted of the concubine and titled it "Baoyuan tu" 抱鴛圖 (literally, a portrait of someone holding in arms a mandarin duck), probably a double entendre referring to the name of his deceased concubine, Jinyuan 金鴛, and the phrase *baoyuan* 抱冤 (being seriously wronged). He began to solicit colophons for the portrait from many of his peers and friends, and it became quite a social event among the literati elite at that time. See Li Shenghua, *Fang Wen nianpu*, 272–274 and, for some of the colophons on the portrait contributed by these friends, refer to Li Shenghua, 526, 529–530, 537, 541–542.
45. *Xiangwan lou yiyu*, *Xiangyan xiaolu*, in Li Baomin, et al., *Ming Qing yuqing xiaopin xiezhen*, 1114.
46. See the respective accounts in *Xiangwan lou yiyu*, 1115 and *Yingmei an yiyu*, 587.
47. *Xiangwan lou yiyu*, 1124.
48. Ruxiang jushi 閏湘居士, "Xu," Chen Peizhi, *Xiangyan xiaolu*, in Li Baomin, et al., ed., *Ming Qing yuqing xiaopin xiezhen*, 1105; see also Ma Lütai's 馬履泰 preface, 1104, in which he compared Chen Peizhi and Wang Zixiang to Mao Xiang and Dong Xiaowan.
49. *Xiangwan lou yiyu*, 1119.
50. *Xiangwan lou yiyu*, 1125.
51. *Xiangwan lou yiyu* 1121.
52. *Xiangyan xiaolu*, Li Baomin, *Ming Qing yuqing xiaopin xiezhen*, 1107–1112.
53. *Xiangyan xiaolu*, in Chongtianzi, comp. *Zhongguo Xiangyan quanshu*, vol. 3, 1454; I am referring to this particular edition of *Xiangyan xiaolu* because these *jiju* poems are not reprinted in the edition in Li Baomin, *Ming Qing yuqing xiaopin xiezhen*.

54. Wang Xuling, "Daowang ji Tang wushi shou," *Shi'en tang shiji*, 10.8b–10.22b. See also note 49, chapter 1.
55. In the twentieth-century writer Qian Zhongshu's well-known novel *Weicheng* 圍城 (The City Besieged), the narrator satirizes one of the characters as a *wenren* thrilled at the opportunity occasioned by the death of his first wife because now he could write various kinds of elegies to showcase his literary talents. Qian Zhongshu, *Weicheng*, 234.

Chapter 8

1. Of course, some brothers might deliberately play down the significance of the sibling relationships between themselves and their deceased sisters when they wrote about them. The Ming writer Tu Long 屠隆 (1552–1605), for example, in his biography of his deceased sister, written at the request of his nephews, only began to briefly acknowledge at the end of the biography that the biographical subject was his sister, as if it had been an after-thought. She was presented as a member of her husband's family only, whereas her natal family was hardly mentioned. "Li ruren zhuan" 李孺人傳, *Tu Changqin wenji* 屠長卿文集, *juan* 4, in *Tu Long ji*, vol. 1, 255.
2. "Wangmei taixuesheng Zhang Yuling fu ruren Wangshi muzhiming" 亡妹太學生張與齡婦孺人王氏墓誌銘, *Yanzhou sibu gao*, 93.8a.
3. "Wangmei taixuesheng Zhang Yuling fu ruren Wangshi muzhimig," 93.8b.
4. "Ku wangmei Wangshi wen" 哭亡妹王氏文, *Yanzhou sibu gao*, 105.20a.
5. "Ku wangmei Wangshi wen," *Yanzhou sibu gao*, 105.18a.
6. The brother-to-brother relationship was one of the so-called "five cardinal human relationships" (*wulun* 五倫) and is an important topic in many collections of household instructions (*jiaxun* 家訓) produced in imperial China; for a brief discussion, see Wang Changjin, *Chuantong jiaxun sixiang tonglun*, 115–120.
7. "Fangshi zi muzhiming" 方氏姊墓誌銘, *Tianjian wenji*, 447.
8. "Fangshi zi muzhiming," *Tianjian wenji*, 447.
9. "Xianmu Pang anren xinglüe" 先母龐安人行略, *Tianjian wenji*, 29.554–29.556.
10. "Xianmu Pang anren xinglüe," 29.555.
11. "Fangshi zi muzhiming," 447.
12. "Fangshi zi muzhiming," 446.
13. "Fangshi zi muzhiming," 446.
14. "Fangshi zi muzhiming," 448.
15. "Fangshi zi muzhiming," 447.
16. "Fangshi zi muzhiming," 448.
17. "Fangshi zi muzhiming," 448–449.
18. In fact, compared with his biographical sketch of his own wife, which I have discussed in detail in chapter 3, Qian Chengzhi, in this epitaph on his elder sister, showed more emotion. Perhaps this is because he wrote the biographical sketch for a future hagiographer to present his late wife as chastity martyr while here he was just writing about an ordinary woman rather than a Confucian saint. Another possible contributing factor is that he wrote this epitaph not too long after the death of his sister, while the pains of loss was still fresh, whereas his biographical sketch of his late wife was composed several decades after her death, a result of the difference between the acts of mourning and commemorating.

19. "Wangzi Sun ruren muzhiming," *Wenjian ji*, 57.16b–57.18a.
20. "Wangmei Yanshi ruren hezangzhi" 亡妹嚴氏孺人合葬誌, *Chuxue ji* 初學集, *Qian Muzhai quanji*, vol. 3, 1646.
21. Cf. the early Qing scholar Zhao Yi, "Bei biao zhi ming zhibie" 碑表志銘之別, *Gaiyu congkao, juan* 32, 655.
22. For a much broader discussion of the close relationship between a married woman and her natal family in the latter half of the long imperial period, see Beverly Bossler, "A Daughter is a Daughter All Her Life": Affinal Relations and Women's Networks in Song and Late Imperial China," 77–106.
23. "Shen shi gu sheng kuangming" 沈氏姑生壙銘, *Fang Bao ji*, 485.
24. "Baoshi zi aici" 鮑氏姊哀辭, *Fang Bao ji*, 498–499.
25. "Xie Jifang zhuan," *Fang Bao ji*, 501–502.
26. "Shu Zhili Xinan Zhang liefu Jingshi xingshi zhuang" 書直隸新安張烈婦荊氏行實狀, *Fang Bao ji*, 129.
27. "Nüdi Suwen zhuan" 女弟素文傳, *Xiaocangshanfang wenji* 小倉山房文集, *juan* 7, *Yuan Mei quanji*, vol. 2, 133.
28. "Nüdi Suwen zhuan," 133.
29. "Ji mei wen," *Xiaochangshanfang wenji," juan* 10, *Yuan Mei quanji*, vol. 2, 229.
30. It is interesting to note that although compared with his peers Yuan Mei was not particularly enthusiastic about the idea of female chastity. He nevertheless authored quite a few epitaphs praising chaste widows; see, for example, "Yang jiefu muzhiming" 楊節婦墓誌銘 and "Yuanmu Han ruren muzhiming" 袁母韓孺人墓誌銘, *Yuan Mei quanji*, vol. 2, 100–101 and 458–459. Of course, most of these were written at the requests of others, an act of social obligation.
31. "Ji mei wen," 229.
32. "Ji mei wen," 230.

Epilogue

1. Wang Duan, "Mengyu sheng shilüe," appended to Chen Peizhi, *Chenghuai tang shiji*.
2. In premodern China, in contrast to men, women produced relatively few biographies. As discussed in the preceding chapters, biographical sketch was one of the favorite elegiac genres many grieving literati husbands turned to when they mourned their deceased spouses. On the other hand, women usually turned to the more private genre, poetry, to remember their deceased husbands, although the extant number of women-authored *daowang* poems from that period is not large. Wilt Idema provides a brief general review of women's elegiac writings in premodern China in his article "The Biographical and the Autobiographical in Bo Shaojun's One Hundred Poems Lamenting My Husband," 230–233. At the end of this article (244–245) he also briefly discusses the biographical writings authored by late imperial women, pointing out how rarely they wrote biographies of men. The Song poetess Li Qingzhao's (1085–1115) "*Jinshi lu* houxu" 金石錄後序 (A Postscript to *Records on Metal and Stone*) is one of the better-known memoir-like essays on a husband authored by a woman during the premodern period (it is primarily recollections of the collecting activities she and her deceased husband pursued together), even though strictly speaking it is not an elegiac work since it is in the form of a postscript

to a book. For a discussion of this work, see Stephen Owen, *Remembrances*, 80–98, and for an English translation of this essay, see Idema and Grant, *The Red Brush*, 207–214. The Late Ming poetess, Shen Yixiu, Ye Shaoyuan's wife, authored two interesting biographies to respectively mourn her daughter and her cousin. One characteristic shared by the two biographies is the attention the biographer gave to the appearances of her biographical subjects and her admiration of their physical charms. See Shen Yixiu, "Jinü Qiongzhang zhuan" 季女瓊章傳 and "Biaomei Zhang Qianqian zhuan" 表妹張倩倩傳, *Lichui*, in Ye Shaoyuan, *Wumeng tang ji*, 201–207.

3. One of the more common forms of elegiac writings women turned to was *jiwen* (sacrificial litany). See, for example, Liu Lingxian's 劉令嫻 (ca. 525) "Ji fu Xu Fei wen" 祭夫徐斐文 (In Memory of My Husband Xu Fei). For the Chinese texts of Liu's litany as well as other *jiwen* works authored by Ming women (including quite a few dedicated to their deceased husbands), see Jiang Yuanxi 江元禧, comp., *Yutai wenyuan* 玉臺文苑, 8.21a–8.28a and Jiang Yuanzuo 江元祚, comp., *Xu Yutai wenyuan* 續玉臺文苑, 4.22a–4.36b. For an English translation of Liu Lingxian's litany, see Idema and Grant, *The Red Brush*, 151–152.

4. Xu Shangzhi, "Chen Xiaoyun sima zhuan" 陳小雲司馬傳, 23a. Xu's biography, like Wang Duan's "Mengyu sheng shilüe," was appended to this same edition of *Chenghuai tang shiji*. Since Xu must have known Chen very well as his close friend, it was likely that his biography was not based on Wang Duan's biographical sketch. This was probably why both pieces were appended to Chen's collection of poems.

5. "Mengyu sheng shilüe," 38b–39a.

6. In classical Chinese, *jun* is a personal pronoun of respect. It can be translated as the second-person pronoun "you" or a third-person pronoun "he" or "she," depending on the context. With the knowledge that the biographer Wang Duan was Chen Peizhi's wife, the reader might have the impression that she is addressing Chen directly as "you" by virtue of the use of *jun*, as in a sacrificial litany when the author typically addresses directly the deceased with this same term (for example, in Zhu Bangxian's litany in honor of his second wife, discussed in chapter 2). However, the generic convention of biography dictates that "*jun*" be read as a third-person pronoun. *Jun* is also used as a third-person pronoun to refer to Chen Peizhi in Xu Shangzhi's "Chen Xiaoyun sima zhuan." By the same token, in Wang Duan's biographical sketch of Chen here, *jun* must be read as the third-person pronoun "he" despite the possible ambiguity as a result of the conjugal relationship between the biographer and her biographical subject.

7. This is consistent with Wang Duan's intention to avoid presenting herself as the wife of her biographical subject in the context of the overall rhetoric of this biographical sketch. This enabled her to avoid the need to use the more common first-person pronouns such as *yu* 余 or the feminine first-person pronoun *qie* 妾 (the self-deprecating first-person pronoun a woman was supposed to use to refer to herself).

8. "Mengyu sheng shilüe," 24b.

9. "Mengyu sheng shilüe," 35b.

10. Wang Duan was much more emotional elsewhere in describing her reactions to the death of her husband. In a note to the four poems dedicated to him on the occasion of the publication of his collected poems, she was more forthcoming in describing the impact of his death on her: "In the early spring of 1826 I received the shocking news of the death of my husband. I cried so much that my bloody tears were exhausted. I was

barely alive. I stopped composing poetry for almost a year. During the mid-spring of 1827, while still sick, I compiled the final draft of the *Chenghuai tang shiwen quankao*. With spring rain falling outside and tears in my eyes, deeply moved, I respectfully composed these four poems to express my sad feelings and did not really care whether these poems were written properly. "Ti *Chenghuai tang yiji* hou" 題澄懷堂遺集後, *Ziran haoxue zhai shichao*, 444.

11. Xu Shangzhi, "Chen Xiaoyun sima zhuan," 23b–24a and Chen Wenshu, "Peizhi shilüe," *Yidao tang wenchao*, 13.23b–13.24. Note Xu Shangzhi's biography is also reprinted together with the former's "Peizhi shilüe" as its appendix in Chen Wenshu, *Yidao tang wenchao*, 13.28a–13.34b.
12. It is said that whenever Wang Yuan had poetic inspiration during the middle of the night, his wife would light the candle and prepare the ink for him. See the biographical note provided in Zhong Xing 鍾惺 (1574–1624), comp. *Mingyuan shigui*, 22.1a.
13. "Mengyu sheng shilüe," 25a.
14. "Mengyu sheng shilüe," 27b–28a.
15. Chen Wenshu's biography of his daughter-in-law, "Xiaohui Wang yiren zhuan," which is full of superlative praises and which I have briefly discussed in chapter 4, may provide ample justifications for such self-confidence on Wang Duan's part.
16. See, for example, the *daowang* poem by Yang Shuzhen 楊淑貞 (fl. early eighteenth century), where she as a widow swore to her deceased husband that she would never remarry; reprinted in Fu Ying, comp., *Ming Qing Anhui funü wenxue zhushu jikao*, 100.
17. "Mengyu sheng shilüe," 28b. As we have discussed in chapter 4, in his biography of his wife "Xianshi Gong yiren zhuan," Chen Wenshu points out (15b) that his wife was very tolerant of their daughter-in-law. She did not get upset even when Wang Duan did not show up to pay respects to her for more than a month.
18. Chen Wenshu, "Xiaohui Wang yiren zhuani," Wang Duan, *Zi rang haoxue zhai shichao*, 316–317.
19. "HuangQing zuizeng Taipushiqing xian Jiangxi Ji'an fu zhifu Zengjun muzhiming" 皇清追贈太僕寺卿銜江西吉安府知府曾君墓誌銘, Zuo Xijia, *Lengyin xian guan wencun* 冷吟仙館文存, in Hu Xiaoming, et al. eds, *Jiangnan nüxing bieji: erbian*, 1417–1420.
20. Such self-confidence on Wang Duan's part was also partly based on the kind of respect she had won from many others, including her own father-in-law, Chen Wenshu. Chen presented his daughter-in-law in his biography of her as his intellectual equal and sometimes even as a person of superior intellectual wisdom, from whom he often sought advice on various matters (see chapter 4).
21. The poetess and painter Fang Weiyi 方維儀 (1585–1668) authored an interesting prose essay titled "Nishi shu" 擬諡述 (A Draft Essay to Request a Posthumous Title) to commemorate her husband, who had died thirty years earlier, just one year after their marriage. It is a brief biography of her husband, focusing on the causes that contributed to his death and his dying moments. In addition, Fang authored a short autobiography titled "Weiwang ren weisheng shu" 未亡人微生述 (An Account of the Humble Life of a Widow); see Fu Ying, *Ming Qing Anhui funü wenxue zhushu jikao*, 161–162. This was quite unprecedented given that very few imperial Chinese women authored autobiographies. The term *weisheng* (humble life) in the title betrays her acute awareness that she was attempting something quite remarkable in claiming her life as a woman was

important enough to merit an autobiography, albeit a very brief one. In other words, she had to go out of her way to appear extra humble when authoring an autobiography as a woamn. According to Fang, she wrote it so that her future epitaph writer would have a record of the important facts of her life. It centers on her life as a widow, explaining the reasons she as a widow moved back to live with her natal family and never returned to her husband's family (*dagui* 大歸), something a typical Confucian widow would not easily decide to do at that time (another exception of a somewhat different nature, discussed in chapter 8, is one of Fang Bao's married sisters returning to live with her natal family even though her husband was still alive). However, the immediate justification for her to write this autobiography was to prepare for her future burial in the joint grave with her deceased husband. It is meant in part to vindicate her virtues as a widow despite her unusual decision to live with her natal family after the death of her husband. Of course, Fang Weiyi was remembered by many for her contributions to her natal family, especially in her role as the aunt who raised and tutored her nephew, the famous Ming loyalist poet and scholar, Fang Yizhi 方以智 (1611–1671). The case of Fang Weiyi once again reminds us of the importance of the natal family in the life of a married woman in late imperial China, an issue discussed in chapters 5 and 8.

22. Grace Fong, "Private Emotion, Public Commemoration: Qian Shoupu's Poems of Mourning," 30.

BIBLIOGRAPHY

An Zhiyuan 安致遠. *Jicheng wengao* 紀城文稿 (*Siku quanshu cunmu congshu* ed.).
Barr, Alan. "Marriage and Mourning in Early Qing Tributes to Wives." *Nan Nü* 15, no. 1 (2013), 137–178.
Bei Jing 貝京. *Gui Youguang yanjiu* 歸有光研究. Beijing: Shangwu yinshu guan, 2008.
Bernardt, Kathryn. *Women and Property in China: 960–1949*. Stanford, CA: Stanford University Press, 1996.
Bossler, Beverley. "A Daughter Is a Daughter All Her Life: Affinal Relations and Women's Networks in Song and Late Imperial China." *Late Imperial China* 21, no. 1 (2000), 77–106.
———. "'Concubines' in Song and Yuan Funerary Inscriptions," paper presented at the International Conference on "The Textual Analysis of Sung Mu-Chih and Its Application as Historical Evidence 宋代墓誌史料的文本分析與實証運用." Soochow University, Taipei, October 18–19, 2003.
———. *Courtesans, Concubines, and the Cult of Female Fidelity: Gender and Social Change in China, 1000–1400*. Cambridge, MA: Harvard University Asia Center, 2013.
Cai Jingping 蔡靜平. *MingQing zhiji Fenhu Yeshi wenxue shijia yanjiu* 明清之際汾湖葉氏文學世家研究. Changsha: Yuelu shushe, 2008.
Carlitz, Katherine. "Mourning, Personality, and Display: Ming Literati Commemorate Their Mothers, Sisters, and Daughters." *Nan Nü* 15, no. 1 (2013), 30–68.
———. "Advertisements for Ourselves: The Reproduction of Elite Status in 16th-Century Chinese Epitaphs," paper presented at the conference on "Lifewriting," Sheffield, England, March 2008.
Chen Chao 陳超. "Mindai nüxing beizhuangwen yu pin'guang mingfu yanjiu" 明代女性碑傳文與品官命婦研究. PhD dissertation, Dongbei shifan daxue, China, 2007.
Chen Gongyin 陳恭尹. *Dulu tang ji* 獨瀘堂集. Guangzhou: Zhongshan daxue chubanshe, 1988.
Chen Jianhua 陳建華. "WanMing wenxue de xianqu: Li Mengyang" 晚明文學的先驅—李夢陽. *Xueshu yuekan* (1986.8): 38–44 and 21.
Chen Jicong 陳繼聰. *Zhongyi jiwen lu* 忠義紀聞錄, rpt. in Zhou Junfu 周駿富, comp. *Qingdai zhuanji congkan* 清代傳記叢刊. Taipei: Mingwen shuju, 1985.
Chen Lai 陳來. "Mengxue yu shisu rujia lunli" 蒙學與世俗儒家倫理, in Chen Lai, *Zhongguo jinshi sixiang shi yanjiu* 中國近世思想史研究, 409–455. Beijing: Shangwu yinsuguan, 2003.
Chen Lancun 陳藍村 et al. *Zhongguo zhuanjiwenxue fazhanshi* 中國傳記文學發展史. Beijing: Yuwen chubanshe, 1999.

Chen Peizhi 陳裴之. *Chenghuai tang shiji* 澄懷堂詩集 (1827 ed.).
———. *Xiangwan lou yiyu* 香畹樓憶語; in *Xiangyan xiaolu* 湘煙小錄; rpt. in Li Baomin, *Ming Qing yuqing xiaopin xiezhen*, 1113–1126.
Chen Que 陳確. *Chen Que ji* 陳確集. Beijing: Zhonghua shuju, 1979.
Chen Shangjun 陳尚君. "Tangdai de wangqi yu wangqie muzhi 唐代的亡妻與亡妾墓誌." *Zhonghua wenshi luncong* 中華文史論叢 (2006), vol. 82, 43–81.
Chen Weisong 陳維崧. *Chen Jialing wenji* 陳迦陵文集 (*Sibu congkan* ed.)
Chen Wenshu 陳文殊. *Yidao tang wenchao* 頤道堂文鈔 (*Xuxiu Siku quanshu* ed.)
———, comp. *Xiling xianyong* 西泠仙詠; rpt. in Ding Bing 丁丙, comp. *Wulin zhanggu congbian* 武林掌故叢編, vol. 3. Taipei: Tailian guofeng chubanshe and Huawen shuju, 1967.
Chen Yongzhen 陳永正, comp. *Qu Dajun shici biannian jianzhu* 屈大均詩詞編年箋注. Guangzhou: Zhongshan daxue, 2000.
Chen Zi 陳梓. *Shanhou wenji* 刪後文集 (*Qingdai shiwenji huibian* ed.)
Chongtianzi 蟲天子. *Zhongguo xiangyan quanshu* 中國香艷全書. Beijing: Tuanjie chubanshe, 2005.
Chow, Kai-wing. *Publishing, Culture, and Power in Early Modern China*. Stanford, CA: Stanford University Press, 2004.
Cox, Harvey. *The Secular City: Secularization and Urbanization in Theological Perspective*. New York: Macmillan, 1966.
Dunstan, Helen. "If Chen Yun Had Written about Her 'Lesbianism': Rereading the Memoirs of a Bereaved Philanderer." *Asia Major*, 3rd series, 20.2 (2007), 103–122.
Ebrey, Patricia. *The Inner Quarters: Marriage and the Lives of Chinese Women in the Sung Period*. Berkeley: University of California Press, 1993.
Fang Bao 方苞. *Fang Bao ji* 方苞集. Shanghai: Shanghai guji chubanshe, 1983.
Fang Junyi 方浚頤. *Erzhi xuan wencun* 二知軒文存 (*Xuxiu Siku quanshu* ed.).
Fang Wen 方文. *Fang Tushan shiji* 方嵞山詩集. Hefei: Huangshan shushe, 2010.
Fang Xiangying 方象瑛. *Jiansong zhai ji* 健松齋集 (*Siku quanshu cunmu congshu* ed.)
Fei Siyan 費絲言. *You dianfan dao guifan: Cong Mingdai zhenjie lienü de bianshi yu liuchuan kan zhenjie guannian de yangehua* 由典範到規範：從明代貞節烈女的辨識與流傳看貞節觀念的嚴格化. Taipei: Taida chuban weiyuanhui, 1998.
Feng Menglong 馮夢龍. *Xingshi hengyan* 醒世恆言. Hong Kong: Zhonghua shuju, 1987.
Fong, Grace. "Signifying Bodies: The Cultural Significance of Suicide Writings by Women in Ming-Qing China." *Nan Nü* 3.1 (2003), 105–142.
———. *Herself an Author: Gender, Agency, and Writing in Late Imperial China*. Honolulu: University of Hawaii Press, 2008.
———. "Private Emotion, Public Commemoration: Qian Shoupu's Poems of Mourning," *Chinese Literature: Essays, Articles, Reviews*, vol. 30 (2008), 19–30.
———. "Writing and Illness: A Feminine Condition in Women's Poetry of the Ming and Qing," in Grace Fong and Ellen Widmer, eds. *The Inner Quarters and Beyond: Women Writers from Ming-Qing China*, 19–47.
Fong, Grace, and Widmer, Ellen, eds. *The Inner Quarters and Beyond: Women Writers from Ming-Qing China*. Leiden: Brill, 2010.
Fu Ying 傅瑛, comp. *Ming Qing Anhui funü wenxue zhushu jikao* 明清安徽婦女文學著述輯考. Hefei: Huangshan shushe, 2010.
Geng Chuanyou 耿傳友. "Yige bei wenxueshi yiwang de zuojia: Wang Cihui jiqi shige yanjiu" 一個被文學史遺忘的作家：王次回及其詩歌研究. PhD dissertation, Fudan University, 2005.

Gu Dashao 顧大韶. *Bingzhu zhai gao* 炳燭齋稿 (*Siku jinhuishu congkan* ed.)
Guan Tong 管同. *Yinji xuan wen chuji* 因寄軒文初集 (*Xuxiu Siku quanshu* ed.).
Guan Ying 關瑛. *Sanshi liu furong guan shicun* 三十六芙蓉館詩存. In Hu Xiaoming, et al. eds, *Jiangnan nüxing bieji sibian*, 1453–1502.
Gui Youguan 歸有光. *Zhenchuan xiansheng ji* 震川先生集. Shanghai: Shanghai guji chubanshe, 2007.
He Xiazheng 賀夏征. *Wenzhang bianti huixuan* 文章辨體彙選 (*Siku quanshu* ed.)
He Yuchun 何愈春, comp. *Shuohai* 說海. Beijing: Remin ribao chubanshe, 1997.
Hou Hanshu 後漢書. Taipei: Dingwen shuju, 1981.
Hu Xiaoming 胡曉明, et al., eds. *Jiangnan nüxing bieji erbian* 江南女性別集二編. Hefei: Huangshan shushe, 2010.
———. *Jiangnan nüxing bieji sibian* 江南女性別集四編. Hefei: Huangshan shushe, 2014.
Hu Xu 胡旭. *Daowang shi shi* 悼亡詩史. Beijing: Dongfang chuban zhongxin, 2010.
Huang Guoquan 黃果泉. *Yasu zhi jian: Li Yu de wenhua renge yu wenxue sixiang yanjiu* 雅俗之間：李漁的文化人格與文學思想研究. Beijing: Zhongguo shehui kexue, 2004.
Huang Jingren 黃景仁. *Liangdang xuan ji* 兩當軒集. Shanghai: Shanghai guji chubanshe, 1983.
Huang, Martin. *Desire and Fictional Narrative in Late Imperial China*. Cambridge, MA: Harvard University Asia Center, 2001.
———. *Negotiating Masculinities in Late Imperial China*. Honolulu: University of Hawaii Press, 2006.
———. "Male Friendship and *Jiangxue* (Philosophical Debates) in Sixteenth-Century China" *Nan Nü* 9.1 (2007), 146–178.
Huang Zongxi 黃宗羲. *Huang Zongxi quanji* 黃宗羲全集. Hangzhou: Zhejiang guji chubanshe, 2005.
Huangfu Fang 皇甫汸. *Huangfu sixun ji* 皇甫司勳集 (*Siku quanshu* ed.)
Huntington, Rania. "Memory, Mourning and Genre in the Works of Yu Yue." *Harvard Journal of Asiatic Studies*, 67.2 (Dec. 2007), 253–293
Idema, Wilt. "The Biographical and the Autobiographical in Bo Shaojun's 'One Hundred Poems Lamenting My Husband.'" Joan Judge and Hu Ying, eds. *Beyond Exemplar Tales: Women's Biography in Chinese History*, 230–245.
Idema, Wilt, and Grant, Beata. *The Red Brush: Writing Women of Imperial China*. Cambridge, MA: Harvard University Asia Center, 2004.
Jiang Yin 蔣寅. "Daowang shige xiezuo fanshi de yanjin" 悼亡詩歌寫作範式的演進. *Anhui daxue xuebao* 安徽大學學報3 (2011), 1–10.
Jiang Tan 蔣坦. *Choulan ji* 愁鸞集, rpt. in appendixes to Guan Ying, *Sanshi liu furong guan shicun*, in Hu Xiaoming, et al., eds., *Jiangnan nüxing bieji, sibian*, 1508–1518.
———. *Qiudeng suoyi* 秋燈瑣憶, rpt. in appendixes to Guan Ying, *Sanshi liu furong guan shicun*, in Hu Xiaoming, et al., eds., *Jiangnan nüxing bieji, sibian*, 1519–1530.
Jiang Yuanxi 江元禧, comp., *Yutai wenyuan* 玉臺文苑 (*Siku quanshu cunmu congshu* ed.)
Jiang Yuanzuo 江元祚, comp. *Xu Yutai wenyuan* 續玉臺文苑 (*Siku quanshu cunmu congshu* ed.)
Jin Huihan 金蕙涵. "Qing yu de: lun Mingdai jiangnan diqu de ceshi hezang mu" 情與德：論明代江南地區的側室合葬墓. *Guoli Zhengzhi daxue lishi xue bao* 國立政治大學歷史學報. 37 (2012), 1–42.
Jin Zhaoyan 金兆燕. *Zongting guwen chao* 棕亭古文鈔 (*Xuxiu Siku quanshu* ed.)

Judge, Joan, and Hu, Ying, eds. *Beyond Exemplar Tales: Women's Biography in Chinese History*. Berkeley: University of California Press, 2011.
Katkov, Neil Ennis. "The Domestication of Concubinage in Imperial China." PhD dissertation, Harvard University, 1997.
Ko, Dorothy. *The Teachers of the Inner Chambers: Women and Culture in Seventeenth-Century China*. Stanford, CA: Stanford University Press, 1994.
Lai Zhide 來知德. *Zhouyi jizhu* 周易集注 (*Siku quanshu* ed.)
Legge, James, trans. *The She King*. *The Chinese Classics*, vol. 4. Hong Kong: Hong Kong University Press, 1960.
———, trans. *Li Chi: Book of Rites*. New York: University Books, 1967.
Li Baomin 李保民 et al., eds. *Ming Qing yuqing xiaopin xiezhen* 明清娛清小品擷珍. Shanghai: Xuelin chubanshe, 1999.
Li Chengzhong 李澄中. *Baiyunchun wenji* 白雲春文集 (*Siku quanshu cunmu congshu* ed).
Li Huiqun 李匯群. *Guige yu huafang: Qingdai Jiaqing Daoguang nianjian de Jiang'nan wenren he nüxing yanjiu* 閨閣與畫舫：清代嘉慶道光年間的江南文人和女性研究. Beijing: Zhongguo chuanmei daxue chubanshe, 2009.
———. "*Qiudeng suoyi* xinkao" 秋燈瑣憶新考 *Dianji yu wenhua* 典籍與文化 (2005.1), 47–48.
Li Kaixian 李開先. *Li Kaixian quanji* 李開先全集. Beijing: Wenhua yishu chubanshe, 2006.
Li Le 李樂. *Jianwen zaji* 見聞雜記. Shanghai: Shanghai guji chubanshe, 1986.
Li Mengyang 李夢陽. *Kongtong ji* 空同集 (*Siku quanshu* ed.)
Li Panlong 李攀龍. *Cangming xiansheng ji* 滄溟先生集. Shanghai: Shanghai guji chubanse, 1992.
Li Shenghua 李聖華. *Fang Wen nianpu* 方文年譜. Beijing: Renmin wenxue chubanshe, 2007.
Li Yu 李漁. *Li Yu quanji* 李漁全集. Hangzhou: Zhejiang guji chubanshe, 1992.
Liu Zongzhou 劉宗周. *Liu Zongzhou quanji* 劉宗周全集. Hangzhou: Zhejiang guji chubanshe, 2007.
Long Qirui 龍啟瑞. *Long Qirui shiwen ji jiaojian* 龍啟瑞詩文集校箋, anno. & comp. Lü Bin 呂斌. Changsha: Yuelu shushe, 2008.
Lu, Weijing. *True to Her Word: The Faithful Maiden Cult in Late Imperial China*. Stanford, CA: Stanford University Press, 2008.
———. "Personal Writings on Female Relatives in the Qing Collected Works." In Clara Wing-chung Ho, ed., *Overt and Covert Treasures: Essays on the Sources for Chinese Women's History*, 403–426. Hong Kong: Chinese University Press, 2012.
Lü Kun 呂坤. *Lü Kun quanji* 呂坤全集. Beijing: Zhonghua shuju, 2010.
Luo Hongxian 羅洪先. *Luo Hongxian ji* 羅洪先集. Nanjing: Fenghuang chubanshe, 2007.
Mann, Susan. *Precious Records: Women in China's Long Eighteenth Century*. Stanford, CA: Stanford University Press, 1997.
———. "The Virtue of Travel for Women in the Late Empire." Bryna Goodman and Wendy Larson, eds. *Gender in Motion: Divisions of Labor and Cultural Change in Late Imperial and Modern China*, 55–74. Lanham, MD: Rowman & Littlefield Publications Inc., 2005.
———. *The Talented Women of the Zhang Family*. Berkeley: University of California Press, 2007.
Mao Jike 毛際可. *Anxu tang wenchao* 安序堂文鈔 (*Siku quanshu cunum congshu* ed.)
———. *Huihou xiansheng wenchao* 會侯先生文鈔 (*Siku quanshu cunmu congshu* ed.)
Mao Qiling 毛奇齡. *Xihe ji* 西河集 (*Siku quanshu* ed.)

———. *Manshu liuying (fu ming zhuan bing mingren tiba)* 曼殊留影 (附銘傳并名人題跋). Shanghai: Shangwu yinshu guan, 1930.
Mao Wenfang 毛文芳. *Tucheng xingle: Ming Qing wenren huaxiang tiyong xilun* 圖成行樂：明清文人畫像題詠析論. Taipei: Xuesheng shuju, 2008.
Mao Xiang 冒襄. *Chaomin wenji* 巢民文集 (*Xuxiu Siku quanshu* ed.)
———. *Yingmei an yiyu* 影梅庵憶語; rpt. in Li Baomin, et. al ed. *Ming Qing yuqing xiaopin xiezhen*, 575–592.
———, comp. *Tongren ji* 同人集 (*Siku quanshu cunmu congshu* ed.)
———, et al. *Yingmei an yiyu, Fusheng liuji, Xiangwan lou yiyu, Qiudeng suoji* 影梅庵憶語，浮生六記，香畹樓憶語，秋燈瑣憶. Changsha: Yuelu shushe, 1991.
Nie Bao 聶豹. *Nie Bao ji* 聶豹集. Nanjing: Fenghuang chubanshe, 2007.
Pan Lei 潘耒. *Suichu tang wenji* 遂初堂文集 (*Siku quanshu cunmu congshu* ed.)
Owen, Stephen. *Remembrances: The Experience of Past in Classical Chinese Literature*. Cambridge, MA: Harvard University Press, 1986.
Qian Chengzhi 錢澄之. *Tianji shiji* 田間詩集. Hefei: Huangshan shushe, 1998.
———. *Tianjian wenji* 田間文集. Hefei: Huangshan shushe, 1998.
———. *Cangshan ge ji* 藏山閣. Hefei: Huangshan shushe, 2004.
———. *Zuozhi lu* 所知錄. Hefei: Huangshan shushe, 2006.
Qian Qianyi 錢謙益. *Chuxue ji* 初學集. *Qian Muzhai quanji* 錢牧齋全集. Shanghai: Shanghai guji chubanshe, 2008.
Qian Zhongshu 錢鍾書. *Weicheng* 圍城. Hong Kong: Jiben shuju, 1974.
Qingdai shiwenji huibian 清代詩文集彙編. Shanghai: Shanghai guji chubanshe, 2009.
Qu Dajun 屈大均. *Qu Dajun quanji* 屈大均全集. Beijing: Renmin wenxue chubanshe, 1996.
Raphals, Lisa. *Sharing the Light: Representations of Women and Virtues in Early China*. Albany: State University of New York Press, 1998.
Rolston, David. ed. *How to Read the Chinese Novel*. Princeton, NJ: Princeton University Press, 1991.
Ropp, Paul. "Introduction." *Nan Nü* 3.1 (2001), 2–21. A special issue on "Passionate Women: Female Suicide in Late Imperial China."
Rouzer, Paul. *Articulated Ladies: Gender and Male Community in Early Chinese Texts*. Cambridge, MA: Harvard University Center, 2001.
Shen Fu 沈復. *Six Records of a Floating Life*, trans. Leonard Pratt and Su-hui Chiang. Harmondsworth, England: Penguin, 1983.
———. *Fusheng liuji* 浮生六記, in Mao Xiang 冒襄, et al. *Yingmei an yiyu, Fusheng liuji, Xiangwan lou yiyu, Qiudeng suoji* 影梅庵憶語，浮生六記，香畹樓憶語，秋燈瑣憶. Changsha: Yuelu shushe, 1991.
Shen Xinlin 沈新林. *Li Yu xinlun* 李漁新論. Suzhou: Suzhou daxue chubanshe, 1997.
Sibu congkan chubian 四部叢刊初編 (suoben 縮本). Taipei: Taiwan shangwu yinshu guan, 1967.
Siku jinhui shu congkan 四庫禁毀書叢刊. Beijing: Beijing chubanshe, 2000.
Siku quanshu 四庫全書. Shanghai: Shanghai guji chubanshe, 1987.
Siku quanshu cunmu congshu 四庫全書存目叢書. Ji'nan: Qilu shushe, 1997.
Siku quanshu cunmu congshu bubian 四庫全書存目叢書補編. Ji'nan: Qilu shushe, 2001.
Song Xiren 宋希仁. "Guanyu shisuhua de duanxiang" 關於世俗化的斷想. *Hunan keji daxue xuebao* 湖南科技大學學報 1 (2005), 34–39.

Stockard, Janice. *Daughters of the Canton Delta: Marriage Patterns and Economic Strategies in South China, 1860–1930*. Stanford, CA: Stanford University Press, 1989.
Struve, Lynn. "Song Maocheng's Matrixes of Mourning and Regret" *Nan Nü* 15.1 (2013), 69–108.
———. "Chimerical Early Modernity: The Case of 'Conqeust Generation' Meomoirs." In Lynn Struve., ed. *The Qing Formation in World-Historical Time*, 335–380. Cambridge, MA: Harvard University Asia Center, 2004.
Sui'an xianzhi 遂安縣志 (a facsimile reprint of the 1930 edition). Taipei: Chengwen shuju, 1975.
Sui Jun 眭駿. *Shi Yunyu nianpu* 石韞玉年譜. Beijing: Guangming ribao chubanshe, 2009.
Sun Cheng'en 孫承恩. *Wenjian ji* 文簡集 (*Siku quanshu* ed.)
Sun Xiaoli 孫小力 and Cai Weiyou 蔡維友. "Hanfu yu yiyou: WanMing Jiangnan funü de jiating juese xinbian" 悍婦與益友：晚明江南婦女的家庭角色新變. *Shenzhen daxue xuebao* 深圳大學學報 14:6 (2007), 142–145
Taiping guangji 太平廣記. Beijing: Zhonghua shuju, 1961.
Tang Shunzhi 唐順之. *Jingchuan xiansheng wenji* 荊川先生文集. (*Sibu congkan* ed.)
T'ien, Ju-kang. *Male Anxiety and Female Chastity: A Comparative Study of Chinese Ethical Values in Ming-Ch'ing Times*. Leiden: Brill, 1988.
Topley, Marjorie. "Marriage Resistance in Rural Kwangton," in Margrey Wolf and Roxane Wike, eds., *Women in Chinese Society*, 67–88. Stanford, CA: Stanford University Press, 1975.
Tu Long 屠隆. *Tu Long ji* 屠隆集. Hangzhou: Zhejiang guji chubanshe, 2012.
Twitchett, D. C. "Chinese Biographical Writings," in W.G. Beasley and E.G. Pulleyblank, eds., *Historians of China and Japan*, 95–114. London: Oxford University Press, 1960.
Volpp, Sophie. "Literary Consumption of Actors in Seventeenth-Century China." In Judith Zeitlin, Lydia H. Liu, and Ellen Widmer, eds., *Writing and Materiality in China: Essays in Honor of Patrik Hanan*, 153–183. Cambridge, MA: Harvard University Asia Center, 2003.
Waltner, Ann. "T'an-yang-tzu and Wang Shih-chen: Visionary and Bureaucrat in Late Ming China." *Late Imperial China* 8.1 (1987), 105–133.
Wang Changjin 王長金. *Chuantong jiaxun sixiang tonglun* 傳統家訓思想通論. Changchun, Jilin renmin chubanshe, 2006.
Wang Cihui 王次回 (Wang Yanhong 王彥泓). *Yiyu ji* 疑雨集. Shanghai: Shaoye sanfang shuju, 1926.
Wang Duan 汪端. *Ziran haoxue zhai shichao* 自然好學齋詩鈔. In Hu Xiaoming, et al. *Jiangnan nuxing bieji erbian*, 299–576. Hefei: Huangshan shushe, 2010.
Wang Fupeng 王富鵬. *Lingnan san da jia yanjiu* 嶺南三大家研究. Beijing: Renmin wenxue, 2008.
Wang Ji 王畿. *Wang Ji ji* 王畿集. Nanjing: Fenghuang chubanshe, 2007.
Wang Maoling 汪懋麟. *Baichi Wutong ge wenji* 百尺梧桐閣文集. Shanghai: Shanghai guji chubanshe, 1980.
Wang Meng'ou 王夢鷗, anno. and ed. *Liji jinzhu jinyi* 禮記今註今譯. Taipei: Taiwan Shangwu yinshu guan, 1971.
Wang Shizhen 王世貞. *Yanzhou sibu gao* 弇州四部稿 (*Siku quanshu* ed.).

———. *Yanzhou xugao* 弇州續稿 (*Siku quanshu* ed.).
Wang Shizhen 王士禛. *Wang Shizhen quanji* 王士禛全集. Qi'nan: Qilu shushe, 2007.
Wang Shunmin 汪舜民. *Jingxuan xiansheng wenji* 靜軒先生文集 (*Xuxiu Siku quanshu* ed.)
Wang Wan 汪琬. *Wang Wan quanji jianjiao* 汪琬全集箋校, comp. and anno. by Li Shenghua 李聖華. Beijing: Renmin wenxue chubanshe, 2010.
Wang Yingzhi 王英志, et al., eds., *Qingdai guixiu shihua congkang* 清代閨秀詩話叢刊. Nanjing: Fenghuang chuban chuanmei jituan and Fenghuang chubanshe, 2010.
Wang Youdun 汪由敦. *Songquan wenji* 松泉文集 (*Qingdai shiwen ji huibian* ed.).
Wang Xuling 王頊齡. *Shi'en tang shiji* 世恩堂詩集 (*Siku quanshu cunmu congshu bubian* ed.).
Widmer, Ellen. *The Beauty and the Book: Women and Fiction in Nineteenth-Century China*. Cambridge, MA: Harvard University Asia Center, 2006.
———. "Xiaoqing's Literary Legacy and the Place of the Woman Writer in Late Imperial China" *Late Imperial China* 13.1 (1992), 111–155.
Widmer, Ellen, and Sun, Kang-I, eds. *Writing Women in Late Imperial China*. Stanford, CA: Stanford University Press, 1997.
Wu Dingzhong. 吳定中, *Dong Xiaowan huikao* 董小宛匯考. Shanghai: Shanghai shudian, 2001.
Wu Na 吳訥 and Xu Shizeng 徐師曾. *Wenzhang bianti xushuo Wenti mingbian xushuo* 文章辨體序說, 文體明辨序說. Hong Kong: Taiping shuju, 1965.
Wu, Pei-yi. *The Confucian's Progress: Autobiographical Writings in Traditional China*. Princeton, NJ: Princeton University Press, 1990.
Wu Qingye 鄔慶葉. *Qu Dajun nianpu* 屈大均年譜. Guangzhou, Guangdong renmin chubanshe, 2006.
Xiang Qiao 項喬. *Xiang Qiao ji* 項喬集. Shanghai: Shanghai shehui kexue yuan, 2005.
Xie Zhazhe 謝肇淛. *Wuzazu* 五雜組. Shanghai: Shanghai shudian, 2001.
———. *Xiaocao zhai ji* 小草齋集. Fuzhou: Fujian renmin chubanshe, 2010.
Xu Jiacun 徐葭村 and Gong Weizhai 龔未齋 *Qiushui xuan, Xuehong xuan chidu* 秋水軒雪鴻軒尺牘. Shanghai: Shanghai shudian, 1986.
Xu Zhen'e 徐震堮, ed. & anno. *Shishuo xinyu jiaojian* 世說新語校箋. Hong Kong: Zhonghua shuju, 1987.
Xuxiu Siku quanshu 續修四庫全書, Shanghai: Shanghai guji chubanshe, 1995.
Ye Shaoyuan 葉紹袁. *Wumeng tang ji* 午夢堂集. Beijing: Zhonghua shuju, 1998.
Yi Ruolan 衣若蘭. *Shixue yu xingbie: Mingshi lienü zhuan yu Mingdai nuxing shi zhi jiangou* 史學與性別：明史列女傳與明代女性史之建構. Taiyuan: Shanxi jiaoyu chubanshe, 2011.
You Tong 尤侗. *Xitang shiji* 西堂詩集 (*Xuxiu Siku quanshu* ed.).
———. *Xitang wenji* 西堂文集 (*Xuxiu Siku quanshu* ed.).
Yu Yingshi 余英時. "Zhongguo jinshi zongjiao lunli he shangren jingshen" 中國近世宗教倫理與商人精神, in Yu Yingsi., *Shi yu Zhongguo wenhua* 士與中國文化, 441–570. Shanghai: Shanghai renmin chubanshe, 1987.
Yu Zhanghua 俞樟華 and Xu Jingpin 許菁頻. *Gudai zazhuan yanjiu* 古代雜傳研究. Changchun: Jilin wenshi chubanshe 2005.
Yuan Mei 袁枚. *Yuan Mei quanji* 袁枚全集. Nanjing: Jiangsu guji chubanshe, 1993.
Yuan Zhen 元稹. *Yuan Zhen ji* 元稹集. Beijing: Zhonghua shuju, 1982.
Zhang Jie 張傑. *Zhongguo gudai tongxin lian tukao* 中國古代同性戀圖考. Kunming: Yunan renmin chubanshe, 2008.

Zhang Minghua 張明華 and Li Xiaoli 李曉黎. *Jiju shi shanbian yanjiu* 集句詩嬗變研究. Beijing: Shehui kexue chubanshe, 2011.

Zhang Ruiqing 張蕊清. "*Qiudeng suoyi yu Fengsheng liuji*" 秋燈瑣憶與浮生六記. *Mingqing xiaoshuo yanjiu* 明清小說研究 (1997.4), 221–223.

Zhang Xuecheng 章學誠. *Wenshi tongyi xinbian* 文史通義新編, ed. Chang Xiuliang 倉修良. Shanghai: Shanghai guji chubanshe, 1993.

Zhang Zhen 張貞. *Qitian ji* 杞田集 (*Qingdai shiwen ji huibian* ed.)

Zhao Yi 趙翼. *Gaiyu congkao* 陔餘叢考. Shijiazhuang: Hebei renmin chubanshe, 2003.

Zhong Xing 鍾惺, comp. *Mingyuan shigui*. The Ming Qing Women's Writings electronic database, McGill and Harvard Yenching Library, http://digital.library.mcgill.ca/mingqing/search/details-poem.php?poemID=32869&language=eng

Zhu Bangxian 朱邦憲. *Zhu Bangxian ji* 朱邦憲集 (*Siku quanshu cunmu congshu* ed.)

Zhu Jianmang 朱劍芒. "Qiudeng suoyi kao" 秋燈瑣憶考, *Qiudeng suoyi* 秋燈瑣憶, in Zhu Jianmang, comp., *Meihua wenxue mingzhu congkang* 美化文學名著叢刊 Shanghai: Guoxue zhengli she, 1935 (rpt. ed. Shanghai shudian, 1982).

Zhu Yizun 朱彝尊. *Pushu ting quanji* 曝書亭全集. Changchun, Jilin wenshi chubanshe, 2009.

Zhu Zejie 朱則傑. "Sanzhong tiyong lei Qingshi zongji yizhu xuba jikao" 三種題詠類清詩總集佚著序跋輯考. *Yuejiang xuekan* 閱江學刊 6 (2010), 76–80.

Zuo Xijia 左錫嘉. *Lengyin xian guan wenchun* 冷吟仙館文存. In Hu Xiaoming, et al., eds. *Jiangnan nüxing bieji erbian*, 1416–1420.

INDEX

An Zhiyuan, 60, 197n16
Autobiography, 9, 35, 76f, 116, 120, 199n10; women authors of, 211–212n11

Ban Zhao, 44, 194–195n18
Barr, Allen, 188n39, 189n15, 190n14, 197n16
Biographical sketch (*xingzhuang*), 4, 15f, 32f; vs. biography 32, 43, 155, 187n7, 209n2. *See also* biography and individual authors
Biography (*zhuan*), 18ff; vs. biographical sketch, 32, 43; vs. epitaph, 153, 177. *See also* individual authors
Bo Shaojun, 184

Carlitz, Katherine, 189n20, 194n10, 196n42
Chen Gongyin, 141
Chen Jicong, 98
Chen Peizhi, 35, 74, 98, 107; on his late concubine, 152–155, 210n6, 207n48. *See also* Chen Wenshu, Mao Xiang, Wang Duan
Chen Que, 18, 73
Chen Weisong, 142, 150, 155
Chen Wenshu, 22, 35; and his concubine, 204n34; and his late daughter-in-law (Wang Duan), 73–74, 183, 211n15, 211n17, 211n20; on his late wife (Gong Yucheng), 73–75, 153, 180, 202n31
Chen Yuanyuan, and Mao Xiang, 122ff
Chen Zi, 18
Companionate marriage, 7, 65, 188n15, 194n11, 200n1
Conjugal attachment, 2, 26, 28, 49, 52. *See also* intimacy

Chow, Kai-wing, 190n8
Cox, Harvey, 6
Cult of *qing*, 47

Daowang (mourning the dead), 187n5; definitions of, 3, 5–6, 13, 23ff, 76, 78; the need to justify, 26ff. *See also daowang shi*, biographical sketch, biography, epitaph, memoir, memory, sacrificial litany
Daowang shi (elegiac poetry), 5ff; compared with other elegiac genres, 9, 28, 30f, 101–103, 105, 109, 111ff; and *jiju* (compiling an elegiac poem using poetic lines from other poets), 136, 154, 193n49; quantification of, 137fl, 141f, 155, 184f, 192n41, 192n48, 209n2
Dong Xiaowan. *See* Mao Xiang

Epitaph (*muzhiming*), 3f, 15–18, 31, 33, 155; circulation of, 18, 31. *See also* individual authors

Family tension, 9, 11, 36, 43, 75f, 96f, 110–112, 175
Fang Bao, 13; on his late wife 21, 47; on his sisters, 168–170, 212n21; on husband-wife relationships, 24; 45, 51–52, 56; on women's epitaphs, 16
Fang Junyi, on his late concubine, 129ff; on his late wife, 129ff
Fang Weiyi, 211n21
Fang Wen, and his late concubine, 207n44
Fang Xiangying, 18, 23; on his late mother, 55, 143, 148; on his late wife, 22

Fang Yizhi, 211n21
Female chastity, 8, 11f, 17, 55–71, 170, 172f, 182, 190–191n16, 194n18, 196–197n5, 209n30
Feng Pu, 144f
Feng Xiaoqing, 146
Fong, Grace, 106, 184f
Fusheng liuji (*Six Records of a Floating Life*). *See* Shen Fu

Gong Yucheng. *See* Chen Wenshu
Gong Weizhai, 74
Guan Tong, on *daowang*, 25f
Guan Ying. *See* Jiang Tan
Gui Youguang, 20, 95, 191n22
Guilt, survivor's, 1, 4, 7, 20, 27, 37, 41f, 48–52, 68f, 71, 104, 130, 142, 159, 168f

Hagiography, 8, 55ff, 59–62, 64, 68–71, 156, 170f, 194n18
Hanan, Patrick, 203n18
Honglou meng (*The Dream of the Red Chamber* or *The Story of the Stone*), 126f
Huang Jingren, 200n23
Huang Zongxi, 16; views on women's biography 20, 31, 56, 59–61, 69–70, 198n22
Huntingon, Rania, 187n8

Idema, Wilt, 184
Intimacy, 3, 5, 7f, 24ff, 46, 105, 184

Jealousy, 7, 40, 42, 52, 94, 118, 128, 131,145f, 169, 182, 194n6
Jiang Tan, compared with Shen Fu, 97f, 101, 111f, 182, 201n11, 202n31; on his late wife (Guan Ying), 9, 97–112
Jiang Yan, 136f
Jiaxun (household instructions), 13, 23f, 192n33, 208n6
Jin Zhaoyan, on his late wife, 73
Jiwen. *See* sacrificial litany

Ko, Dorothy, 65, 188n15, 191n20, 194n12, 200n1

Li Chengzhong, on his late wife, 21
Li He, 78
Li Huiqun, 98
Li Kaixian, 28f, 192n42, 192n43
Li Mengyang, on his wife, 4, 29–30, 37, 116, 192n45; justifying *daowang*, 26f
Li Panlong, defending a wife's shrewishness, 19, 181
Li Qingzao, 209n2
Li Yindu, 138
Li Yu, 94, on his late concubines, 116–121, 129, 132, 145, 156, 178, 184, 200n24; 203n14, 203n16 203n18
Lienü zhuan (*Biographies of Women*), 172, 189n17, 192n36. *See also* Liu Xiang
Lienü zhuan (*Biographies of Female Chastity Martyrs*), 55, 191n16, 194n18
Liji (*The Book of Rites*), 4, 194n15, 204n33
Lin Lan Xiang (*The Three Women Named Lin, Lan and Xiang*), 200n24
Lisao (*Encountering Sorrows*), 19
Liu Ling, 74
Liu Lingxian, 210n3
Liu Xiang, 44, 189n17, 194n15
Liu Zongzhou, 189n19
Long Qirui, on his late wife, 76, 96
Lu, Weijing, 187n8
Luo Hongxian, on his late wife, 47, 195n23
Lü Kun, 24ff

Manhood, 47, 86ff, 92
Mann, Susan, 189n18
Mao Jike, on his late daughter, 198n27; on his late mother, 21
Mao Qiling, on his late concubine, 144–150, 153, 155–156, 207n41, 205n12; and literati networking, 147–149
Mao Xiang, on his late wife, 128–130; and literati networking, 142, 193n53; and his influence, 76, 151–152, 207n48, 204n30; and his memoir on his late concubine (Dong Xiaowan), 10, 34–36, 74, 76–77, 98–99, 120–130, 132, 136–137, 151, 203n20, 205n15
Masculinity, 87, 195n26. *See also* manhood

Memoir, 9f, 12, 23, 33–36; and Chen Peizhi, 151f; and Jiang Tan, 99f, 112; and Mao Xiang, 121f, 130; and Shen Fu, 76f; vs. memoirs on historical events, 188n14

Memory, 4, 13f, 15, 42, 126f; and forgetfulness, 8, 42, 62, 127, 198n21; intimate 3, 7ff, 13; redeeming function of, 42, 125ff; secularization of, 6f, 12, 17–19, 22f, 27, 30, 33, 36, 71, 188n13, 188n14, 190n8

Mourning rituals, 38, 43, 51, 131f, 165. *See also daowang*

Muzhiming. See epitaph

Mubiao. See epitaph

Natal family, 9, 56, 77, 101–112, 138, 157–160, 162, 166–172, 190n12, 208n1, 209n22, 211–212n22

Nie Bao, on his late concubine, 115–117; on his late wife, 115–117

Nüjie (Precepts for Women), 44, 195n18

Pan Lei, 143
Pan Yue, 30, 138

Qian Chengzhi, on his late mother, 161–163; on his late sister 12, 33, 159–164, 168, 208n18; on his late wife, 8, 31, 61–68, 70–71, 156–198n22

Qian Qianyi, 181; on his late sister, 116f; on women's biography, 191n21

Qian Shoupu, 184
Qian Weilu, 198n22
Qian Zhongshu, 208n55
Qin Guan, 201n11

Qiudeng suoyi (Fragments of Memory under the Autumn Lamp). See Chen Peizhi

Qu Daqun, on his late wives, 138–141; and literati networking, 141–142, 153, 155; 205n15

Raphals, Lisa, 189n17, 194n15
Ruan Ji, 74

Sacrificial litany *(jiwen)*, 4, 32f, 38, 41f, 76, 127, 158, 170, 195n23; women authors of, 210n2. *See also* biographical sketch, epitaph, individual authors

Shen Fu, and *Fusheng liuji*, 9, 13, 35–36, 71, 73, 76–97, 101, 111, 193n56, 194n9, 199n16, 200n24

Shen Shanbao, 200n2

Shen Yixiu, 43–47, 65, 79, 194n12, 195n22, 196n36, 209–210n2. *See also* Ye Shaoyuan

Shi Yunyu, 90f

Shiluë. See biographical sketch

Shuihu zhuan (Water Margin), 195n26

Song Maocheng, 194n9

Struve, Lynn, 188n14

Su Shi, 153

Suicide, by wife, 8, 55–61, 63, 65, 67–79, 170, 196–197n5, 197n20, 198n34

Sun Cheng'en, on his late concubine 114–115; on his late sister, 164–166; on his late wife 115; on women's epitaphs 19, 21

Tang Shuzhi, 17, 29, 190n8
Tanyangzi, 107
Tu Long, on his late sister, 208n1

Wang Chideng, 37
Wang Cihui, 30, 102m, 111
Wang Duan, 14, 73–75, 107, 151–152; on her late husband (Chen Peizhi), 177–185. *See also* Chen Wenshu, Chen Peizhi
Wang Ji, 47
Wang Maolin, 18
Wang Shenzhong, 28; on his late wife, 33f
Wang Shizhen (1529–1590), 18, 37, 57; on his late sister, 157–159; 164, 174, 175, 181
Wang Shizhen (1640–1688), 18, 73, 137, 142
Wang Shunmin, on not remarrying, 55
Wang Wan, on women's biography, 15–16, 18, 194n18
Wang Xuling, 154
Wang Youdun, 198n21
Wifely virtue, 12, 19ff, 24ff, 27, 30, 34, 37–40, 44–50, 55, 57–60, 64, 69, 71, 94, 114f, 124, 128, 158, 169, 175, 182, 189n17, 212n27. *See also* womanhood

Womanhood, 3, 14, 19, 44, 152, 157, 172, 191n20. *See also* wifely virtue
Wu Wenying, 178

Xiang Qiao, on his late wife, 195n24
Xiangwanlou yiyu (*The Remembrances of the Tower of the Fragrant Garden*). *See* Chen Peizhi
Xie Zhaozhe, on biography of women, 19f, 189n17
Xinglüe. *See* biographical sketch
Xingshi. *See* biographical sketch
Xingshu. *See* biographical sketch
Xingzhuang. *See* biographical sketch
Xu Ziyun, 150. *See also* Chen Weisong
Xun Fengqian, 102, 137, 139, 201n16

Ye Feng, 143
Ye Shaoyuan, 18–19, 32; on his late wife (Shen Yixiu), 43–48, 51, 65, 73, 76, 79, 96, 135–137, 152, 182, 194n15, 196n36, 196n37, 201n16; womanhood redefined, 19, 44f
Ye Xiaofan, 196n36
Yingmei an yiyu (*Remembrances of the Convent of the Plum Shadow*). *See* Mao Xiang

Yiyu. *See* memoir
You Tong, 1–3, 7, 18, 22–23, 73, 127, 137; on his late wife, 1–3, 48–50, 52, 61; and literati networking, 142–144, 155
Yu Yue, 187n8
Yuan Mei, on female chastity, 71, 170–173, 209n30; on his late sister, 71, 171–176
Yuan Zhen, 30, 36, 38, 43, 95, 138, 193n56

Zhang Cai, 178
Zhang Chao, 147, 206n36
Zhang Xuecheng, 188n17
Zhang Zhen, 8; on his late wife, 57–63, 68–71
Zhao Yun, 153
Zhu Bangxian, on his first wife 37–38, 40–41, 194n6, 194n10; on his second wife, 37–43, 194n10
Zhu Jianmang, 98
Zhu Xi, 194n15
Zhu Yizun, 18, 148, 181
Zhuan. *See* biography and biographical sketch
Zuo Xijia, 183

www.ingramcontent.com/pod-product-compliance
Lightning Source LLC
Chambersburg PA
CBHW030649230426
43665CB00011B/1012